The Basic Arts of
MARKETING

The Basic Arts of
MARKETING

PRABHU S. GUPTARA

Hutchinson
Business Books

To Pia

First published in Great Britain by
Business Books Limited
An imprint of Century Hutchinson Limited
20 Vauxhall Bridge Road, London SW1V 2SA

Century Hutchinson Australia (Pty) Limited
20 Alfred Street, Milsons Point, Sydney,
New South Wales 2061, Australia

Cetury Hutchinson New Zealand Limited
PO Box 40–086, 32–34 View Road, Glenfield,
Auckland 10, New Zealand

Century Hutchinson South Africa (Pty) Limited
PO Box 337, Bergvlei 2012, South Africa

Photoset by Deltatype, Ellesmere Port
Printed and bound in Great Britain by
The Guernsey Press Co. Ltd, Guernsey, Channel Islands

British Library Cataloguing in Publication Data

Guptara, Prabhu S.
 The basic arts of marketing.—3rd ed
 1. Marketing
 I. Title
 658.8
 ISBN 0-09-174165-3

Contents

Introduction

What is marketing?

The word 'marketing' can be confusing, because it is used in two different ways.

First, marketing refers to particular activities or functions. That is why people suffer from the illusion that marketing is concerned mainly with selling or advertising. Or that it has something to do with people carrying clipboards. Of course, there is a data-collecting, number-processing, planning and promotional side to marketing – but that is not all there is to it.

Marketing is also an essential and utterly simple philosophy of business: no customers, no business. Simple common sense? Perhaps. (But don't forget the proverb: Common sense is not very common.) Certainly, there are too many businesses that don't appreciate the full force of that simple philosophy.

Put the attitude of mind together with the functions and techniques and you begin to understand marketing. The book is mainly about the marketing mentality, orientation or philosophy. The second part introduces you to some of the techniques of the field. The aim of the whole is to give you an introduction to the principal techniques or functions of marketing, as well as to get you to begin to think like a marketer.

Here are a few exercises to introduce you to the discipline, practice and fun of thinking like a marketer.

Think about someone in a shop or office who served you within the last 24 hours. What aspects of their manner reflected a marketing orientation? Think, for example, of their physical behaviour, choice of words and the way those words were said. Did any of these things reflect a lack of concern with getting the right product to the customer at the right price?

Think about a shop or office which you visited in the last 24 hours. What aspects of the layout and design of the place reflected a marketing orientation? What additional features might improve their marketing orientation?

Think about a manufactured product which you purchased

1

recently. Which of its features demonstrate a marketing orientation? Examine the product: see if any features of its design make it particularly easy to use. What features reflect the lack of a marketing orientation? Perhaps you bought the product at least partly because of its prestige value. What features of the product give it that prestige value? What features might enhance its prestige value?

Have you purchased anything from a mail order firm recently? Think back to that experience as a whole. You will probably recollect anything that upset or irritated you, such as a delay in delivery, or some mix-up about the order or payment. (We rarely recollect things that go right.) Examine the catalogue: see what features make it easy to use, such as the way it is organized. How simple is it to find your way around it? What is the position of the order form in the catalogue – or outside it? How is the order form laid out? Does it allow you to pay by a variety of methods? How does it use incentives to make you want to buy the products?

One final word of explanation. The examples given in many marketing books, lectures and courses are drawn from the consumer goods business. This is for a very simple reason: almost everyone buys soap and chocolate. Relatively few people buy steel from a stockholder. Much of what is said about a particular sector of business applies to other business sectors. However, all illustrations need to be accepted only after thoughtful consideration: marketers believe that while many products from different industries have a lot in common so far as marketing is concerned, different business sectors require different approaches to marketing.

1
Thinking like a marketer

People who work in marketing have certain characteristic habits of mind: they always want to know why things happen the way they do in the market; they constantly ask what the implications of their actions will be; they are intensely interested in investigating the inter-relationships of the various bits of their own enterprise.

Marketing people believe that if they can ensure a constant stream of such information, then the potential of a business can be developed to the full. Business disasters can be predicted, anticipated, prepared for – and therefore avoided. Those are big claims. They need explanation and qualification, which the rest of this book provides.

However, two aspects of marketing which begin to illustrate the force of that claim will be explored in the rest of this chapter: understanding and action.

1.1 Understanding and action

The first point may surprise you: any business will be the better for fully understanding what exactly it is about. 'But,' you may respond, 'don't all businesses already know what they are about?' Unfortunately, the answer to that question has to be 'No, too often they do not'.

Actually, understanding exactly what business a company is in is not as simple as you might think. A company specializing in hand-creams was celebrating its diamond anniversary and invited a marketing specialist to take part in a special seminar for retailers. During the course of his talk, the specialist mentioned another company which had discovered that it was marketing its product to only a relatively small section of the market. Its real opportunity lay in promoting its product in another sector.

This stimulated several of the managers present to mention that thoughts of the same sort had been going through their minds about

3

their own company and its product. Now, keep in mind that the company was celebrating 60 years of success. It knew that its product could also be used as body lotion and as a sun-barrier cream, and that the market for these other categories was much larger, but it had not promoted its product in this way because of the fear of damaging its prime market.

Prompted by the seminar, the company undertook extensive studies into the use of its product. To its surprise, it discovered that the prime use to which its product was put was actually as a body cream! And the second most popular use of its product was for avoiding sunburn. Its product's use as a hand-cream was, in fact, its least popular use. The company had been in business for 60 years – successfully – without fully understanding what its business was about.

If you do not understand the nature of your business accurately, then naturally, you will not be able to take appropriate management and marketing action. But there is not much point in merely obtaining information of the sort that this company did: you have to do something with the data. What sorts of things should you do if you are in this kind of situation? That depends on a number of things, which we will consider in a moment, but let's look at a different sort of example first.

A few years ago, one of Britain's largest publishing groups launched a new magazine aimed at women. The concept of the magazine was not based on any research, and the research which was there suggested that the magazine would not succeed, though the publishers thought that their publishing flair would enable them to sell the magazine successfully. And, when the magazine was launched, it did sell very well, confounding the sceptics. But follow-up research revealed an alarming number of first-time buyers who said they wouldn't buy the magazine again, and when they didn't, the magazine had to be withdrawn. It was an expensive failure. The only credit to the management lay in their swift action to restrict losses on the venture. However, if management had done their marketing homework, they could have avoided a costly failure by not launching the magazine in the first place. Indeed, they might have had a success on their hands if they had launched a magazine which more closely matched the needs and interests of potential readers.

So, what does the marketing department of an organization do? It gets the right product to the right customer at the right price and at the right time. Marketing is a philosophy of business which puts customers and potential customers at the centre of business strategy. It is also the umbrella title given to those operational activities which aim to:

- identify the needs of existing and potential customers
- determine the best product strategy
- ensure the effective distribution of products
- inform customers of the existence of products, and persuade them to buy these products
- determine the prices at which they should be sold
- ensure after-sales service of the right quality.

Everyone in every organization needs to be, and should be, encouraged to 'think marketing'. That is, to remember that in the long run it is customers who keep companies in business. Specialists may fulfil important marketing roles, but there are many more people who, often without knowing it, make significant contributions to the effectiveness of the marketing performance of their organizations. But 'marketing' is not just a description for the world of people who have the word 'marketing' in their job titles. Marketing is a basic way of thinking and caring about a business. It is often regarded as the chief executive's responsibility, though it needs to be practised by everyone with total support at a senior level so that effective action can be guaranteed. Otherwise, the best marketing people in the world will not succeed, even when armed with the most advanced techniques, the best salesforce and the most effective promotion.

Marketing thrives in the right conditions, but requires understanding and commitment. It cannot grow on fallow ground, of course, but neither does it respond to hot-housing. It provides policies for profitable action, which someone has to ensure. That is where senior management comes in. But if the marketing attitude permeates the whole business, then action will be swifter, more soundly based, and more certain. What that means is that everyone in your company needs to be a marketing person, beginning with complete commitment from the top.

1.2 Definitions of marketing

Virtually every writer and lecturer on marketing has felt the need to phrase his or her own definition of marketing. So there is no shortage of definitions. Let's take a few of these to see how far they enlighten us. Here is one of the simplest:

Marketing takes the guesswork out of hunch

Any new business starts with an idea. Any change of business direction has the same beginning: an idea. We have already seen that untested ideas can be very expensive. If an advertising agency creates a purely speculative campaign for one of its clients, the cost is mainly time, a few materials and some share of total overheads: not a vast sum, and similar to a small gamble. But it can save you a fortune: imagine trying to build a nuclear reactor hoping that someone might want to buy it! Even door hinges are expensive to produce, if you consider the cost of the machines you may need to buy, the cost of the iron or plastic, the cost of the machine operators, the property, and all the ancillary costs of book-keeping, selling, and so on.

If you have a hunch, whether about nuclear reactors or door hinges, you can test that hunch through appropriate market research. This will not eliminate risk entirely. Nor will it by itself reduce the risk that you may take. But it may *help* you to reduce the risk by giving you information about the needs and preferences of potential customers, which you can then attempt to match. More importantly, market research can help you to quantify the risk that you will be taking and give you some idea of the potential rewards, so that you can make a more informed choice about whether it is worth proceeding.

Professor Peter Drucker puts the same idea in a more straightforward way:

'Marketing is the whole business seen from the point of view of its final result, that is, from the customer's point of view.'

Or, if you like something more punchy, try this:

'Marketing is the creative process of satisfying customer needs profitably.' (Author)

The most widely-accepted definition of marketing is provided by the Chartered Institute of Marketing (CIM):

'Marketing is the management process of identifying, anticipating and satisfying customer requirements profitably.'

Marketing is a management skill. It is not a science. Nor is it a technique that can be taught in the way that, say, woodturning on a lathe can be. Marketing is a matter of identifying opportunities and of deciding what risk to take when anticipating how customers might act or be persuaded to act. Appropriate techniques can and should be used but, in the end, it is a matter of judgment. You seek to satisfy consumers' requirements for the purpose of making a profit, not just today, but in the future, and, against reasonable yardsticks, to ensure the validity of the company.

The CIM's definition is sometimes criticized for dealing inadequately with social marketing – that is, the application of marketing philosophy and marketing techniques to non-commercial activities. However, the concept of 'social profit' or 'welfare benefit' can easily be included under the heading of 'satisfying customer requirements profitably'.

1.3   Philosophy and techniques

Marketing is not a precise art with easily defined skills, even though it is taught and examined. It is not a business confined to certified practitioners (although it is going that way and the process may well be completed in the not-too-distant future). After all, some 300 years ago, no one could see why an accountant should be different from any other businessperson: everyone in business had to keep accounts! Nowadays, accountants are licensed to practise, yet that has not in any way stopped efficient businesspeople from realizing that a basic knowledge of the principles of accounting is essential. Similarly, it is essential for every businessperson to have a basic knowledge of the principles of how most effectively to give customers satisfaction. Fundamentally, marketing is an attitude of mind which is appropriate for everybody in business – and, indeed, in any other sort of work.

However, just as the manager with a sound awareness of the principles of accountancy still requires a qualified accountant to attend to the highly skilled aspects of the work, as well as the detail, so you may need experienced specialist marketers in your enterprise. True, some businesses are too small or too specialized to require the full-time services of a professional business manager. In the same way, many businesses will not find it appropriate to employ specialist marketers. It is not necessary to develop the whole infrastructure of a marketing department or organization, but it is necessary to accept that a marketing approach is essential if your enterprise is to fulfil its potential. Nowadays, a lot of help is available to managers who cannot specialize in marketing, especially from the CIM, which is the main body in this field.

There is one further thing which needs to be understood. Marketing people are of two distinct sorts. The first is the marketing generalist. It was marketing generalists who began and grew the function of marketing. Initially, therefore, marketing people tended to be jacks-of-all trades within the area of marketing – and perhaps masters of some aspects. Their mastery tended to be in sales and advertising, and that is what created some of the misconceptions surrounding marketing today. However, as the study of consumer behaviour advanced, the need for specialists grew. So did the need for people who could understand and communicate the new specializations. That is why we now have generalists with titles such as Marketing Director, Marketing Manager, Brand Manager, and Product Manager. We also have marketing specialists. These specialists, in turn, can have a relatively broad specialization (eg, market research managers) or rather narrow specializations, (eg, psychological research, industrial or medical market research, and so on).

The widespread employment of such specialists, and the use of these techniques is very reassuring to marketers. It indicates an acceptance of the notion of marketing as a federation. But this acceptance does not mean that there is necessarily an acceptance of the marketing philosophy. In other words, there is a distinction between the *philosophy* of marketing and the *techniques* of marketing. You can have the philosophy without many of the techniques, of course; but, surprisingly, you can also have the techniques without the philosophy. Under many circumstances, the first can make sense; but the second makes no sense in any circumstance.

The ideal, naturally, is to have both. Whether one adopts the techniques or not is a matter of judgment about profitability. In any business, what we are trying to do is to maximize profit over chosen periods of time. There are occasions when the techniques will not add anything to our profitability, because the techniques are not cheap to apply.

1.4 Market research

Customers are less articulate, less inventive and less inclined to take risks than those who supply them. You cannot sit back and wait for customers to tell you what they want. Moreover, actually asking potential customers what they want is seldom rewarding. If you ask a thousand people to describe their ideal car, you will get a great many divergent answers. If you then put all the answers together and design a car to those specifications, you may end up with something that has a long boot, a long bonnet and plenty of room inside the car. There is then a strong possibility that those who wanted the long boot didn't want a long car. You have the design of a car that has elements of what everyone wants, but which no one will buy. The case of the Edsel car in the USA is a prime example of this. There is also a British manufacturer which has a research finding 'proving' that the ideal car has a roomy, separate boot – with estate car doors! In short, research tends to deal in average consumers. Average consumers seldom lead to highly successful products. It is the above-average product that attracts customers. So what we need to do is to assess consumer needs and satisfactions, and check our ideas against them – not the other way around. By keeping a check on consumer response, business will be in harmony with customer needs: guesswork will be reduced, risk minimized and repeat business enhanced.

1.5   Types of company

There are, broadly, three types of company, and most pass through the first two stages before reaching the third:

1   Production-orientated
2   Sales-orientated
3   Marketing-orientated

A company starts with an idea for goods or services, which it then produces and goes out to sell. As sales grow, the salesforce creates pressure for the addition of other products which could be sold – the company begins to be sales-orientated, though if surplus capacity exists, it may ensure that production continues to dominate. There comes a time, however, when the company may begin to run into sales difficulties. That is when it looks to marketing as a sort of instant solution for getting back into full gear. However, marketing should be an essential part of a company's outlook and structure from the beginning.

1.6   Production-orientation

Production-orientated companies rely on the salesforce to sell their

9

products. Such companies believe that their products are the best in the world. So if their products don't sell as well as the owners anticipate, it is easy for them to think that there can be only two reasons:

1 The sales force isn't up to scratch
2 The customer is ignorant.

Not so long ago, a company designed a completely new form of roof insulation material which was supposed to offer significant consumer advantages. Made of re-cycled waste paper, it was in flat panels made up as squares to fit the space between roof rafters. It was far more efficient in retaining heat than other forms of insulation, provided at least three layers were used. Unfortunately, the product did not sell. The manufacturer's explanation was that the people in the trade were just stupid and did not realize what advantages the product offered the householder. But the company had ignored two things: the cost of the new panels was markedly higher than that of existing products, and they took at least three times as long to lay. Neither the dealers nor the householders were as stupid as the producers thought.

That is only one example from hundreds which could be quoted of marketing failure. It illustrates two things which all providers of goods and services should appreciate:

1 The customer is the main arbiter of quality.
2 An 'improvement' which the customer cannot understand or does not appreciate or want is no improvement at all.

If the story of the roof insulation panels was an example of an improvement which customers didn't understand, here is an example of an improvement which customers didn't want.

The term 'quality tea' is used to describe teas which retail over a certain price. Since price is a fair reflection of ingredient cost, the feeling that price indicates quality is not entirely unreasonable, though that does not always follow. The interesting thing is that the average British householder has a nickname for these quality teas: he or she calls them 'funny teas'. So far as the customer is concerned, they taste 'funny' – that is, different from what he or she usually buys. What customers buy reflects their opinion of quality, and that is the only thing that means anything to them.

A parallel case is that of an institution's dining hall near Grimsby, from where there was a rash of complaints when truly fresh fish was introduced for the first time: having never tasted fresh fish in their lives, the officers thought it was 'off'.

10

The case of *The Daily Mirror* is also worth considering in this context. The newspaper thought that it could gently move its readers a little more upmarket. Gradually, the theory was, readers could be weaned from the trivial and sensational content of the paper as it then was. While it was gradually doing this, it also gradually lost sales. Finally, the ailing paper had to be sold to Robert Maxwell, who promptly restored flesh and gossip, and had the paper flourishing again.

Whatever personal views you may have about newspapers such as *The Daily Mirror* and *The Sun*, it is difficult to deny that they do show what a very large number of people in Britain want from their daily paper.

Such knowledge may not feel comfortable. Most people feel a sort of moral obligation to help other people to something approaching their own level, or at least to desist from pandering to what they regard as such low levels. Marketing frequently involves the individual in quasi-moral dilemmas until marketers learn to accept that it is not possible to impose their standards on others. We are all human, we all have lives to live outside our work, and the division between personal and professional life into which marketing can divide our lives (if we allow it to) can lead to dissatisfaction, discomfort and anxiety.

The way out of this dilemma is to see that it arises from a hangover of Victorian moralism, which is best countered by an appreciation of the freedom which has been granted to all human beings to live their individual and communal lives according to their own notions of what is good, proper, beautiful, and so on. Everything is *not* relative, but some things certainly are. Quality lies in the beholder's eye, so quality is one of the things that is relative: it means very different things to different people.

If those are the perils of production-orientation, what is the difference between that and marketing-orientation? Perhaps this example will help clarify the difference. A British company achieved spectacular growth in the do-it-yourself market. Aware of the growth in popularity of polystyrene tiles, it decided to enter the market and build a plant. However, it wasn't long before this venture began to look very sick. Capacity was badly underutilized. The company began offering sales discounts, running promotions and, when those did not produce the desired results, searching for new markets. Its attitude was: 'We've got a very good product; there must be someone, somewhere we can sell it to'.

In fact, its market analysis was faulty. It was true that the market

11

for ceiling tiles had grown exponentially. However, there is a significant difference between initial demand and annual repeat buying, which it had not understood. Its executives had not asked themselves how often they expected that people would replace their ceiling tiles, and the rate of growth had in fact peaked. The question they should have asked was: 'We can obtain the technical skill to manufacture and mould polystyrene: how can we match those skills to existing profitable markets, preferably without any change in our facilities and capacity or with only minor modifications?'

1.7 Sales-orientation

The cardinal sin with a sales-orientation is the pursuit of volume. This can be turned to advantage, as the Japanese have demonstrated, but only if it is part of a wider plan. By itself, the pursuit of volume is counter-productive.

Why? Because profit and volume are hardly ever maximized at the same point. There are some exceptions: for example, professionals with more demands on their time than they can meet, can afford to raise their fees till all their hours are filled at the maximum price, and all the work is done in their own office or consulting room. Most businesses, however, find that various practical factors prevent them from maximizing profit and volume at the same time. For example, they usually have distribution costs which vary with load and distance, and they can seldom impose differential prices to cover the variance in costs.

The fact of the matter is that a few important customers always account for the bulk of profits, while a large proportion of customers yield only a low proportion of profits. (You will usually find that the proportions work out as 80:20. This is sometimes called Pareto's Law, and applies in practically all areas of life.) Increasing the number of customers may not necessarily cover increased costs of distribution, especially when the majority of such customers may represent low profit.

One other problem is that sales and marketing tend to develop in opposite directions. Increasing the scale of production usually leads to economies of scale. However, increased sales tend to result even more quickly in diminishing returns due to sales costs and human inefficiency. So, at precisely the same time that the factory pushes for more sales to improve factory costing, the salesforce will be increasing its costs by spending more time gaining conversions, taking more time in travelling, making several visits to obtain an order, and making special runs to deliver. Economies of scale in *manufacturing* can easily go hand-in-hand with dis-economies of scale in *selling*.

Would a marketing approach help? Yes, in two ways. First, it would seek to improve profitability by concentrating efforts on influencing the major customers and finding more cost-effective ways of servicing the rest. For example, both Lyons-Tetley and Brooke Bond Oxo once used to sell tea from vans which called on virtually every retailer who might have sold tea. Both now concentrate their efforts on the top end of the grocery trade, leaving the wholesalers and cash-and-carry outlets to cater for the rest of the trade.

Second, a marketing approach would have embraced a greater awareness of the inter-relationships and implications of apparently separate decisions. The first of these is 'What is our market?' Then 'How many do we want to serve direct?', and then the key question, 'How do we maximize profit?' Examining these three questions might have led to decisions about production capacity at an early stage. It is emotionally difficult for a sales-trained manager to decline to serve any potential customers, but you may well have to decline to serve categories of potential customers in order to be profitable. We shall see why in a moment.

1.8   What marketing does

Implicit in the above questions about marketing is an awareness of what you are doing, why you are doing it and what the implications are – now and in the future. It is very difficult to be certain about anything in business. Given the same facts, one company will make one decision and another will take an entirely different direction. One may well be wrong, or both may be right. However, if each company knows why it is doing what it is, the chances of remedying an unfavourable situation and avoiding a similar error in the future will be far greater.

So what is marketing? Marketing isn't just common sense. It is more than selling or advertising. It is not wholly what business is about, but it is concerned with the essential matter of investigating the most profitable direction for any business. It therefore:

1   Assesses markets. It measures existing and potential markets, defines market segments, recommends which to attack, monitors progress, and so on.
2   Specifies products and services. Taking both market

13

assessment and product potential into account, it ensures that the end-user's views and opinions are adequately represented in the goods and/or services offered. That is, the way in which customers are offered products or services emphasizes *benefits* rather than production *features*.

3 Evaluates pricing policy. Based on the preceding points, marketing recommends policies which will afford maximum profits at least risk. It will also consider possible competitive reactions and devise responses to them.

4 Recommends channel policy, or how goods/services should reach the end-user. Marketing establishes the levels through which the goods/services will pass. It asks whether sales are to be entirely direct, only indirect, or some combination of the two. It establishes how intermediaries will be selected, remunerated, trained, motivated and retained.

5 Evaluates sales and physical distribution policy, on the basis of the functional consequences of channel decisions; the size and duties of the sales force; the number and location of warehouses and departments; call and delivery rates, and so on. In other words, marketing examines the question of profit versus volume.

6 Makes recommendations regarding advertising and promotion – how much (if any), when, to whom? Such areas as packaging, service manuals and training (as part of product promotion) need to be analyzed and researched.

7 Co-ordinates the work of the different areas of the business and ensures total quality management. This is vital. If there is any single role that transcends all others in distinguishing a marketing person from other managers it is that of co-ordinator and quality ensurer. Marketing can be seen as a sort of federated union. The component states include selling, market research, advertising, public relations, promotion, merchandizing, and so on. But marketing also co-ordinates the efforts of those components with production, accounting, buying, etc. In this way, it relates to all the ramifications of every business action.

Only by studying their market continuously can anyone speak for their customers – using their words. That is the work of people in marketing. They know that there is a fate which will overtake them unless they act, but they dare not act too quickly or with insufficient knowledge of the market.

1.9 Summary

Marketing is a way of thinking that links a host of separate activities and unifies them in the search for profit. Because marketing people are always asking questions about the market, a number of techniques have grown up. Ideally, the techniques go hand in hand with the philosophy of marketing. Often the techniques cannot be afforded or are inappropriate to a particular industry or situation. That is no barrier to adopting the marketing way of thinking, of continually wanting to understand what the company is doing, why and what the consequences might be now and in the future.

The underlying concept behind all marketing thinking is that profit can ony be created from satisfying customer needs.

1.10 Checklist

1 Who is the ultimate marketing authority in your company? Who should it be? *No-one . HODs have control*
2 Is this authority delegated? Wholly or partially? How? *To field staff*
3 How is the company organized to:
   a. identify customer requirements?
   b. anticipate them?
   c. satisfy those needs?
4 Do any mechanisms exist to check continuing levels of satisfaction; monitor quality complaints; deal with service complaints? *No*
5 How thoroughly is the marketing philosophy accepted in the company? That is, how thoroughly is it accepted that the company must produce what the customer wants rather than what the company wishes to make? *Not at all*
6 Is your company:
   a. Production-orientated? *Yes*
   b. Sales-orientated? *No*
   c. Marketing-orientated? *No*
7 Key areas for marketing attention: *that I can hope to influence*
   a. Assessing markets *✗*
   b. Specifying products and services to meet market needs
   c. Pricing policy
   d. Channel policy *✗*
   e. Sales and physical distribution policy *✗*
   f. Advertising and promotion *✗*
   g. Co-ordination of the separate activities of company *✗*

departments to achieve corporate marketing goals, and total quality control

h. After-sales service and analysis.

2

The foundation: comparing businesses

No two businesses are precisely the same. However, businesses that appear to be very different from each other behave in rather similar ways in certain key respects. On the other hand, some businesses that appear to compete in the same market operate, in fact, in quite different markets.

How useful is it, then, to compare businesses? Such comparisons are, in fact, the heart of marketing. They are what enable you to understand what business you are in, as against your competitors. The usefulness of such comparisons will become evident when we consider particular marketing techniques and ideas for action.

We begin with a difficulty. All attempts to categorize industries and services with any degree of finality are doomed to failure. Some consumer durable products, for example, are almost industrial in their complexity but sell to individuals for private use (think of electric drills). On the other hand, there are many products that appear to be obviously industrial but are sold through shops to individuals as well as to companies, who are the final users (eg, certain kinds of stationery and office equipment).

This ambiguity is precisely what makes the exercise of thinking through what sort of business you are in and how it compares with other businesses so useful. Difficulty can often be fruitful. In relation to our case at present, it can help us to look at the situation from different points of view, enabling us to see different advantages and disadvantages, possibilities and limitations.

Let us first look at some categories in popular use. For example, we could separate companies into small, medium and large (and nationally-sized, and internationally-sized). But do we mean small in terms of capital employed? Or do we mean small in terms of turnover or profitability? From a marketing point of view, moreover, there is no correlation between size and the nature of a company's operations in the marketplace.

One other popular method of categorization is by the nature of the final product. This method is not watertight either: service industries could be stretched between consumer and industrial services, and each of these would be worth sub-dividing further. For simplicity, however, companies can be divided into:

- Mass-market consumer businesses
- Suppliers to other companies
- Service businesses
- Export businesses
- Small businesses.

2.1 Mass-market consumer businesses

The marketing philosophy has been accepted relatively slowly in the UK. This is probably for two major reasons: first, the belief that marketing only applies to consumer products – especially soap powders; second, the idea that marketing techniques are readily transferable from consumer marketing to marketing in quite different areas. Techniques and tactics are not always transferable, even between different parts of the consumer market: newspapers are obviously consumer products, but they do not have '3p off' promotions. There is still a widespread belief that marketing is really only effective when you spend millions of pounds on television advertising, have hordes of product managers, spend a fortune on market research and do all your sales analyses on a mainframe computer. And if you've got all that, goes the argument, consumer marketing is dead easy.

On the contrary, that kind of consumer marketing is the hardest of the lot. That is why all those techniques need to be used. That is why so much money has to be spent making potential consumers aware of your products and encouraging their sale. At its crudest, the difference between consumer markets and other markets is the difference between trying to address your message once a week to 16 million householders, and contacting 300 buyers four times a year. If you like, it is the difference between a sane, rational discussion with a buyer about objective matters such as price, performance, delivery and service, on the one hand, and on the other, dealing with emotive and unpredictable purchasing behaviour by someone confused by a shelf-full of competing hair shampoos, all at around the same price. It is the difference between trying to convince the householders that his or her family will love

18

this new flavour that you have just invented, and responding to the demands for new processes, new ingredients or new performance standards from a long-standing customer.

Both positions are obvious extremes. But they do help to kill the myth that consumer marketing is easy. They also help to explain part of the confusion that exists between different types of marketing.

Consumer businesses do use advanced techniques and spend large sums on promotion, but they do it because they have to – not because they enjoy doing it. Groceries, confectionery, cigarettes and other fast moving consumer goods (FMCG) are marked by the problems of what might be termed 'distance' and 'frequency'.

'Distance' is, simply, the number of steps (or people) between the manufacturer and the final consumer. Distance is also compounded by the sheer number of consumers, because communication difficulties multiply geometrically as numbers rise arithmetically. But the key factor is the amount of effort you have to invest in persuading wholesalers, buying groups, store managers and other links in the chain from manufacturer to consumer to stock your goods, promote them and be generally enthused by them. Indeed, many food products for example, are promoted only to the grocery trade. The producer relies on retailers to pass on part of the deals they receive in the form of price promotions. These make the product attractive to the consumer at the moment of purchase.

'Frequency' can also complicate the problem. The more often a product is purchased, the greater the reliance on customer loyalty and on regularity of repeat purchase. The great bulk of consumer promotion is aimed at first creating, and then maintaining, customer loyalty. To achieve this, it is necessary to have a considerable quantity of sophisticated market research. Companies need to be aware of buying rates ahead of that awful day when orders on the factory simply dry up. Other characteristics of this sort of market are that the average volume purchased tends to be low; turnover is relatively high; and profit margins are relatively low. Goods are bought for personal or family use and satisfaction, and the group that makes the buying decision is usually the user. Businesses in this sort of market tend to be widely dispersed.

However, it must be remembered that many consumer products and services have quite different characteristics. Many of them are far less frequently purchased, far more expensive, subject to careful consideration and have technical features and attributes. Washing machines, refrigerators, cars and television sets fall into this category. However, foreign holidays and financial services from banks and insurance companies may have the same sorts of characteristics. The buyer will look around, compare performance, check prices and possibly try out the product. In many cases, purchasers will carry skills and disciplines from their working life into the purchasing situation. People who work all day in a scientific atmosphere will not simply switch off their analytical and logical abilities when buying something for themselves. A great deal of fairly skilled consideration has to be given to many consumer purchases if satisfaction is to be ensured. Packaged holidays, for instance, involve consideration of destination, of a hotel within the resort, of length of holiday, type of room, price and activities which might be pursued while there. Quite apart from the complex inter-relationships between these decisions, there is the all-important consideration that the holiday involves a large outlay of money but cannot be seen, touched or experienced at the moment of decision.

Some people would argue that a packaged holiday is a product that involves putting together a number of services rather than a service in its own right. The special positions of services will be examined later in this chapter. At the moment it is sufficient to point out that consumer services can be sub-divided into three categories:

1 Domestic services
2 Direct personal services
3 Public personal services.

Examples of the first category might be window cleaning, plumbing and milk delivery. Direct personal services are those which are rendered to one person at a time, such as haircutting, bank accounts and life assurance. The opposite is the service which a person receives as an individual, although it is actually performed simultaneously with many others (or is intended to be). A train journey is an example of this kind, as are all other services performed by public utilities. Thus, commercial marketing merges gradually into the spheres of social services and what is beginning to be recognized as 'social marketing' – the application of the principles of consumer satisfaction and the awareness that the effects of inter-related yet separate activities upon the user as an individual have some bearing on them as members of society at large.

2.2 Industrial businesses

It is comparatively easy to produce a definition of industrial marketing, though it is very difficult for any definition to include all appropriate cases. (Indeed, if a properly pedantic view is taken, it is impossible to produce any kind of definition at all.)

The classic, and most useful, description of industrial businesses is that they are concerned with *derived* demand. That is, they are in the business of supplying companies who use the products bought to produce other goods and services which are supplied to the ultimate customer. At times, the distance between the first producer and final user may be enormous. These industrial services are performed for other companies in the manufacturing field, but they may also be performed for institutions, local and central government and farmers. Even when the product is identical the selling method of each of these kinds of customer will have to be very different.

Many of the industrial products that are involved in the production of other goods are completely consumed. Many food products that are clearly consumer items (such as cooking fat) are only used as an aid to the production of an end-product. Obviously, products and services fall into a length spectrum of which the two ends are light years apart, yet near neighbours, with some overlaps.

So the classic definition is useful but not entirely satisfactory. Just as we could distinguish sub-divisions of consumer markets, so we can provide other categories for industrial markets. We can look at businesses by the length of period over which they provide a benefit and by the degree of interdependence they have with other producers.

First, benefit. What most people in consumer industries think of as industrial products are really capital items whose benefit lasts over a very lengthy period, covering a considerable number of production cycles (often millions). Such products are often regarded as epitomizing the industrial market. Where the products are tangible, they are capitalized in the balance sheet and depreciated over relatively long periods of time. Intangible items cannot be dealt with in the same way, so are written-off very shortly after purchase.

Other kinds of product provide their benefits over a much shorter time-span – typically, one production cycle. So they are charged against revenue and, because demand is usually closely derived, are regarded as variable costs in the purchaser's accounts. An example of such an item is fertilizers. (In many cases, agricultural products fall between the two definitions, in that demand is not closely derived from a single product and does not vary directly with output in all cases. The farmer will regard the expenditure as a fixed cost,

21

but the benefit will be effectively confined to one growing season.)

The other way in which we can look at industrial businesses is by the interdependence between products. We can distinguish between three types of product which are technically linked in some way. There is also one type of product which is not. Stationery, for example, is not usually technically linked with an end-product or process – the letters and forms a company employs are an essential part of being in business but have no direct connection with an end-product (unless it is for a printer). In cases like this, other considerations determine the buying cycle, and we will look at these later. Services, such as contract plant maintenance, would also fall into this category.

One type of technically-linked service or product, such as a chemical, is vulnerable to substitution by another product. Products in this category live and die by their appeal to their direct customer on the conventional industrial grounds of cost, efficiency, reliability and service. Where the ingredient or component is firmly associated with a company or brand name, the owners of that name can take steps to defend their position as a supplier as well as to develop the end-user market, safe in the knowledge that they will benefit from the derived demand. This is known as 'back-selling' and classic examples in Britain are the promotion of synthetic fibres, on the one hand (Terylene and Crimplene, for example), and the efforts of the International Wool Secretariat, on the other, to promote products made of pure wool.

Slightly different are other technically-linked products for which the demand is closely derived and where the end-user is aware of the generic product, but not necessarily aware of the company who supplied it. A good deal of switching gear comes into this category. Back-selling would be obviously wasteful here and substitution is again much more possible than would be the case if the supplier's name were important to the customer. Control over one's destiny is obviously more difficult and it is clear that the fundamental problems of industrial marketing are precisely connected with the amount of influence a company can have over its own market.

Many of the characteristics of buyer behaviour in industrial markets will be the mirror opposites of those we saw for final consumers. Such is the diversity of businesses that come under this heading, however, that it becomes near impossible to tabulate any distinctions without constant qualification.

The term 'business-to-business' is now being increasingly adopted to cover a far wider area of activities than can be included under the traditional description of 'derived demand' items. For the moment, it is enough to say that the principal considerations of industrial marketing concern the question of control over one's own destiny, the greater concern with selling through, rather than to, one's customers and the increasingly complex nature of the decision-making process before placing an order.

2.3 Service businesses

Businesses which have the function of providing services to others may do so to private individuals, to companies and to local and central government. A characteristic of a service is that it is intangible. Most are very difficult to describe and to measure. Frequently, a tangible product is the direct result, as when a decorator papers your walls. Often, the tangible aspect is several stages removed (as is the case with most services provided by banks and insurance companies), and in many instances the service is performed in order to *prevent* something tangible happening: a chimney sweep may prevent a fire, a marketing consultant may prevent bankruptcy. In many such cases, there may be little visible evidence of any kind. This often leaves the door wide open for criticism of the service on subjective grounds. This is especially true of preventive servicing of all kinds. In a well-maintained car, as with a regularly serviced piece of machinery, there is nothing to show. Criticism will be prompt if a mishap occurs soon after servicing, but few bouquets are offered when nothing untoward happens between services.

Payment often has to be made well before the benefit is obtained – holidays and life assurance are good examples – and in many cases, the benefit will be received by someone else. Frequently, as with most kinds of insurance, there is always the hope that no one will benefit in any tangible way – except the insurance company of course – what it has sold is 'peace of mind'.

People are fundamental to the performance of services. When a highly efficient engineer turns up two days late, the fact that the engineer did a good job can easily be overlooked. The performance of employees can harm any business of course, but services suffer especially in this respect.

It is quite understandable that criticism, and occasionally praise, should be directed at the people who represent the company providing the service: after all, that is what the customer pays for. The 'production costs' of services are principally the labour costs, though goods and other services associated with them also add to the bill. This leads to some features – which can also be problems – of service industries. The performance of people is less predictable and more variable than the output of machines: differences between individuals performing identical tasks are invariably greater than between the same types of machinery. People usually need more breaks from work and, themselves, break down fairly often. On the other hand, they are capable of exercising initiative, intelligence and adaptability. As the famous sign in the IBM office in Tokyo puts it:

Man – Slow, Slovenly, Brilliant
IBM – Fast, Accurate, Stupid

In many service industries, an almost identical end-product can be supplied by many different suppliers. The main joint stock banks in the UK offer the same basic services at the same time and with very little variation between them in price. In cases like these, real differences are found in the highly personal qualities of the people who perform these services: their reliability, helpfulness, honesty and cheerfulness. In many service industries, from banks through advertising agencies to highly personal services such as hairdressing, one even finds that personal qualities among staff can actually overcome a poor end-product. Research conducted into ladies' hairdressing repeatedly shows that the majority of women complain that their favourite hairdresser 'can't cut hair'. The reasons for continuing to go to that salon are mainly to do with a liking for the staff and especially for a particular stylist.

Highly personal services like that are clearly at one end of a spectrum. At the other end would be mainly industrial services. Preventive servicing is clearly a long way from ladies' hairdressing, although the services of a hair clinic and a trichologist could be classified as preventive servicing. In general, industrial services are bought for one or more of the following reasons:

- To reduce cost
- To improve profits
- To promote and maintain efficiency
- To improve morale
- To provide welfare benefits for staff
- To comply with laws, codes and regulations.

Service industries generally lag far behind the rest of British business in the adoption of the marketing philosophy. The very fact

24

that the services offered are personal has tended to incline service industries to the belief that they are in touch with their customers and that marketing has nothing more to offer. Although the phrase 'The customer is always right' originated in the service industries, we all know far too many cases where this has not been integrated into the practice of the businesses. There are numerous reasons for this (many of them summed up in the earlier paragraph on the differences between people and machines). One big difference is that machines are indifferent to time. People place an increasing value on their time. People want more money for the time they are working, so that they can use it in the time when they are free. This fact frequently leads to differences in the value placed on time by the employee and the worth of that time to the customer.

By and large, we are badly out of line in the cost-of-time in services. It has taken hairdressing businesses many years to come to a position of putting anything near the true worth of time into their prices. The do-it-yourself home decorating boom is based entirely on unwillingness to value a craftsman's time as highly as the householder's own time. Homeowners look at the capital cost of the *total outlay* on decorating a room and compare it with the *cost of materials*. Implicit in that decision is a refusal to measure how the cost of the paper-hanger's time compares with their own hourly rate.

In a very real sense, the under-valuing of time is one of the major harvests from the ignorance of marketing thinking in service industries. In all services, from hairdressing to service engineering, there have been examples of intuitive marketers who have been ahead of their time in gauging the readiness of the market to pay a realistic price for a well-performed service. The alternative, and far more frequent response, has been to excuse the inadequate service and justify it by a chain of logic that says: 'The service is poor because the staff won't work in an industry that pays less than others, and which pays less than others because customers will not pay the price that good service should cost if the wages were right!'

That is the sort of thing which the novelist Joseph Heller called 'Catch 22'. An unfortunate result of this phenomenon is a tendency for some people to look down on people who provide services. When this attitude is combined with the demand for such services at hours during which other people don't work – and often in conditions that the person who pays for the service wouldn't tolerate – the major problems confronting this sector of business are readily appreciated. The absence of good marketing must bear a large part of the burden for allowing these attitudes to prevail. It may well take a long time for the underlying sociological problems to be reduced to tolerable levels.

2.4 Export businesses

International marketing is difficult to discuss adequately as a small part of one chapter, but let us begin by looking at the whole spectrum of what goes under the name of international marketing.

In the initial stages of the growth of a small company, that company may be unwilling to be involved in trade internationally, because of the extended lines of communication; the additional problems created by foreign languages and ways of doing business; the increased difficulties in collecting payment; the risks created by currency fluctuation; and the greater amount of work necessitated by working internationally.

Later, the company may become willing to accept orders from abroad, though it may still be unwilling to do anything to cultivate markets outside its own country.

In a third stage of development, it might export experimentally to one or two countries. Next, it might become experienced in a few countries, and begin to look systematically at choosing and working in particular markets abroad. It is only at this stage that it is proper to describe this company as being involved in international marketing, though the term is sometimes applied to companies at earlier stages of growth.

International marketing implies that the same care is being taken in assessing opportunities, wherever the market, as against the attitudes: 'We can make it, all we've got to do is go out and sell it' or 'If it's good enough for us, it is certainly good enough for foreigners'. Though there are certain similarities between human beings everywhere, the *reasons* for using a product, and the purposes to which products are put, can vary enormously. Methods of selling, distribution, production and promotion are quite different in other parts of the world. So the natural tendency – to try to sell existing products to profitable foreign markets in the same way as we sell them at home – will not lead to the best results. Experience soon teaches those willing to learn that there are better ways of developing markets abroad.

Exporting is extremely hard work. It involves all the effort of a domestic market plus the many new disciplines of dealing with different languages, new systems of distribution and operation,

26

different laws and regulations, and the vagaries of public opinion and politics abroad.

In a company which starts selling internationally, the most important new emphasis will be that of market research: this is important in a domestic market, of course, but it is possible to get away with a minimum of pre-testing because the company's reputation will always do something for its products – for example, when a new one is launched. Sheer experience in a domestic market enables one to slot a new venture into a known pattern. This in turn gives the company a fair chance of anticipating customer reaction as well as competitive reaction. In foreign markets, the very opposite is true: a business needs to pre-test not only the product, but the product with the name of the supplier – and the country of origin.

The last point may seem academic, but there are countries which will not take easily even to British-made goods, with our long history of manufacture and service internationally. Similarly, there are areas of the world which will not buy from Jewish companies. There are countries which refuse to trade with those who deal with people whom they consider their enemies – or to whom they object for some other reason. When entering a country for the first time, it is usually necessary to find some way of testing the sales, distribution and servicing arrangements. The example of the Japanese motorcycle manufacturers is a salutary one: they built up their servicing and spares capability before they started to hard sell, and this was one essential ingredient in their winning the market from American and British motorcycle manufacturers.

This didn't come about by chance. Marketing teaches us to take a broad look at the skills we have which induce our customers to buy from us rather than from someone else. Frequently, it is something other than the product itself, such as the skill of the salesforce, the speed of delivery or a rapid trouble-shooting service. When a company with these sorts of attributes operates in other countries through agents, factors, contractors or indeed foreign employees with different values and attitudes, many of those advantages disappear – certainly, they are out of the company's control. Often the failure to identify just what it is that your customer is buying from you starts at home.

A division of ICI, manufacturing and selling industrial paints, had been remarkably successful in Britain but very unsuccessful in selling abroad. Its product was superior to the local ones and it afforded significant value in its protective qualities and fire-proofing. So why was its product doing badly? Marketing analysis –

27

of the domestic situation – revealed that although the product-claims had always been based on its protective qualities and fire-proofing, the product had two other important qualities: ICI produced the widest range of colours on the market, and were able to guarantee almost 100 per cent availability. These were the very things which could not be provided under sales arrangements in the majority of ICI's foreign markets.

A sound reason for searching for markets in other countries is to utilize existing capacity and know-how or to justify longer production runs to maximize production efficiency. The typical question asked by the company involved in international marketing is: 'What foreign markets may exist for the skills we possess, either exactly as they are now or reasonably adapted?'

This is, however, only the start of the road to growth.

2.5 Multinational, global and cross-cultural businesses

In the next stage in a company's international growth, it finds itself dealing with many countries. Not only is the marketing department organized in such a way as to function across national boundaries, but manufacturing plants and management teams may also come to be located in several countries. Whereas international marketing tends to imply that trade develops from a home base, multinational marketing describes a situation where there are several bases, and where each country or region (often acting semi-autonomously within broad corporate objectives) may market different products. Unilever is a good example. It markets different products in Africa from those it markets in Europe, though it also markets some products simultaneously in several regions or countries. In some parts of the world, it uses different brand names for the same product, in other parts of the world it uses one familiar name for quite different products.

Global marketing is the next step up from international market-ing. It treats the world more or less as one unit. A company involved in international marketing may still consider itself to be producing goods or services principally for a domestic market, with orders from abroad being seen as a useful and lucrative additional source of income. With global marketing, a company will have moved to considering the whole of the world as its market. The product may be manufactured at several locations, but each of these locations will be supported by a worldwide programme of research and communications. The intention is to flatten, as far as possible, the

28

cultural differences between nations. The famous Coca Cola television and film campaign around the theme of 'It's the real thing' is a good illustration of the global marketer's mentality: the campaign featured a musical score chosen for international appeal and acceptability; the visual was the same wherever you saw the advertisement (the models were deliberately chosen from several different ethnic backgrounds); none of the actors said anything of course, but the written communication at the end of the ad was in the language appropriate for the country. So, while the international marketing operation seeks to build on a domestic model, the gobal marketing operation takes the world as a whole as its basic building block.

Until recently, global marketing has been seen as the pinnacle of development in terms of the internationalization of a company. Now, however, it is becoming increasingly accepted that there is a step beyond global marketing. This is called trans-national or cross-cultural marketing.

Cross-cultural marketing is a step beyond global marketing. It takes what it sees as a global product or service, and tries to tailor the whole chain of marketing effort in a way that is highly sensitive to the cultural differences between countries and indeed between regions.

Economies of scale are on the side of the global marketeer, but greater penetration is on the side of the cross-cultural marketer. The challenge of the future will be whether it is possible to combine the insights and strengths of global marketing with those of cross-cultural marketing.

2.6 Small businesses

The successful small business is a prime example of a marketing-oriented business, for a very simple reason: perhaps 95 per cent of the small businesses that fail do so for a basic marketing reason. People working on their own find it difficult to undertake the analysis that a large company would require before entering a new market. Indeed, the inclination may be lacking. The subsequent failure is usually for one of two reasons:

1   the product (or the particular quality of product or service) was not required, or
2   if it was required, it was not required at a price that justified the time involved.

Small businesses are remarkably similar to the service industry. Their major resource is people. The capacity to expand is limited by the capacity of people to multiply their own efforts because of the lack of funds to employ more people. In the early days at least, personal qualities tend to dominate, even where the final product is from a machine. The very personal qualities of reliability, punctuality and honesty are often the reasons why people buy from a small firm rather than a large one. The standards set by the owner-entrepreneur are important too – things such as final quality, after-sales service, care and attention – all these things can be instilled into operatives and carefully monitored in a small business.

However, those very qualities lead to two big problems:

1   the time to contemplate and plan for growth is severely limited by the need to be continually involved in the setting and maintenance of standards in the business
2   growth takes place beyond the capability of the owners to monitor the kind of performance that caused them to grow.

How often do you hear, 'Now they've got big, they don't seem to bother any more'? Often there is a failure to appreciate what it is that attracts customers to the business: all too frequently, owners of small businesses just do not realize exactly what satisfactions their customers are getting from the total service they provide. Consequently, when the business grows, incorrect priorities are assigned and senior people tend to become involved in, say, finance – to the neglect of the very skills and qualities that made the company grow.

Certainly, the vast majority of ladies' hairdressers in the country regard themselves as skilled craftspeople and recruit staff on that basis, but the research quoted earlier shows that women do not see the great majority of hairdressers in that light at all. When salon owners employ artistic directors who behave like prima donnas, they may be throwing the baby out with the bath-water. They may be emphasizing a production quality which their customers do not buy, in place of a very different one of pleasant service, which they do buy. Yet other hairdressers may succeed simply because they do employ talented prima donnas. The secret in all cases is to *know your market*. Often the sheer size of a big company enables mistakes and sheer bad practice to be overcome in the marketplace. This is not a factor which helps small businesses. The methods of many big companies would kill the small business. Many of the techniques of marketing may be beyond most small businesses, but the mentality or philosophy of marketing is absolutely vital for the small business. It needs constantly to analyze what it is that its customers buy from it, and to question every potential step in terms of the consequences for the business now and in the future.

2.7 Marketing for all

It isn't easy, as we have seen, to divide businesses into watertight compartments. It is easier to imagine that all businesses fall along a continuum. Some products that seem to be highly industrial, actually behave in ways that are similar to fairly frivolous consumer products. Others, clearly aimed at consumers in their own homes, have more in common with a nuclear reactor. In fact, an energy authority is far more likely to buy two nuclear reactors at a time than a householder is to buy two washing machines.

In Figure 1, an attempt has been made to illustrate this continuum. If your business fits the characteristics of the 'consumer' end of the spectrum, for example, it means that techniques commonly used in those areas will probably be right in your business. You may have thought that because you were selling, say, paint through builders' merchants to the building and decorating trades, you were primarily industrial. However, the fact that you have wholesale and retail channels; deal with an industry in which there are large numbers of small firms and effectively no national operators; and have few large customers among end-users means that you have to deal with the same kinds of problem that Heinz do when they sell baked beans.

One of the routine objections to marketing people is that they want to sell everything as though it were a can of baked beans. If, in fact, there are any such marketing people around, they must be very poor at their job. All problems are not capable of similar solutions: at least, not if we take the philosophy of marketing seriously. What good marketers will say is that a surprising number of different businesses look alike from a marketing point of view but, on the other hand, a surprising number of apparently similar businesses are quite different. For example, builders, doctors and farmers act in many ways just like householders: there are millions of them, they act individually or in small groups, they do not have separate buying functions (or only very few of them do) and the bulk of them work from home. So, all kinds of businesses have a great deal to learn from each other. Much of the knowledge we normally gather together under the heading of marketing is applicable to all kinds

Highly localized markets

Short life in use

Narrow product definition

Standardized product

Large no. potential customers

High frequency

Fashion content

Impulse

Standardized/Relatively cheap/Wide demand/Frequent purchase

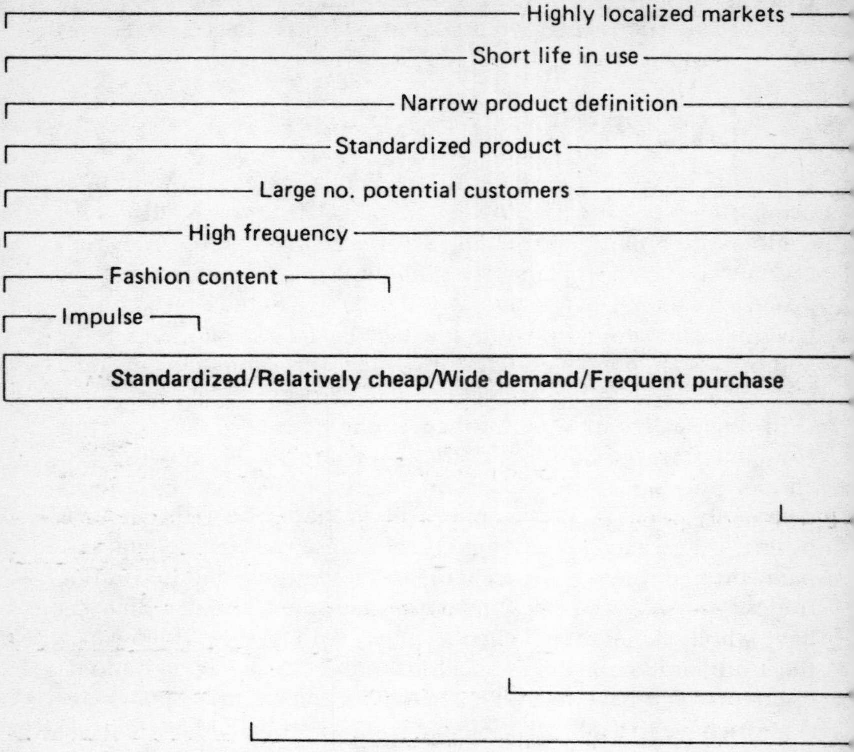

Typical marketing methods:

| Mass media | Consumer offers | Emphasis on packaging | Sales force calling on wholesalers/retailers | After-sales service |

Examples of typical industries:

| Toys Confectionery | Records | Luxury foods | Staple foods | Necessary consumer durables (e.g. cookers) | Luxury consumer durables |

Examples of problem fits:

| Consumable industrial supplies (e.g. electricity, stationery) | High-frequency ingredients and components | Basic bulk items (e.g. cement, fertilizers, chemicals) | Packaging machinery |

Figure 1   *The marketing progression*

(Note: Each of the attributes named is commonly assumed to have its opposite on the other side of the dividing line. For example, it is normally assumed that no industrial buying decision is ever made on impulse.)

Specialized/Relatively expensive/Narrow demand/Infrequent purchase

Alternative product uses Complexity of product 'Heaviness' of product

Buying decisions by group Direct contact buyer/seller

High unit cost

Derived demand

High cost of mistakes

Buying for stock

Rational buying motives

rature, ibitions, posia	Subsidized initial orders	Trade-ins as part of 'deal' price	High-level negotiations	Trade credit, leasing, export guarantees
mponents	Computer systems	Major plant		Factory buildings

| nestic | Domestic deep-freeze | Larder stock (cooking fat, dried fruit, etc.) | Private cars | Packaged holidays | Life assurance | Houses |

33

and sizes of businesses. That is the approach we will take in the rest of this book. Readers will profit from asking continually how appropriate any particular statement or example is to them.

2.8 Summary

Attempts to categorize industries are doomed to failure. Although attempts are frequently made, and there can be profit and use in such an exercise, the categorization of one's own business on any conventional lines will reveal how futile is the quest for definition.

There is, however, one use in such an exercise: it can help correlate techniques and methods of approach *between* product groups, as well as *for* products from other fields which share the same marketing characteristics. This will often show that industries, generally classified in one way, in fact behave more like a totally different kind of industry, and are amenable to similar treatment.

2.9 Checklist

1 Consumer markets
- distance from producer
- number of intermediaries
- frequency of use
- need to create and maintain customer loyalty
- buying decisions often highly subjective.

2 Consumer durables
- greater objectivity in purchasing
- more 'shopping around' to compare specifications, performance, price, etc.
- buying decision often has complex inter-relationships
- more likely to involve group decisions (eg, in the family).

3 Customer services
- domestic: applied to the home
- direct personal: one at a time to individuals
- public personal: used individually, but by means which are made available simultaneously to many people.

4 Industrial goods
- technology is not necessarily the best way to describe the market

34

- this is because the market varies from high-value but low-frequency to low-value but high-frequency ones
- direct contact between supplier and customer is more common
- demand is derived
- markets defined by benefits and by the time-span over which that benefit is obtained
- markets defined also by interdependence, that is, by being technically-linked
- selling efforts are affected by the degree of 'branding' or identification of the item.

5 Service industries
- sell to private individuals, companies and institutions
- offer benefits without a tangible product
- offer benefits which may produce a tangible result, though this may be several stages removed
- offer benefits that cannot be stored or kept for later use
- the most tangible part is often the people involved in providing the service
- industrial services:
  reduce costs
  improve profits
  promote or maintain efficiency
  provide welfare benefits to staff
  help companies to fulfil their legal obligations
- have the problem of how to value the time employed from the viewpoint of the customer.

6 Exporting
- attempts to see if there is a market abroad for products which have been produced essentially for a domestic market.

7 International marketing
- places as much emphasis on understanding, choosing and working in foreign markets as in domestic ones.

8 Multinational marketing
- products may be manufactured in and marketed from several different countries
- products may be marketed under different names; further, different products may be marketed under the same name in separate parts of the world

- often seeks completely different markets in different parts of the world.

9   Global marketing
- may manufacture products in and market products from several different countries, as well as seek different markets in different parts of the world, but its chief distinguishing characteristic is that it treats the world as one unit in its search for markets.

10 Cross-cultural marketing
- designs marketing effort to cope with the cultural differences between countries and regions.

11 All marketing across national boundaries
- may involve the same techniques as marketing domestically, but the solutions arrived at are likely to be radically different
- operates through different and more distant channels when compared to marketing within one's own country
- searches for markets in which existing skills and capacities can be used, or for which they can be adapted.

12 Small businesses
- have a higher failure rate, principally due to insufficient demand at the price required to make a reasonable profit
- find it difficult to cope with the organizational problems created by growth
- find it difficult to maintain quality and standards as they grow.

3

How do customers decide what they will buy?

The sole purpose of production is consumption. And a business has only costs until it has customers. So any business ought to know as much as possible about its customers, who often behave in ways that are quite different from those in which their suppliers think they behave.

There are some generalizations which can be made about the way in which customers decide to buy. These are the principal concern of this chapter, which will also indicate how some techniques of understanding customer behaviour can be applied to a particular product or service.

Clearly, people behave differently when circumstances change, and we would expect customers to change buying behaviour too. However, most people are confronted with very different kinds of buying problems even when the situations appear very similar. For example, decisions about a choice of washing machine have certain similarities to decisions about the choice of washing powder to use in it, but the decisions are clearly of different value. The choice process will therefore be different. Again, the choice of location for a new factory is different from the choice between alternative production processes, or between competing suppliers of paint for a new factory. So it becomes difficult to see that there are any similarities at all in buying decisions.

However, some distinctions are more important than others. In marketing, the most important distinctions are between the very broadest categories: consumers and industrial buyers. By and large, decisions about purchasing services involve the same sorts of considerations as industrial products or consumer durables. There are also a few special categories, such as pharmaceuticals, which we will consider in due course.

3.1 Consumer purchases

Some conventional descriptions of consumer markets indicate a belief that consumers are not very rational. However, buying decisions are usually made according to a sequence that can be understood, though they are made at a very low level of consciousness. Indeed, some appear to be taken with no thought at all. Certain buying decisions seem to revolve around the question of finance – can the product be afforded; should money be spent on one product or on another; which product offers better value for money; and so on. Other buying decisions involve considerations of product performance, belief, fashion, 'fit' (eg, 'will it match my curtains?'), etc. Yet other decisions are those which are inherently more interesting as decisions: deciding on the family's new colour television is likely to rank far higher as an interesting decision, than which brand of butter to buy. Obviously, some decisions are highly complex, involving a good deal of logical analysis and considerable financial risk – in fact, some personal buying decisions carry far more risk than is involved in a great many decisions made in industry.

However, only very few buying decisions in the consumer market form true parallels to industrial buying decisions. Such decisions are the ones that most clearly involve decisions by a buying unit (such as a family) rather than an individual. Generally, individuals do not have the time for the buying process that groups and industrial purchasers need to go through. Just think about all the decisions that a householder has to take every day – decisions about how best to use; the amount of money to be spent; what to buy for immediate use: what to cook today; what to cook for stock; and so on. If each of these decisions was a mathematical problem which needed to be run through, every home would need a computer, and a pretty powerful one at that. Every brain is a supercomputer, of course, and what is more it copes with problem-solving on the basis of far less information. A computer would find that there was too little usable information, and an enormous number of decisions in any case. If a computer is likely to blow a fuse or two, what about the poor householder?

Without a great deal of conscious thought on any particular decision, he or she arrives at methods of decision-making which make life a little more tolerable. Compare the following with your own behaviour in other contexts.

First, the householder allows habit to take over wherever

possible. Watch someone in a supermarket. It is remarkable how often their arms seem to reach out almost automatically. These habits can become so strong that new information is not merely rejected, it is totally ignored: you always buy Typhoo Tea; what does it matter that PG Tips have 3p off this week? Or maybe you do notice but are pulled back by the strength of the habits of others in the family. Habits can affect buying decisions at the level of the shopper, as well as the level of the constraints placed upon the shopper by the habits of others on whose behalf he or she shops. This second level, of course, involves slightly more thought than the first level.

Next, the householder allows his or her brain to make what can be called 'maps of available options'. Some trigger pulls the appropriate map to the forefront of the mind and selection takes place.

Let's say you are driving along, referring to an old road map, and discover that the road you wanted to take has now been built over, or become a one-way road, or terribly crowded due to changed conditions. What do you do? You make a note of the changed conditions mentally or perhaps on the map itself. A similar thing happens with these option-maps which we all use for making decisions. The maps are very susceptible to outside influences. New pressures can disturb them. A price reduction might trigger off the thought that the product is very good but normally too expensive. This new information reshuffles the information in one's head and quickly produces a new map. There may be a dozen other items on the map, but they may all pale into insignificance compared with this new relationship of price to quality. This factor also helps to explain some of the strange phenomena which occur in consumer markets.

The third little trick used by the householder in helping to lighten the load of decision-making is that decisions are grouped into 'families' on the basis of links between products. For example, buying a turkey involves a near automatic purchase of stuffing, sausage meat, peas, gravy browning, potatoes and roasting fat. Eggs and bacon similarly go together in Western countries. A standard razor needs blades. A fountain pen needs ink. Such decision-clusters are, to a certain extent, habit-decisions. They are also a sort of map. But they are slightly different, and all three are used to ease the burden of decision-making. The problem is that while these make the task of decision-making easier for the consumer, they make the task of promotion more difficult for the marketer.

Ideally, marketers need to isolate which of these kinds of mental tricks applies to decisions relating to their particular products. Then they need to ask: is that the sort of mental trick which is reachable by promotion, advertising and the rest? Does it respond to rapid efforts (such as money off) or does it need the slow, steady drip of mass media messages over a long period? Much promotion aimed at the consumer market is based on a naîve belief that all consumers react to particular stimuli in similar ways and that the buyer cares about the product as much as the producer does.

There was a time not so long ago when marketeers used to compare tea to oxygen. If people are stopped in the street and asked what is the most important thing in their life, they will give answers such as 'the family', 'love', 'work', 'God', and so on. No one will say 'oxygen', because no one thinks about it. Similarly, if you ask the people on the street about the most important product in their lives, very few will say tea, or eggs, or butter, or sugar or any other staple item. All these are classic examples of products which have become as essential as air, and to which we assign the same degree of conscious thought.

Yet the 11 items that grocers know are the great draw-lines to their store are included in this list of products about which we don't think a great deal. This leads us to think about a new kind of cluster. These 11 classic everyday items are of a sort on which the householder wants to spend as little effort as possible. So decisions about these become clustered into one, and the householder looks for a shop to which he or she can trust these habits. The decision about which shop to buy from at a particular time is crucial. It channels a host of other decisions. That is one of the reasons why most people shop at different stores even when they may all supply the same range of goods. They go to one shop for its price, another for range, yet another for quality, one out of habit, one for convenience and one for 'last resort purchases' (such as when one unexpectedly needs more of something than one had planned, or outside normal shopping hours). The more rational householder tries to group these decisions further, so that shopping hours are optimized.

Some kinds of decisions, as we have seen, are left to others. When one goes into a public house and asks for a pint of beer, it is very seldom that one is asked what brand one wishes to have. At the most, the only question will be about price (expressed in terms of 'Best?'). In cases like this, the brand has in effect been chosen by entering the particular outlet. In fact, there is a great deal of

40

evidence that there is no conscious brand decision involved in choosing an outlet: the motorist is more likely to need a tankful of petrol than a tankful of BP petrol. The householder asks for a pound of apples; the greengrocer asks whether he or she wants cooking apples or eating apples and then which kind. It is the grocer who has chosen between competing suppliers of the same kind of apple with different qualities, sizes and prices. Such decisions have, in effect, been delegated by us to the company or individual that controls the outlet. In each of these cases, the physical position of the pub or petrol station, and its attractiveness, will be prime influences on the purchasing decision.

On the other hand, there isn't much point in going into a well-sited, attractive confectionary outlet and asking for a 'bar of chocolate' or 'a packet of cigarettes': a brand name is clearly required. It is in this sort of decision that buying behaviour may be more understandably described, even though 'irrational' or impulsive behaviour is only to be expected from time to time – as when you feel like having a Mars bar or Lyons Kunzle Cake, and if that isn't available, you may not want anything else at all. Generally, however, purchasing behaviour does follow certain steps in more or less comprehensible order.

3.2 Purchasing behaviour

Marketing knows few laws, though there are many generalizations – and some of them are helpful. This isn't surprising. Experience gives rise to many observations of consumer behaviour and many of them are at variance with the ways in which companies approach the sale of their products. Although the bulk of these observations comes from consumer fields, they are applicable to almost any kind of repeat-purchase item.

Many products, which appear to be aimed at middle- to upper-income families, are actually bought by much lower-income groups. The reasons are often to be found in the fact that the lower down the socio-economic scale the measurement is taken, the more likely there are to be several wage-earners in the family. They are less likely to have regular calls on their income (like mortgages, insurance policies, children's education) and thus have a higher level of discretionary income (the economists' term for cash available for spending). Small families may be heavier consumers than larger ones. Small companies often buy more of a given product than larger ones. As we shall see later, the use of standard classifications is a valuable tool in defining markets and deciding which position a company might adopt in the marketplace, but it should not be followed too slavishly: Pareto's Law applies again (see page 12), and a small proportion of customers will probably account for a high proportion of turnover and profit. Analysis in terms such as heavy, medium and light users is a worthwhile addition to other kinds of classification, even where it does not replace them completely. These terms can be particularly useful when deciding on the media to use to contact a target audience. Many consumer product companies have been alarmed to discover that heavy viewing of television and high rates of buying of their products do not necessarily go together.

In consumer markets, the realization that the more usual standard classifications of age, sex, class, family size and family life cycle may not distinguish buyers sufficiently has led to a search for other useful categories. One of the more important is 'psychographics' of life-style research. As the name implies, this is an attempt to discover whether there are psychological characteristics that link people together irrespective of their age, sex or class. Obviously, in almost all kinds of buying situations, there are some people who are more adventurous than others, those who tend to be leaders of fashion, whether it be in clothes, hair-styles, cars or new machinery. Any manufacturer of the more expensive kinds of office equipment will be aware that there are many companies who are the first to have the latest computers, the first with vending machines, the first with water fountains – and the desire to be a leader often transcends economic considerations. Researchers have distinguished five categories of people, and the proportion of relevant people who fall into them:

Category	per cent
Innovators	2.5
Early adopters	13.5
Early majority	34
Late majority	34
Laggards	16

Marketing to each of these categories clearly calls for different approaches: an approach which will be successful with the innovators will highlight its novelty; this is precisely the sort of approach which will turn off each of the other categories of people.

3.3 Brand loyalty

One of the favourite phrases in marketing is 'brand loyalty'. The uninitiated may imagine that this refers to unswerving or total adherence to one brand or company, but it doesn't take much thought to see that this almost never happens in real life. Brand loyalty simply means, at best, the brand to which a particular individual or group returns most often. Many buyers purchase from more than one company, and often in a reasonably short period. What are often seen as non-buyers are, in reality, infrequent buyers. The most successful approach to improving market position will often come from upgrading infrequent users to more regular buyers and this is usually far easier than the attempt to switch non-users to users.

Total quality management helps to create brand loyalty, as in the case of the Marks and Spencer 'St Michael' brand. But people who set out to create brand loyalty often set their sights too low. Table 1 shows why. Householder A may not be perceived as brand-loyal because he or she switches about with abandon – but buys Sugar Puffs five times in ten weeks. Householder B is the opposite; he or she is absolutely brand-loyal even though he or she only buys two packets of Sugar Puffs. Householder C is neither brand-loyal to Sugar Puffs nor a regular buyer – but does buy more than the brand-loyal householder. Householder D is a non-buyer of Sugar Puffs. He or she is the only person who is worth less to Sugar Puffs than the brand-loyal householder! Clearly, it would be better to make householder B buy with greater frequency even if he or she also bought some other breakfast cereals at the same time.

Table 1   *Examples of buying frequency*

House- wives	Week 1	2	3	4	5	6	7	8	9	10
A	SP	R	SP	SW	SP	PW	SP	R	SP	PW
B	SP	-	-	-	-	-	SP	-	-	-
C	R	SP	-	PW	R	SP	PW	SW	-	SP
D	R	R	SW	R	SW	SW	PW	R	R	SW

SP = Sugar Puffs   SW = Shredded Wheat
R = Ricicles   PW = Puffed Wheat

A brand of instant coffee, searching for a form of consumer promotion that would build brand loyalty, asked a marketing company to organize a scheme. A great deal of research information was supplied, which showed clearly that both the frequency of buying and the quantity bought at each purchase were significantly lower than was the case for its main competitor. If a brand-loyalty exercise had been pursued, the brand might have levelled off at something close to the rate of sale at that time. Instead, by aiming for increased usage, sales were increased significantly. Lack of loyal customers is often seen as an affront, but what makes the till ring is the *quantity* of your products that your customers – loyal or disloyal – buy.

In this context, the importance of buying for stock is worth understanding. This is an area where consumer and industrial purchasing are similar. Not much grocery and industrial purchase is for immediate use. By far the greatest number of grocery items are bought to release or replace a similar item from stock. This is a more or less conscious decision: 'I am going to make a meat pie for dinner today and there is one tin of stewing steak in the cupboard – better get another one to replace the one I am going to use'; 'flour is a bit low – better get another bag'. Marketing efforts aimed at increasing *consumption* result in the reduction of stock and thus in motivating buying.

Over a wide range of goods and buying situations, the householder acts in precisely the same way as a retailer. Therefore, awareness of the level of larder stock and the average length of replacement time is as important to a manufacturer of grocery items as it is to a supplier of repeat components to industry. Changes in those levels will mean new levels of sale. One of the most significant features in times of economic recession is a reduction in industrial, consumer and retail stock levels, not necessarily associated with a change in patterns of use. Just as the householder reduces his or her larder stock cover from two tins of meat to one, retailers may find themselves having to reduce their stock cover from three weeks to two.

So one major task of marketing is to stimulate usage as well as purchase. Sales can be successfully stimulated by promoting new uses: Kelloggs' emphasis on recipes which included cornflakes added to the standard quantity consumed at breakfast. Similarly, Weetabix extended sales of the product by promoting summer use as well as the more usual winter consumption. Carbonless copy-papers moved beyond order forms into accountancy forms, computer print-outs and other systems' uses. Existing users normally constitute the soft underbelly of any market. A non-buyer is less likely to change to a new product; but a person who already knows and appreciates the quality and performance of a product is more likely (other things being equal) to use more of a product.

Research conducted on behalf of tea-producing countries has shown that the best potential markets for their produce are existing markets and present buyers, rather than new buyers. It is always something of a gamble to try to approach new buyers. A person who already drinks three cups of tea a day is an easier prospect for an extra cup than someone who drinks three cups of coffee a day: starting to take one cup of tea a day may require efforts to change the habits of a lifetime, and may involve disruption of the family routine.

In other words, from what we have learnt so far about buying behaviour, we can take the following steps, and in this order, if we wish to increase sales systematically:

1 Persuade existing users to buy more often
2 Persuade them to use more of the product
3 Turn occasional users into regular buyers
4 Increase their frequency of purchase
5 Convince them that they should use more
6 Increase brand loyalty
7 Seek new users from the total non-user market.

However, all this does rather pre-suppose that there is a single dominant buying influence over items that are purchased fairly frequently. This is seldom the case in the next kind of market which we are going to look at.

3.4 Industrial buying

It is in this sphere that the most revealing discoveries about buying behaviour have been made over the last two decades. Successive pieces of industry-wide research, backed up by product-specific investigations, have shown that there is a clear separation between deciding what to buy and placing the actual order. Over a considerable part of industry, companies had been concentrating their efforts on order-placers without realizing that the people who _determined_ what to order were quite different, and that it was much more difficult to gain access to them.

The great bulk of industrial buying is dictated by a group

decision-making process with final decisions about the supplier most frequently being taken at chief executive or board level. The decision-making group, as distinct from the person who places an order, is so important that it has become commonplace to refer to it as the DMU (Decision-Making Unit).

Unlike many buying decisions by consumers, a great deal of industrial purchasing involves a complex operation in which a number of people are likely to be concerned in a number of defined stages. A fairly typical pattern is for senior management to commission a thorough examination, say, of a new process, a piece of replacement equipment, or a trial of new components. A project team or some kind of sub-committee under a technically qualified person (or with significant contributions from such a person) will be set up and will consider literature and specifications, visit exhibitions, study advertisements and possibly even visit other firms using the product or process. It will make recommendations to the board as a whole and a decision will be taken at that level. It is exceedingly rare for the chief executive to actually place an order: that process will be delegated. However, it is also extremely rare for purchasing managers to have discretionary limits allowing them to change supplier or specification without reference to some other authority.

Of course, the process varies according to the product or service being considered, the size of the company, and often the position of the managers involved. Certain industries have conventional patterns of behaviour which produce other sequences of buying decision-making. Nevertheless, decisions involving major capital items are likely to be taken at the highest levels. The chief executive, the board as a whole or individual directors will make the decision to buy in principle, possibly leaving the detailed consideration and evaluation to department managers. Final decisions will go back to where the first decision was taken. (Needless to say, more delegation occurs in larger companies than in smaller ones: there are simply more people, and more who can be trusted with important decisions which involve considerable risk.)

The buying of materials is the only significant area which is still within the direct control of the purchasing manager. Typically, the choice of material is made at a very senior level, but the choice of supplying company is left to the buyer. Components are treated in a similar way.

Obviously, any company should consider how relevant these findings are to their area of business. Research does tend to deal in averages, and it is always possible for 95 per cent of a business to act one way and for the companies making up the other five per cent to behave differently, not only from the 95 per cent but also among themselves. If your company's major buyers are located within the five per cent, it is not necessarily much help to know how the 95 per cent behave.

However, the realization that so much of British sales effort has been misdirected for so long may have important lessons for any business. There is an enormous number of cases where a firm has ceased to call on purchasing managers (or reduced the frequency of its calls) without any consequent loss of sales. This is also dramatic confirmation of the automatic nature of a good deal of industrial purchasing. Industrial buyers, like domestic consumers, may use habit for making decisions as routine as possible.

Another important factor arising from the concept of the DMU is that the people who have to be influenced may be too widely dispersed throughout an organization to be reachable by sales-people. They may also include people who traditionally do not see representatives. This frequently produces a case for forms of advertising which otherwise would appear to be unjustified.

In the last chapter, we demonstrated the difference and overlap between industrial buying and consumer buying (see pages 32-3). At the right-hand end of the scale – the 'heavy' end of industrial marketing – much more considered decisions will be taken. Complex equations may be operated, advanced decision theory may well be involved, and tendering comes into its own. Any of these methods might well be used anywhere else along the scale – for example, institutional canteens adopt tendering as a way of life, often to the apparent exclusion of considerations of quality.

3.5 Models of buyer behaviour

Research in this field is most interesting. However, no systematic ways of understanding buyer behaviour have been discovered yet, so the research merely tends to confirm that buyer behaviour can be very complex and is influenced by many variables. The models of buyer behaviour that have been developed are therefore useful in describing that behaviour, but are useless for helping us predict how people are going to behave. However, understanding the models does have one important use: it can enable us very carefully to consider our actions and the possible reactions to them.

One of the most elementary of such models is the 'Black Box

Figure 2   *The Black Box model*

model' (Figure 2). On the left are the various stimuli and on the right are the various observable responses possible. Stimuli include internal ones induced by physiological needs such as food, warmth and protection, as well as external stimuli such as the effect of family, friends, media, promotional offers, etc. The output variables are relatively easy to measure. On the other hand, the input variables are rather difficult to measure – some of them may even be immeasurable.

Equally difficult to measure are the contents of the Black Box and what goes on inside it, since these are entirely individual and personal. The inclusion of a Black Box in any model is an admission that 'something is going on here, but we don't know what it is'. To relate the Black Box to what we have already discussed, the Black Box doesn't have much of a place in the objective decision-making, regarding purchases of the sort one finds in industrial markets.

One of the best known and most widely accepted models of buyer behaviour is the Howard-Sheth model. A simplified version of the model is shown in Figure 3. The Black Box is found here disguised as 'Hypothetical Constructs'. In other words, the model tells us that we don't know how individuals see and receive stimuli, and we don't know how they construct them into a learned behaviour pattern which produces buying responses. The full version of the model proposes external stimuli additional to the perception and learning elements. These include how important the purchase is to prospects, their financial position, the socio-economic class to which they belong, and the influences that class imposes. The full model is detailed, with considerable attention being given to each of the terms used in the simplified version of the diagram in Figure 3.

It is worth spelling out the input and output variables of the Howard-Sheth model a little more fully. The stimuli side has social as well as commercial inputs. Social inputs arrive via the family, peer groups, reference groups and the dictates of one's socio-economic class. Commercial inputs include price, availability, service, etc. However, they may be 'significative' or 'symbolic'. 'Significative' inputs are the actual attributes of the product in the

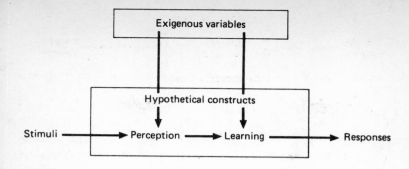

Figure 3   *Simplified Howard-Sheth model*

way it is marketed and presented to customers. 'Symbolic' inputs are the ways in which attributes and concepts are generated by the supplier and communicated to customers – for example, through advertising, brand image, corporate identity, etc.

The 'output' stages of the Howard-Sheth model are shown in Figure 4. Notice the number of feedback loops, which indicates a hierarchy of effects. For example, the producer or marketer somehow has too succeed first of all in persuading you that a product you have never used earlier may be suitable for you. After you become interested, any knowledge you pick up about the product is fed into what might be described as a 'bank' of information about the product category. Comparisons are then made against target specifications, competitive claims and performances, knowledge of availability, etc. As a result of that comparative examination, you form an attitude towards the product which may create either a negative or positive intent. One

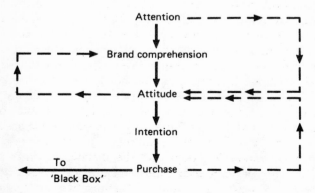

Figure 4   *Output stages of Howard-Sheth model*

49

possible response may be to include the product on a mental list of those from which a final purchase might be made. Eventually, you may decide to purchase the product.

If you decide to buy it at some stage, you can then judge its performance. Your attitude towards the product and its provider will change or be confirmed, and you can use your experience of the product to make further decisions about possible purchases from that source. A product may become recognized as 'my brand'. Alternatively, it may become a product, brand or manufacturer to which you become very resistant.

A very similar model is proposed by Engel, Kollat and Blackwell. Again, reduced to its simplest form, it is based upon five groups of variables (Figure 5). The 'input information' stage begins once a problem or need is recognized. A prospect generally starts with stored information and/or a set of perceptions, and reviews these before going any further. If this produces strong, positive inputs, prospects tend to search for products or suppliers capable of confirming the buying hypothesis they have formed. If the information is insufficient, a search begins for the purpose of filling the gaps. From here on, the stages of Figure 5 resemble those of Figure 3.

At the 'decision process' stage, alternatives are critically assessed and a choice made. 'Product brand evaluations' involve 'testing' the criteria used in the previous stage against our attitudes and beliefs and the intentions we may have for the product in use. The major 'general motivating influences' are our individual motives, personality and lifestyle, and the 'degree of normative compliance' involved.

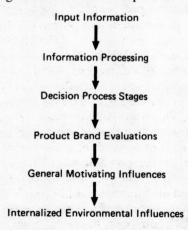

Figure 5 *The Engel, Kollatt and Blackwell variables*

'Degree of normative compliance' is an important concept, which can be simply explained as the degree to which individuals comply with what are perceived to be the norms of their group. We all know people who are rebels in their social group, or indifferent to it, or aspire to leadership of it. The results of normative compliance can be seen in fashion and the notion of 'keeping up with the Joneses'.

The 'internalized environmental influences' featured in the Engel, Kollat and Blackwell model, include cultural norms, and those derived from our reference group (often family or friends, through whose eyes we measure ourselves).

A criticism of both the models we have discussed so far is that they leave out any consideration of the role of the manufacturing or marketing company. The Nicosia model (Figure 6, page 52) actually begins with the firm. The analysis in this model is similar to those in the previous two models. The differences are that:

1 buying is seen as an adaptive process in that the actions of one party may influence those of the other, and
2 purchasing does not result directly from attitudes formed, since other influences may also be important.

Most choices involve an element of compromise. This involves an element of disturbance, because we have had to compromise our standards in some way. We seek to justify our compromise to ourselves, so that we may feel more comfortable with the decision we have taken. The lady who has just bought a dress in a sale may be unable to resist looking in all the other sale windows to see if she could have bought it cheaper. Naturally, she hopes she cannot find a cheaper version. If she does, she may well try to justify the purchase: 'Perhaps it is not my size', 'It looks dirty', 'I prefer the sales assistants where I bought it'. As an old, once-popular song used to say: 'Accentuate the positive, eliminate the negative'. In other words, we reduce our inner conflicts by concentrating on the positive elements in our choice, and on the negative aspects of the rejected purchase. This is why an important function of advertising is to reassure customers that they made the right choice.

We can all recognize the need for such reassurance in our own behaviour, say, after the purchase of a car – when we tend to scrutinize car advertisments even more than we did before the purchase! This kind of disturbance is likely to be highest when the risk is greatest and the opportunity to buy again is relatively distant. Purchase of capital equipment, houses and major consumer durables is therefore subject to extensive pre-purchase examination.

51

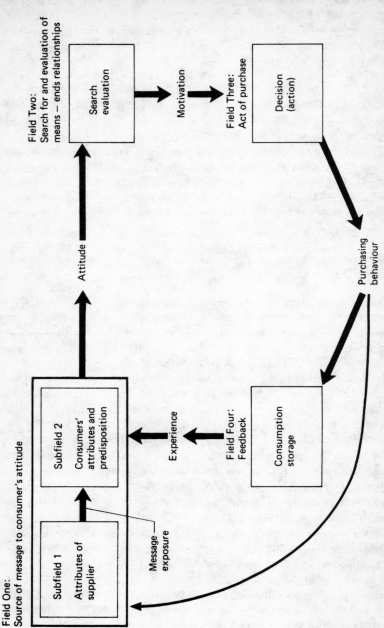

Figure 6 *Nicosia model of consumer behaviour*

52

We will look in a moment at one final, very simplified, model of the buying process. But, before we do so, it is worth discussing a major piece of work into attitudes and beliefs: Fishbein's theory. This has two key elements:

AO   or the attitude towards an object, and
A act   or the attitude towards performing a specific activity.

According to Fishbein, each of these is a function of several factors: the strength with which beliefs are held about an object, brand or activity; how those beliefs are evaluated; and how many beliefs there are about the object or activity. Imagine we take a set of beliefs about a camera, then ask respondents to assign scores to the importance of those attributes. Each is then asked to give an evaluation score about the belief (using a technique known as 'semantic scaling' which is, broadly, a scale ranging from 'very good' to 'very bad'. Normally, five or seven points are used, with the central point representing a 'neither good nor bad' neutral opinion). The scores for 'importance' and 'evaluation' are then multiplied together to give a final attribute score. Table 2 gives an example.

Table 2   *Attribute scores for a camera*

Attribute	Importance	Evaluation	$I \times E$
35mm	1	1	1
Coupled exposure metre	1	1	1
Automatic mode	4	3	12
Interchangeable lens	2	2	4
			18

In this analysis, low scores are the more favourable. A total score of 18 is very favourable (compared with what the maximum could be) but it is very clear that a 35mm camera with a coupled exposure meter is the prime requirement. The interchangeable lens would be quite nice but perhaps does not justify the cost for the limited use the buyer might get out of it.

However, the attitude towards a 35mm, coupled-exposure-meter camera will be conditioned by your attitude towards photography. To someone with little or no knowledge or experience, an automatic mode camera might have far greater desirability.

Thus Fishbein's theory has several important consequences for marketing:

- To change the attitude towards a product, it may first be necessary to change the attitude towards the activity it represents. The detergent that advertised 'Washday white without washday red' simply drew attention to the fact that handwashing clothes *could* cause red hands, even though the product claim was emphatically that it wouldn't!
- Changing purchasing behaviour requires the changing of beliefs about the product – although this is seldom easy to do and even more difficult to achieve quickly.
- It may be necessary to change the way in which the beliefs are evaluated. The desirability of a new airport differs dramatically between householders and local shopkeepers. Harmony of interest could possibly be achieved by stressing the benefits to the community from the increased trade the new airport will bring. Similarly, the use of fully automatic cameras has quite dramatically changed the way multi-mode cameras are evaluated by keen hobby photographers.

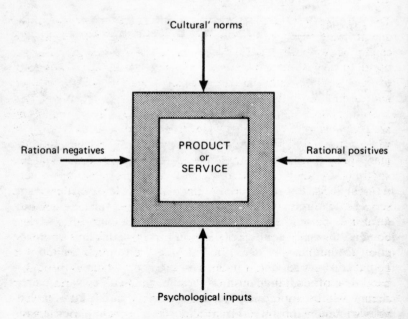

Figure 7 *Simplified buying model*

3.6 A simplified model of buyer behaviour

Many purchasers consider the positives and negatives very carefully before making a purchase (see Figure 7). Industrial buyers may have to arrive at a formula for dealing with the same performance at different prices; with different delivery dates; and with different levels of service. They may also have to take into account the supplier's reputation and experience; the terms on which the purchase is to be financed; plus a number of less objective but highly important factors. They may, therefore, move marginally into the psychological and normative areas.

Marketers of FMCG will be involved primarily with the psychological inputs and the effects of cultural norms, but they will also consider rational factors. The big difference is that high frequency of items purchased means that detailed consideration will not occur every time, and the purchasing decision will be relegated to the habit area as rapidly as possible until some new information (or new product) comes along to challenge it.

3.7 Changes in buyer behaviour

The purpose of this section is to draw attention to buying processes and attitudes that may seem somewhat surprising at first sight. We cannot be comprehensive in the course of this short chapter, but it is useful to suggest that all kinds of buying behaviour can be reduced to two simple umbrella categories. (The exceptions will be addressed later in the book.)

Some people make conscious decisions nearly all the time. They are probably very difficult to live with and they would certainly be wise to stay out of supermarkets. There are probably just about as many people who never take a really considered decision about anything. Neither case is normal. Most people make some very serious decisions some of the time about some products and services. Serious decisions that are obvious include: house, furniture, cars, certain kinds of clothing. Others are far less obvious. Often a great deal of the most serious consideration will be given to the change from a 'habit' brand to another, which it is hoped will become a new habit. Householders often go through a good deal of mental anguish on these occasions, wondering if the change will be appreciated by the rest of the family. It is a well-known phenomenon in food marketing for a householder to change a brand without saying so. If no comment occurs, he or she will go on buying the new product. When the householder is really sure everything is as it should be, then he or she will announce the change. Then it is relegated back to a habit. On the other hand, if the change is noticed, the householder's reaction is often to deny that any change has been made and quickly return to the usual product.

No one is obliged to be either consistent or logical when buying things. We do not divide our lives simply into work and leisure. The habits of leisure may be carried over into work, and vice versa. The industrialist taking an apparently rational and logical decision when considering whether to buy your product may call in at the tobacconists on his or her way home and take a couple of habit decisions. Even people who make conscious decisions most of the time often behave in a totally different way in another aspect of their lives; for example, they may be quite extravagant in connection with a hobby. We all have our blind spots. The managing director who subjects every other buying decision to computer analysis may behave completely self-indulgently when it comes to decorating his or her office. Symptomatic of this is the fact that large company boards often spend a considerable amount of time on the decision about which private cars the company will buy, yet delegate decisions about commercial vehicles!

It should be clear by now that buyers do not optimize their decisions only, or even primarily, in cash terms. For example, a considerable proportion of householders have switched from cheaper 'packet teas' to more expensive tea bags, which offer tea that is less satisfactory in terms of its strength! It must be the case that they value convenience more than they care about buying at the cheapest rate consistent with acceptable quality. In other words, customers seek to optimize their satisfactions: convenience rates so high with these householders that they change the old considerations of quality. We marketers therefore need to discover what is the hierarchy of satisfaction sought by buyers. A good deal of available research tells us that one of the satisfactions sought by many people is that of an easier life – easier not only in terms of convenience products but also in terms of adopting little mental 'dodges' that enable a great deal of complexity to be reduced in everyday life.

3.8 Summary

Buying behaviour is of varying sorts, but can be thought of as a progression. On the one hand, we can place those decisions which are impulsive and habitual. On the other, we can place decisions which are taken with rational, deliberate choice, perhaps involving others in group decision-making. Between these two types of behaviour is an enormous range, with the amount of conscious thought exercised on the purchase decision being dependent on the importance of the product or service. For most people, life is a mixture of both sorts of decisions.

From a marketing viewpoint, one should invest most in trying to reach those sectors of the market where the number of users and the amount they use the product is highest. What matters is not loyalty, but frequency and amount of use.

3.9 Checklist

1 Consumer purchases
- buyers tend to reduce as much buying activity as they can to the level of habit. 'Brain maps', and clustering 'families' of decisions together, are two other devices we use to simplify the nervous strain of making purchase decisions
- purchase decisions are also delegated to others, sometimes wholly and directly, and sometimes partially and indirectly
- buying for stock is important in every area of business, including domestic purchases.

2 Purchasing behaviour
- people do not always buy in the way we think they might
- some customers are more valuable than others (Pareto's Law)
- psychographic research indicates patterns of living (life-style) that frame purchasing decisions
- brand loyalty matters only at acceptable levels of sale.

3 To improve sales
- get existing buyers to buy more often
- persuade them to buy more
- turn occasional users into more regular ones
- persuade them to increase the frequency of their purchases
- persuade them to buy more at a time
- aim for brand loyalty
- seek new users from among the wide world of those who do not use the product or service at present
- seek new opportunities.

4   Industrial buying
- orders are placed by an individual, but the decision to do so is made by a group (the Decision Making Unit) which may not include that individual
- there may be only one ultimate decision-maker, but a number of influences are involved
- it is seldom possible for any salesforce to establish face-to-face contact with the members of the DMU.

5   Models of buyer behaviour
- customers are not always interested in seeking the cheapest acceptable product: they seek rather to optimize their satisfactions
- marketers need to discover precisely what satisfactions and benefits customers are buying, as well as who specifies them, in order to make the most effective sales approach
- 'Black Boxes' are conventionally used in such models to indicate the highly unpredictable and subjective nature of what happens in individual minds between the varying stimuli they receive and the decision to buy
- the Howard-Sheth model clarifies some of the factors which influence individual buying behaviour, such as the individual's financial position and the importance of the purchase
- the Engel, Kollat and Blackwell model is more comprehensive: it shows something of how external influences are adapted and adopted according to individual motivating factors
- the Nicosia model starts with the activity of the manufacturing or marketing firm rather than the buyer; it emphasizes a) that changes by one party lead to adaptive changes by other parties involved in the world of business; and b) that the purchase experience leads to adaptation of buyer behaviour
- the Fishbein theory emphasizes the importance of the activity for which the product or service is needed. It attempts to describe attitudes towards the product or service, the strength of the attitudes being determined by the beliefs held by the potential purchaser. It also helps in understanding the steps that need to be taken to change buyers' attitudes
- our simplified and integrated model shows the importance of both rational and subjective considerations: rational ones being primary in the case of high-risk, low-frequency items; psychological, cultural and normative ones being primary in the case of low-risk, high-frequency items.

4

Six searching questions

Management consultants as well as advertising agencies use questionnaires to gather information for helping their clients. These questionnaires often run into many hundreds of questions. Answering these questions can require a great deal of internal analysis by the client, as well as formal market investigation. Most clients complete such exercises not only with relief but also with the realization that they should have started doing something like this years ago. It can be enormously valuable to look at your business with fresh eyes.

The hundreds of questions in a typical questionnaire are a more detailed way of answering only six basic questions. These questions are memorably rhymed by Rudyard Kipling:

I keep six honest serving men
(They taught me all I know)
Their names are WHAT and WHY and WHEN
And HOW and WHERE and WHO.

There is, in fact, an advantage in dealing only with these six questions: it forces you to concentrate on the fundamentals. Answering hundreds of questions without keeping these six firmly in the forefront of your consciousness can result in masses of information without the necessary business analysis.

What we need to know is: where the business currently stands, what it is all about, and how it got there. Such an analysis will result in many of the company's practices being questioned. If we wish the business to improve as a result of this questioning and analysis, then the questions must be used as an opportunity for creative thought.

4.1 What?

The traditional and proper question with which to start is: 'What are we selling?' Or, more powerfully, from a marketing point of view, we can ask: 'What is the customer buying?'

That, in turn, prompts the question: 'Are our customers buying the satisfactions that we think we are selling, or are they buying other satisfactions?'

If the answer is that customers are buying satisfactions other than the ones we thought we were selling, then we need to ask: 'What business are we really in?'

From these basics will stem a number of other vital questions for the business to ask itself: 'Are you properly geared to be in this business? Is the real business of the company being maximized, or are opportunities being presented which are not being explored?'

Some people are appalled at the possibility that some businesses don't know what business they are in. Experienced marketers, on the other hand, are surprised if any business's attempt to define a market position for itself is right the first time round. Customers have a perverse habit of deciding upon quite different uses for a product from those its creators imagined.

You may recollect the incident quoted earlier in the book, of the hand-cream company which thought it might consider promoting its product in two 'new' markets, but discovered that those were precisely the two markets it was in. Johnson, on the other hand, discovered that their sales of baby powder and baby lotion were far greater than could be accounted for by the number of parents who might conceivably use the correct amount for their babies. The difference was so enormous, that parents were probably using several times the right amount, perhaps bathing the babies in the lotion, and maybe even feeding them with it! Alternatively, the company wondered, was it that 'babies' up to the age of 14 were still having it applied to the appropriate part of their anatomy?

In fact, as Johnson discovered very quickly, the product had become a general cosmetic item. Women had discovered through accident that the product suited their own skins, and probably reasoned that a product good enough for a baby's delicate skin would be good enough for theirs. Moreover, it was cheaper than most branded products which did that job, and much more widely available.

The next step in the Johnson saga is very important, for it is a classic illustration of how to capitalize on this sort of finding. If you ever discover that you are in a completely different market from the one you had aimed at, it is vital that you do two things very quickly:

1 Redefine your market carefully
2 Analyze the strengths that put you there.

As a result of this sort of process, Johnson put themselves into the skin-care section of the female cosmetic market. Much later, they acknowledged that another change was necessary and addressed themselves to the many thousands of males who were discovered to be using Johnson. The company decided that its real strength lay in the word 'baby'. Alternative appeals such as 'Cheaper than most' or 'Available at Boots, Woolworths and all good chemists' were clearly less effective and far less strong than the description 'Baby Lotion' and the now-distinctive labels with the baby on them. Appeals were variants on the theme: 'Baby yourself: be a Johnson's Baby'. Instead of being in a market of roughly 1.5 million children, as it was then, Johnson found itself in a market many times that size, made up not only of children, but also of their older sisters, mothers, and indeed all women – and many men!

Lyons launched Ready Brek as the 'instant hot porridge'. Initial sales produced one of the steepest sales curves ever seen for a new grocery product. However, almost before the salesforce could arrive at a suitably euphoric state about their early success, sales dropped alarmingly. Panic measures were introduced, including a good deal of the research that ought to have been done before the product was launched. The investigations showed two things very clearly. First, confirmed porridge-eaters did not like the taste and texture of Ready Brek. Second, it clearly had a very effective television commercial based on a superb product claim that had produced a high level of initial trial by porridge eaters. The TV commercial had used the claim: 'Now! Porridge you can make in the plate. No more messy saucepans'. A very appealing claim for any householder who has experienced a saucepan of porridge bubbling on the stove for an hour every morning, producing a skin that almost required a blow-lamp to remove from the bottom and sides of the pan!

Hardly had Lyons had time to examine why their product was not selling, when sales started rising again. Who was buying their product? Not the regular porridge eater, as they knew by this time, but those who belonged to the 'variety cereal market' – that is, those who buy a variety of cereals for breakfast.

Further research revealed that not everyone in the variety cereal market was buying Ready Brek. People who were buying Ready Brek seemed to be buying it for families with children. Why was this? Because Ready Brek was being served to children by their parents, even though it was not being asked for by children. In most cases, the children were too young to express an opinion other than

61

outright rejection. Parents had decided that if Ready Brek could be made in the plate simply by adding hot milk or water to it, then its consistency could be controlled. Besides, everyone knows that oatmeal is good for you. Ready Brek became both a post-weaning food and a way of giving a child the nourishment that he or she might not seek of his or her own choice.

At this point, Ready Brek had two competing directions in which it could go. It could become an out-and-out baby food, or it could aim for a wider child market. It chose the latter path. First, the product was described as an instant hot oatmeal breakfast. Like Johnson in the earlier illustration, Lyons was basing its product-claim on the qualities the consumer had identified, even though Lyons itself had promoted the product initially on the basis of other qualities. The second move was to change the pack, from a very adult red to a beautiful golden colour with pictures of children on the front, so that parents would identify it as a product for children. To complete the market positioning, the advertising was now directed at parents to give their children the best possible start to the day in winter, under the banner of 'Central heating for kids'.

Ready Brek has been one of the most successful new product introductions in the cereal market in the last 35 years, yet it was so nearly a failure. Indeed, the porridge market into which it was launched was in decline at the time and went on falling for several years. Lyons was fortunate: its customers chose Ready Brek, so that it continued to grow through a declining market and then grew even more quickly as the whole market grew again.

The same sort of thing can happen in any sort of business. In mid-1975, a consultant did some research into the market for women's hairdressing services in the UK. The question was, 'What real satisfactions do women obtain from a visit to the hairdresser?' It was discovered that the satisfactions could be grouped, like this:

- cut, shampoo, blow dry, set
- beauty, confidence, excitement
- relaxation, rejuvenation, relief
- health, treatment, cure
- ambience, attention, care
- personal service, friendly staff, familiarity

Notice that only the first set contains any reference to the basic craft of hairdressing. Most of the others have to do with atmosphere and other intangible sources of satisfaction. That underlines the key to this sub-section: we have to discover what satisfaction customers take from our service. In the case of hairdressers, the list outlined above indicated that women look at their hairdresser in three different ways: as an artist, as a craftsperson and as a hair care expert (a sort of 'hair doctor'). But how did the women rank these three aspects? The traditional way the trade has looked upon itself (the artistic craftsperson) is the least important. Nine times out of ten a woman doesn't want artistry, she wants a quick, efficient service. Emphatically, she does want healthy hair all the time. Here was a clear opportunity for hairdressing that all but the most go-ahead had failed to discover, under their very noses.

Let's take a different area of activity. Banking and insurance companies offer financial packages of various sorts, each of which can offer different satisfactions to different people. What is a cautious investment to one family can be a speculative one for another family. Where one man is buying security for his family if any disaster overtakes him, another is buying a guaranteed sum of money at the age of 65. The same policy will give them both the things they want. If the family security-conscious man survives to 65, he will benefit from the lump sum. If the investor dies before he can cash in, his family will benefit from an assured sum. These two men will buy for different reasons and need to be sold to in different ways. Certain approaches, publications and sales people will succeed in one case and fail in the other. The whole image of one company can be for one thing, while its competitor provides an exactly similar package yet has a totally different reputation.

Black & Decker is an interesting example of a company whose analysis of what it was selling resulted in it finding a considerably larger market than it had earlier anticipated. The first electric drills were straightforward industrial products used in other industrial companies. It then became clear that the qualities offered by these drills could provide benefits to a larger number of occupations. Their strengths lay in the speed and efficiency with which Black and Decker drills bored holes. The deferred demand was essentially for different kinds of assembly and construction jobs. They weren't selling drills; they were selling to people who wanted ⅛ inch holes. That size hole takes the most commonly-used screw and is therefore required for an enormous range of jobs about the home. The rapid growth of home-ownership led to an ancillary market for attachments (sanders, circular saws, polishing buffs, and so on). There was also a demand from industry for heavy duty drills with larger and longer bits, and then for a range of heavy duty attachments.

Industrial businesses have to look not only at their immediate market, but also beyond or through that market at the nature of the ultimate demand which their goods and services satisfy.

Defining what business you are in, and then seeing who else might be interested in buying from you, can lead to exciting developments in your business. One word of warning, however. You can define your business too widely. Some companies have decided that they are in 'transportation' or 'entertainments' or 'communications'. This is fine as long as no one else comes along and defines a position which may be narrower but gives them a competitive advantage. It was for this reason that what was then the Thomson Organization (now International Thomson) decided to depart from its own formulation of its business as 'communications'. This was a reasonable business definition for a group in newspapers, magazines and books, but they decided to look within that range for what it was they did best. The answer was 'advertising'. That redefinition enabled them to launch a number of new magazines and newspapers and, in the UK, the Yellow Pages with the Post Office.

Here are a couple of other examples of how businesses have defined their area of particular skill:

1   A company manufacturing sealants and 'O' rings redefined its business as 'selling containment'. It then examined those areas where leaks could be disastrous. As a result, it now concentrates on the containment of hazardous chemicals and on the aeronautical business: two areas where premium prices and healthy profit margins are available to companies which meet the exacting needs of those industries.

2   The generally accepted definition of the computing business has been 'information storage and problem-solving'. However, this has been challenged by two major developments: the widespread use of micros and personal computers, and the development of 'user-friendly software' packages which permit sophisticated use without programming knowledge. Company data processing departments have been threatened or indeed eliminated, as more and more functional departments decide on their own data processing needs and solutions, and more and more managers take personal control of data processing through the increasingly powerful computers which are now available for desktop and laptop use. Computer manufacturers are therefore segmenting 'information storage and problem-solving' into software for defined business needs.

Let us move, now, to considering the next question regarding what business you are in.

4.2 To whom? Or, who are your real customers?

In moving to this second question, it is as well to draw your attention to one thing: all the questions inter-relate, and answers to later questions may well cause some change in the way you have treated an earlier question.

The UK package holiday business rates as its biggest competition not holidays abroad but painting the house or buying a new car: painting the house takes up the holiday period, while buying a new car absorbs all the family's discretionary income. Every business is faced by direct and indirect competition, often from sectors that appear unrelated. The trick is to identify the really relevant competition. This is often the clearest indicator of your real market.

What we are interested in discovering is: who influences the purchasing decision? This is easier in consumer markets than in others, though one still has the odd surprise. For example, we all know that the vast majority of razor blades are bought by women, but that the brand is specified by the husband. Marketing effort for razor blades therefore continues to be directed at men. Men's underclothing, on the other hand, is almost entirely a female purchase, with a high proportion bought without any prior reference to the man who will wear it. Brand-name promotion to men is therefore of little use; availability at shops where women normally buy is far more important. The right kind of marketing effort needs to be directed at the most appropriate audience.

In consumer markets, it is often possible to talk simultaneously to both decision-maker and purchaser: mass media inevitably pick up rather more people than simply the prime targets. In industrial markets, as we saw in the last chapter, the purchasing decision often involves several people at different levels. Individual approaches may or may not get you in contact with them. We have already noted the importance of the DMU in non-consumer markets, though the position can be even more complicated.

Industrial markets have a number of potential influences over any buying decision. One of these is trade unions. There was a time not so long ago when sophisticated print machinery was available in Britain but not used in British printing plants even though the DMUs had reached their decisions and the boards had approved the necessary expenditure. Why? Because trade unions refused to accept the new machines. We can show the very considerable problems that any company can face by the use of a simplified diagram.

In Figure 8, you will find the most frequent buying influences set out under four headings: formal and informal, internal and external. The top left block, the internal formal influences, corresponds to the DMU which has already been identified. However, the DMU will have to take into account a number of very significant external formal influences in reaching any decision: one of those is the policy of trade unions. It can be argued whether this should be more correctly described as an internal influence. Strictly speaking, a branch or chapel decision is internal, but official union policy is probably best regarded as external. In any case, legal and other regulations, codes of practice and government inspectors also come under this category.

Informal influences can be every bit as potent. Operatives can express their opinions in other ways than through official trade union action. Typists, on the other hand, are usually consulted about the choice of a new machine. Any supplier of goods and services to other industries will have the final end-user very much in mind as an external influence.

Public opinion can be another powerful influence, whether expressed directly through the media or through the agency of local government. A company buying a new fuel for its factory will have to consider whether deliveries will inconvenience local residents,

	Formal	Informal
Internal	Specifying technologists and managers Purchasing Manager Project Committee Chief Executive Board	Operatives Salesmen
External	Laws Regulations Codes of Practice Industry Standards Government Inspectors Trade Unions	Customers Final end-users Public opinion Local Government Contacts in other companies

Figure 8 *Typical industrial buying influences*

how much they might pollute the air in the neighbourhood, and so on.

Finally, industrial marketing companies should never neglect the value of contacts in other companies. At the investigatory stage, visits to other firms using the items under consideration will be high on the list. Good customers know this and use existing customers to help sell for them, by arranging demonstrations. (This assumes, of course, that the existing customers are satisfied customers.)

The field in which it appears to be most difficult to identify the ultimate buyer is the ethical pharmaceutical industry – that is, that bit of the pharmaceutical industry which is concerned with drugs sold only to medical institutions and to the medical profession for use on prescription. One part of the problem is the existence of hospital management committees and buying committees. Where the latter exist, they perform a role similar to that of the DMU, but these committees may well be made up of lay people who will then rely on the advice of experts.

For most ethical pharmaceuticals, pharmacists are the equivalent of buying managers: they are the people who hold the stocks on which the doctors draw. But if the doctors prescribe something the pharmacist doesn't have, one is going to have to convince the other. Sounds familiar? Well, it is actually even more difficult. The ward doctor makes a preliminary diagnosis and a corresponding prognosis. Then blood samples may be sent to a pathologist, who makes a final prognosis and prescribes treatment. So there may be three distinct and separate people – the doctor, the pathologist and the pharamacist – who can influence a buying decision by insisting on a particular treatment. (There is a painfully hilarious account of some people with an enormous amount of money who still got consistently the wrong treatment as a result of not understanding this problem, in William Shawcross's recent account of the life of the ex-Shah of Iran, *The Shah's Last Ride*.) If the different specialists involved are in harmony, all is well; if not, someone, somewhere is going to be unhappy, unwell or even dead.

A company supplying surgical sutures made a remarkable discovery while researching the effectiveness of a journal they produced for consulting surgeons. Earlier research had revealed that the journal was well-received and widely read. In a new piece of readership research, which was conducted through interviews in the ante-rooms of operating theatres, it was decided to throw in an odd question: 'Which brand of surgical suture did you use in that last operation?' Over 90 per cent replied: 'Ask the theatre sister, she looks after those things'. Subsequent research revealed that theatre sisters did in fact 'look after those things', but they never specified a brand. In most cases, the sutures were supplied on tender to the hospital management committee. There are many cases like this. Kleenex value the influence of nurses so highly that a great deal of their marketing activity for paper sheets and pillow cases is directed at them. Nurses don't buy things for hospitals, but if they keep on at the matron, the matron will get at the management committee, and the bed-linen supplier may well be changed.

The pattern in Figure 8 applies, then, to many different kinds of businesses. In the instance of a hospital, nurses can be considered as the operatives, and the final users are patients.

4.3 Why?

Why do people buy from your company rather than some other? What are your strengths; what attracts customers to you? Conversely, what are your competitors' weaknesses, by which customers are put off?

The third question is less important than the first two. Considering what you are selling and to whom will help you determine why customers are buying: these questions are thoroughly inter-related. One instance of this inter-relatedness is found in the sale of advertising space in quality newspapers, such as the *Financial Times*, *The Guardian*, *The Independent* and *The Times*. A first shot at what is being sold might be: 'advertising space in a quality newspaper'. A more refined description might add something about the kind of reader: more businesspeople and civil servants, say, than any other general daily newspaper. The 'why' and the 'to whom' come very much together when one considers the decision-maker for advertising of this kind. Quality newspapers such as these do relatively poorly in terms of numbers, which is one of the criteria that media planners in advertising agencies like to use in determining where to advertise. So a good deal of space for this kind of advertisment is sold by the newspaper's appeal to the top management of the advertiser. This is a very strong reason why so many very large companies choose *The Times* to carry their advertising.

Often the reason why is to be found in areas other than product performance. Service, delivery times, consistent quality, reliability in service areas, helpful staff, few errors in invoicing – these, and many more like them, can be the deciding factors in the choice between close competitors. A few examples may clarify the point.

When Lyons acquired control of Symbol Biscuits, the sensible thing appeared to be to sell the biscuits through Lyon's grocery salesforce and deliver them with all the other grocery items. The new organization would then be able to offer quite significant advantages over the old. For a start, five times as many salespeople would be selling the lines, calling on a larger number of shops with greater frequency. In reality, it didn't work out that way at all. Symbol were very small in a market dominated by two great biscuit companies, United Biscuits and Associated Biscuits. Yet Symbol sold to particular stores on a regular basis. They also sold regularly to a constantly changing set of larger stores, including some of the leading supermarket chains. Why? Well, apart from certain regional strengths based on a combination of tradition and acquired taste for a different biscuit formulation, the reason lay in speed of delivery. A high proportion of their biscuits were ordered over the telephone and delivered within 24 hours. The giant Lyons grocery organization had a regular salesman's call-cycle and an associated delivery frequency. Incorporating a 24-hour delivery facility in that would have been uneconomic, yet sales of these biscuits needed that particular service. You may think that your company offers all sorts of benefits, but if the key benefit from your customers' point of view is prompt delivery in response to rush orders, then it may be possible to drop several of the supposed features of your goods or services without affecting demand for your product.

Quality can be a very important attribute. However, quality is a word that means something only as a customer accords it significance. Remember the case of the teas which were described as quality teas by the producers, but which were described as 'funny teas' by the householder? Symbol Biscuits tried, at one time, to market 'the best chocolate couverture in the world'. Their consumers, however, thought it was the worst. Why? Because the 'best' product, which was originally aimed at a discriminating market, found no one to appreciate it in the mass market to which Symbol sold. What Symbol thought was excellent quality, and what was excellent quality for the right sort of customer, was poor quality so far as their existing customers were concerned.

It is well-known in the confectionery market that because people have become more used to artificial fruit flavours, they generally prefer them to real fruit flavours. So if you want to sell the purest, freshest fruit sweets on the market, you will probably need a much smaller factory, fewer people in your salesforce, carefully selected outlets – and you probably won't be able to advertise effectively due

69

to the problems of reaching your target market. However, the moment this point has been made, one must be conscious of the rising tide of 'green' consumers, who may change this marketing environment entirely. The market is always in a state of flux, and wise marketers try to stay in tune with the *changes* in their particular markets – neither moving ahead of them, nor lagging behind.

The way you handle people is another factor which can be crucial. This doesn't apply only in the service industries, or only to salespeople. Most salespeople can tell you of the order they almost lost because of unsympathetic handling of complaints by the head office, or because of their prospect being left hanging at the end of a telephone. In most fields today, your customers can find a competing supplier, so the product needs to be looked at in its totality, including its price, after-sales service, competent handling of complaints, discounting procedure, and the rest. The company which performs best over the whole field, or the one which offers the longest list of desirable attributes, is the one which scores.

However, let's not fool ourselves. People *can* hold business, even where the product has fallen below par. Why are they able to do this? Some light was thrown on this question by ladies in the research to which we referred earlier: many of them had expressed discontent with their hairdresser, and when they were asked why they didn't change their hairdresser, they offered a variety of reasons, the majority of which were to do with the relationship they had built up with the stylist over the years: 'She can't cut hair but she's very sweet and always nice and friendly' sums it up. Most salespeople have come across buyers who readily admit that the competitive product they are buying is inferior but 'they've always looked after me and I don't like to let them down when they've never done it to me'.

A company that adopts a sound marketing concept and promotes it at all levels throughout the company is less likely to be dependent upon such generosity than one that has an unfounded faith in the superiority of its product and treats the buyer as fortunate to be allowed to do business with it. Some companies have evolved little promotional tricks that have greatly helped in creating good staff attitudes towards customers. If, like Avis, you pick up the telephone and answer, 'Avis, we try harder', you are not merely keying in to what was a very effective advertising campaign, but you are also forcing yourself into an attitude of being helpful. So make a point of noticing how your own staff answer the telephone to

70

customers, handle complaints, talk about customers: and if it isn't all it could be, do something about it.

If the first two questions, 'What?' and 'To whom?', have been tackled with proper objectivity and creativity, it should be easy to list your competitive strengths and weaknesses. Such a list, of the reasons why you are or are not selling and, therefore, of why your customers are not buying, will inevitably overlap with the question of how you sell and how the customer buys.

4.4 How?

There are a number of ways this question can be tackled. Most companies will want to use them all.

First, you need to ask how customers get to know of you and what you have to offer. Is it by promotions, media advertising, exhibitions, personal recommendation, or simply by waiting for customers to come in? How do your competitors do it? You don't have to follow the leader; it may well be right to go in a completely different direction. You must consider what satisfactions you are both offering and to whom, before you can decide whether a different way of doing things will be a competitive strength or a weakness.

It is always worth paying close attention to your competitors: what are they doing? Why? Why at that time of year? Why in that media? Have your competitors discovered new market opportunities at different times of year or are they simply doing what other companies of a similar size do? Why do they use that particular medium for selling their wares? If they change the media they use, it could indicate a significant change in their strategy – most alternative kinds of approach tend to reach different target groups. If a manufacturer of electric drills suddenly changes from selling through builders' merchants and advertising in trade and technical magazines, to television advertising and selling through electrical shops, departments stores and every retailer that will take them, then it ought to be a reasonable conclusion that they are trying to compete in a different market.

Businesspeople often complain that they would drive themselves mad trying to monitor all competitive activity, fathom the reasons for its variety, *and* work out a reasonable response. On the other hand, the most usual reasons for business failure (after cash shortages) have to do with not knowing how competitors achieve their success and failing to estimate possible customer reactions.

71

It is worth devoting a good deal of attention to the physical act of selling. This is the one area where information is lacking. Not long ago, a company in the grocery field discovered exactly how large one of its competitor's salesforce was. It had always estimated it at around 30, when in fact it was over 600! When this was revealed at the annual sales conference, it turned out that many of the original company's salespeople were much closer than head office to the truth. The trouble was that their estimates of around 800 seemed so wildly exaggerated that no one in head office took them seriously.

Salesforces often know a great deal about the size, location and calling patterns of competitive salesforces. One of the characteristics of modern salesforces is that they work from home, so don't often meet at the depots every morning and night. Instead they meet perhaps once a month at area sales meetings or at specially convened conferences. They very often see more of their competitors than they do of their own colleagues. They meet in the same shops, the same ante-rooms and the same cafes and pubs. Even if no confidential information is exchanged, a great deal can be deduced from piecing together the number of times any salesperson runs up against the same person from the competition, and how often different salespeople are seen on one territory. This sort of exercise may produce nothing, or it may give you ideas for improving your own operation and seizing comparative advantages. Good communication between field and head office is essential: it will happen more promptly and fully when salespeople know why they are passing on information and when they can see resulting action.

There is also the matter of the complete terms of business between you and your customers. In the carbonless paper field in the UK, there is an important distinction in the way the three largest companies do business. One offers no discounts but fairly lengthy credit. Another does it the other way round: generous discounts for quantity and prompt payment, but very tight on credit. The third strikes a fairly conventional balance between the two. Under conditions in which the final user may have considerable difficulty in distinguishing the products of any one of them from another's, a printer might well choose a brand according to the trade-off in that firm between the need for cash discounts and the desire to hold cash in the business as long as possible. 'Long credit terms' may well be the 'how' of selling for Company A.

In the computer industry, training can be the equivalent motivator. Engineering firms frequently offer free servicing for a contract period or a marked degree of subsidy. Kleenex, we saw, paid a great deal of attention to an influential group of non-buyers. Brooke Bond attribute a great deal of their continuing success in tea to the influence of the tea cards inside their packets which create an awareness which is carried through life and into a purchasing situation. All these supposed ancillary marketing devices go towards the concept of total product and help answer the questions, 'How do we sell?' and 'How does our customer buy?'

4.5 Where?

Here once again there is a contrast: 'Where are we selling?' as against 'Where are our customers buying?' You will find that the answers divide neatly two ways: those concerned with geographical location and those concerned with sales through outlets.

One of the standard demographic units used by most business firms is area. In most cases, the Registrar-General's standard regions forms the basis. Sometimes, other standards may be used, such as areas described by certain research companies (usually called 'sales bricks'). Companies which rely on mass media advertising may well use television transmission areas. Some companies create their own sales or distribution units.

More and more companies are finding benefit in the ACORN analysis ('A Classification of Residential Neighbourhoods') which works on the assumption that people tend to choose to live among others with similar life-styles, or that they adopt those habits when they move into a neighbourhood. Twelve ACORN groups are used (such as agricultural areas, multi-racial areas, poor quality older terraced housing) and 39 ACORN types (including areas of farms and smallholdings, multi-let big old houses and flats, private flats with single pensioners). These classifications are also of enormous benefit to companies using direct mail as part of their promotional or selling activities.

Clearly, there is considerable advantage in using a generally accepted standard, since use can be made of a great deal of ancillary data. It is, for example, very difficult to establish the population in one of your own sales areas, so it is far easier to make a sales area conform to a standard region. This is particularly true in times of rapid social and economic change, as has happened in the last ten years, and as promises to continue to happen into the next century, due to the impact of the Single European Market, the building of the Chunnel, the globalization of business and the sclerosis of road and rail transport – in Britain, anyway.

Not every company will find important distinctions in geographical units. Companies which are local, for example, are more interested in individual customer records. In the grocery field, on the other hand, there are very few national supermarket chains. Leading supermarket operators like Tesco have marked regional strengths. It is by no means rare to find that a brand which is number three or four in the country as a whole is the brand leader in a certain area.

It could well appear that the supplier does very well in that region as a whole, though in reality, its strength in the region is due entirely to the number of shops in that region operated by one chain.

So what? Two things. First, success in one area may not be repeatable in others, simply because the conditions which created success cannot be duplicated. Not only is it possible that the store group which has supported you is not in the new area, but it may also be the case that its biggest competitor is strong there – and will not accept your product at any price. Second, it may well mean that the scale of your marketing efforts should be entirely different from area to area, based on *customer* strengths, not purely regional ones.

On the other hand, there are marked regional preferences for certain products, particularly by brands and individual companies. The eating habits of the Scots are very different from those of the English. Scots tend to eat less meat but pay more for it; they eat rather more chocolate biscuits per head and drink more soup.

Particular brands may be better suited to certain areas. Teas and soap powders have one thing in common – they perform in different ways according to the water in which they are used. There is a good reason why Horniman's Tea should have established such a strong foothold in South Wales – the blend was particularly suited to the water there. There was quite a different reason why Black & Green's tea was so successful in the outlying areas of Manchester. It was a local company and, by selling in the local markets around the edge of Manchester, it established a market for a 'gift tea' (one where labels could be exchanged for goods like cutlery, crockery and linen). If you were a company like Horniman, it would suit you to search for other areas of the country with similar conditions – in the case of this particular sort of tea, for places with soft water.

Black & Green, on the other hand, since they have no such factor to look for, would have to look for other areas of the country with similar socio-economic profiles where their selling method and strength might enable them to repeat their Manchester success.

74

Additional factors in the case of international markets include: parity or stability of exchange rates, lack of controls on foreign exchange, political stability, local laws and regulations, and so on. The equivalent to Horniman asking, 'Where else is the water similar to that in South Wales?' might be that of asking in which countries are the laws similar to those in which the product is already a success.

The other matter which needs to be considered in answering the question 'Where?' has to do with customer strengths. Much of British industry took a very long time to realize that some customers are worth considerably more than others. This realization has paid handsome dividends to companies that changed their business practices as a result. Many companies have still not recognized that fact, or have failed to take any resulting action. Nowadays, high volume and value, high frequency of purchase and perishability are the only conditions which justify the very large salesforces which are necessary nowadays being required to call regularly on the vast distribution network. Even medium-life products are not considered worthy of regular contact with the bulk of the retail trade.

This means that the basis of measurement should change: one should be concerned not with the sheer number of customers but with the *value* they represent. That 80:20 rule will rear its head again: a small number of customers will account for the bulk of the trade in any given product, service or commodity. What we should be looking for is: which stores account for the highest proportion of the trade; which bank's current account holders have the highest number of transactions; which socio-economic groups buy the most life insurance; which countries have the highest per capita consumption of Scotch whisky; which farms have the highest consumption of fertilizers, etc.

This kind of consideration gives rise to a very useful concept known as 'sterling weighted distribution'. Normal distribution checks might well tell you that your soap powder is stocked by 60 per cent of the grocery trade. That is a fairly worthless figure unless you have some measure of the importance of those stores. You could well find that the 40 per cent of outlets which your company is missing accounts for 60 per cent of the total sale of soap powders. If so, your distribution figures will begin to look a little sick. What any business really needs to know is:

- What proportion of the total business do your customers account for?

- What proportion of the specific product field do they command?
- What proportion of your sales do they account for?

The first things to ask, for example, might be what percentage of the total retail food business do your customers account for? What proportion of total motor manufacture?; What share of total package holidays booked? Moving on, the question will be refined to enquiries such as: what share of total soap powder do those stores have?; What proportion of tyres do the manufacturers account for?; How much of the all-inclusive tour market to the Costa Brava do they account for? In each case, the aim is to refine the information as closely as possible to useful, actionable data for your specific business.

In Chapter 2 we saw the relative importance of different categories of buyer. It is essential to isolate the heavy user from the light: 'To each according to their worth' should be our credo for maximum profitability. We shall see more evidence of the value of this dictum in other sections of this book. In particular, we shall see that there are many *emotional* barriers to overcome in making the most sensible allocation of resources.

It never comes easy to any salesperson to be forced to consider which customers they are prepared not to supply or even to consider; which they are willing to allow to be out of stock. On the other hand, it is easy to contemplate the possibility of calling on and delivering to every customer precisely when they want it. The optimum will be somewhere between the two. Costs and profit are what need to be weighed against each other. The sooner your company accepts that profitability summaries by region (or product, or whatever other category is appropriate) must become a way of life, the quicker profitable rationalization and exploitation of real opportunity areas can be undertaken.

Ironically, most companies still measure geographical sales when they make all the profit calculations on a global basis. This assumes that a head office located in London exerts the same influence on Glasgow as it does on Birmingham; that Glasgow actually requires the back-up of a London head office; and that the effect of an advertisement in the *Daily Telegraph* is the same throughout the country. Customer records are needed for virtually all the most useful forms of marketing analysis and forecasting. Most businesses would be all the sharper for backing them up with profit calculations made down to the smallest practical unit.

When your customer strengths have been recognized and

recorded, you need to know one more thing: when are you selling? When are they buying? Have you got this in harmony?

4.6 When?

It is natural for any manager to think only of aspects of seasonality under this heading, but there is more than that to consider. A real understanding of regular fluctuations helps with effective sales forecasting, while a completely different but nevertheless vital consideration is that of which periods afford the best opportunities for selling.

Obviously, the time periods chosen for investigation vary dramatically, according to the business. If, for example, your business is selling porridge, the difference between October to March sales and those for the rest of the year will be critical. If you are a hairdresser, you will be much more concerned with days of the week (Mondays are traditionally poor) and with Bank Holidays, when people like to look their best for planned events. The first step is to recognize strengths and weaknesses by day, week, month or season as those may affect your business. Then consider what you might be able to do about it.

Several breakfast cereal manufacturers have promoted summer uses for products previously served mainly with hot milk during winter. (They had discovered that a very high proportion of people used cold milk in winter in any case.) Additionally, some were able to promote the use of their products as ingredients in other meals and in cakes, while most have successfully developed uses at other meals.

Mealtimes can be important under the heading of 'When?' The great strength of tea in the UK is: first thing in the morning, often before breakfast; in coffee-drinking countries, coffee assumes the same role. Many hairdressers have made Mondays their day for children, old-age pensioners, even models. If you are doing no business at all at certain periods, it can make sense to consider marginal costings; things that may not be worthwhile in good times can be very beneficial in poor periods.

Sometimes it is necessary to recognize that there are times when no amount of effort can produce a sale. Closing day is an obvious example. Certain industries close down for annual holidays; in parts of the country your efforts will be affected by annual holidays, extra days at Bank Holidays, etc.

There are two things you can do about this sort of situation.

First, you can stop wasting effort. Perhaps this is the time for your own annual close-down to take place. Certainly, you can plan for these periods in sales forecasting and production scheduling. Second, this may be the time when a valuable service can be provided for customers. While no selling takes place in the average supermarket on early closing days, a great deal of merchandizing of stock goes on. A considerable amount of goodwill is created by giving this kind of assistance at precisely the time when the stores need it most. Industrial companies may send in their technical experts and service engineers at the time when their client company is shut down for annual maintenance. Not every off-season for selling is a problem: many present opportunities.

Notice that our discussion has widened from days, months, and seasons to any regular occurrence. This can be useful to keep in mind when it comes to sales forecasting, and the next time there is an inquest into why sales did not meet a budget. The analysis of regular fluctuations is the foundation of most forecasting techniques. On the other hand, managers do have an alarming tendency to produce budgets which ignore the fact that Easter is in a different month the following year and that Christmas may fall on such a day that many factories will close down for a whole week.

Look at it this way: does your product provide the same satisfaction and meet the same need at all times during the year? Let us consider this question in relation to fountain pens. They come in all shapes, sizes, qualities and prices. They can be considered as necessary writing instruments, gifts, expressions of someone's personality or status symbols. A 22-carat gold pen may write no better than a plastic-barrelled version costing only a tiny fraction of its more status-conscious fellow. A necessary writing instrument can be a 50p pen picked up off a rack, or one costing 20 times as much chosen from a counter with the skilled help of an assistant.

By far the greatest proportion of all types of fountain pen are bought at Christmas. Even the very cheapest sell more at that time, for they provide a much-appreciated and cheap gift. Nevertheless, the cheaper pens do a far higher proportion of business at other times of the year, whereas solid gold ones peak around Christmas-time. The degree of effort, the timing of promotion and selling, as well as the kinds of appeals made either through media advertising or at point of sale will vary considerably by the time of year. If fountain pen manufacturers ask, 'With what are we competing?' they will find that the answer changes with the time of year. A fountain pen for personal use bought at any time of the year will probably compete primarily with ball-point pens and felt-tip versions. The same pen at Christmas was, until recently, more likely to compete with a cigarette lighter – the item then most often used as an alternative gift for a man.

As the timing changes, so the opportunity differs. One of the most popular clichés in marketing is that marketing is concerned with opportunities not problems. What everyone in business should be looking for is the time at which those opportunities are greatest. For example, such an apparently marginal item of information as the depreciation policy of a major customer can be a great help. Depreciation allowances run out with time, and no further claims can be made to offset Corporation Tax. As that time comes closer, boards of directors become increasingly concerned with knowing if the plant is to be replaced, with what, when and at what cost. It becomes even more vital when, as is usually the case, there is no actual cash reserve which represents the annual depreciation. If the plant is to be replaced, the money has to be obtained from somewhere. If reserves are not available, then borrowing will have to be increased. It is obvious that senior management is going to be very concerned as capital equipment nears the end of its scheduled life. This is obviously the time for sales approaches to intensify, to change from simple contact to hard-selling.

A very different example comes from the field of national daily newspapers. In the sense that most people use the word, newspapers are not seasonal. But they tend to behave a little strangely around Christmas. A characteristic of the British is that they like to have a house full of reading matter at Christmas. Probably because the whole family is sitting down together, most families buy extra papers and magazines. Depending where Christmas falls, daily newspapers (or Sundays) may receive a very short burst of sales. However, this is a recent phenomenon.

Up to the period between the wars, there used to be a sharp drop in newspaper sales during July and August. People went on holiday and cancelled their newspapers. (The UK has two unusual characteristics in the newspaper field: it is the only country in the world with truly national newspapers and it enjoys a high level of home delivery.) One enterprising circulation manager noted the number of people sitting in deck chairs doing nothing and thought how much better it would be if they bought his newspaper. He reasoned that if only he could devise a scheme that would get them to sample his paper, a good proportion might stay with it when they went home. Even if they didn't, his overall sales would increase substantially.

He also thought that cancelling a newspaper, and therefore somehow 'escaping' from what was going on in the world, was all part of being on holiday but, on the other hand, by about the first Tuesday of the holiday, Dad would be fretting to know the latest cricket scores and what the favourite was for the three o'clock at Ascot. He could indulge himself on holiday by not buying his usual paper and trying a different one. Perhaps his wife would like one too, thought the circulation manager. After all, she normally got to read the paper – on the rare occasions when she got the chance – only after her husband brought it home from work.

Those thoughts going through the circulation manager's head were the beginning of all the mystery men and women who produce a reward in money when correctly identified – provided the challenger is carrying a copy of the right newspaper. That was the beginning of the now-familiar beach games sponsored by newspapers and a host of other activities at popular holiday resorts. That circulation manager was right: summer holidays were not a problem to the industry – they presented real opportunities. Under normal everyday circumstances, people do not like to change from a familiar newspaper; here was a situation where the very same people, of their own free will, actually wanted to have a change.

The moral of this story is that every business should seek to recognize regular variations, ask why they happen, and decide whether they represent a problem they cannot solve (and so should adapt to) or an opportunity which ought to be seized.

Here is a list of the sorts of things which can present opportunities:

- Announcements of engagements to marry
- Marriage announcements
- Birth announcements
- Children starting school (which can be calculated from the date of birth)
- Students starting at university (they receive their grants in lump sums and may need help in budgeting)
- Job promotions (life assurance and investment scheme opportunities)
- Building of new factories
- Acquisitions (especially where one of the firms involved is already a customer)
- Life of plant or consumer durables (last new car bought three years ago; children should be growing out of the bunk beds bought four years ago; plant superseded by new methods, etc)

These are examples of times when customers are open to suggestions for new goods and services and, in several of the examples, are themselves making fundamental changes in their buying and behaviour patterns. All of these sorts of opportunities should also be considered under the heading of 'When?'.

4.7 Repeating the exercise

When attempted for the first time, the exercise of answering these six basic questions will be quite demanding. Some of them cannot be answered in a satisfactory way without independent outside help. If market research is beyond the budget (or possibly inappropriate to the business), it can be extremely useful to involve an experienced consultant for a couple of days to do no more than act as a catalyst. It is often easier for an outsider to ask apparently naïve questions (which are often the most searching) than it is for an insider – especially when that person is a subordinate.

Each time the exercise is repeated, it gets a little easier for, on subsequent occasions, the examination becomes concerned only with identifying those changes that could prompt fresh initiatives. It is worth recording each new fact and decision in some kind of fact book or data book.

The annual repetition of this six-question analysis is more valuable even than the formal annual plan, for the latter can so easily take place without the necessary preliminary analysis of what the business is, where it has got to, and where it wants to get. The sheer momentum of day-to-day work can keep the nose of senior management firmly to the grindstone. It pays to invest in getting away from the offices for anything from a day to a week, depending on the size of the business, to give uncluttered time to this exercise. The result can be the identification of new opportunities and the launch of bold new initiatives. You may decide to follow what everyone is doing, or you may decide to buck the trends.

The Xerox machine was around for 30 years before anyone with sufficient courage could be found to market it. The basic ingredients in a perfume may cost only 5p per ounce; you can market it at 15p – or £15: the choice is yours. The strategies are entirely different, as are the tactics by which each strategy is achieved.

4.8 Summary

Six simple questions will provide a searching analysis of any business field, and of any product or service within it. Confining the exercise to so few questions can provide a sharper definition than asking for much more detail. The keys to success with using this form of analysis are:

- complete objectivity and lack of bias
- creative approach to the questions and their answers
- being prepared to obtain independent information or obtaining the help of an outside catalyst, rather than relying on what the business has always believed
- recording all new facts for future reference
- acknowledging that all businesses change over time and that the implications of change must be considered openly
- repeating the exercise at regular intervals, under conditions which emphasize its importance to the continuing success of the company.

4.9   Checklist

1   The key business question is 'What are our customers buying?' This is a matter of identifying the ultimate satisfactions they derive from your product or service.

2   Asking the question 'What is our competition?' is usually a reliable indicator of what business one is in. Until one knows the answer to that question, the business has little effective control over its destiny.

3   Those involved in selling their products and services to other businesses need to look not only at the satisfactions their direct customers seek but also at the satisfactions the ultimate end-users derive and what part their product or service plays in that ultimate satisfaction. The greater the part (for example, a Rolls-Royce engine in a Boeing aircraft), the higher the price that can be commanded.

4   Care must always be taken to identify the benefits your customers seek, rather than to catalogue the features your product or service provides. A feature only becomes a benefit when someone has a need which that feature can help fulfil.

5   Next, a business has to ask itself 'Who is buying what I sell?' The buyers are not always the decision-makers, who can be groups or individuals – it is usually possible to identify one key specifier, but it is not usually easy to gain access to him or her.

6   Ultimate purchasing decisions are often affected, however, by 'influencers'. These can be the ultimate users or consumers of

the product or service, but workers, children, families and nurses are all good examples of people who influence certain buying decisions powerfully. It is worth keeping firmly in mind that the different people involved in a purchase may have entirely different viewpoints.

7   Frequently, different segments of the same market have different specifiers as well as different influencers.

8   Why people buy from your company is usually an amalgam of what you are doing right and what your competitor is doing wrong. (The opposite can also be true!) An objective and continuing analysis of comparative strengths and weaknesses is necessary – and this must always be related to the benefits and satisfactions that customers desire.

9   How you get your product or service to its market is as important as what your market is. People are not prepared to search for products, unless they are really exceptional. Your competitors may be doing better than you because they have managed to organize themselves so as to get the right product at the right price to the right place at the right time.

10   The way sales are spread amongst potential outlets and customers is also vital to two things: first, to locating your customers and identifying the best way to achieve the maximum profit; and second, to enabling you to concentrate on selling to the customer groups that account for the bulk of the available business.

11   Two aspects of timing are involved in the question 'When are we selling?' One is that of seasonality, by which we mean any regular variation, however short. The second is that of identifying periods when the need to buy (and thus the opportunity to sell) is greatest.

12   While analysis based on the six questions is a worthwhile exercise, it is also time-consuming and may require expenditure on independent research, analysis and often advice. The exercise becomes easier and more valuable if it is repeated at least annually. It will not be necessary to repeat everything every year. Look for significant changes and search for the new threats and opportunities they present.

5

If it's living, it's dying

Some things go on for so long that it is easy to forget that they are mortal. Nothing lasts forever. Just think of the household names of ten years ago and consider how many have disappeared. Famous companies, old and favourite sweets and toys, fashions that were all the rage – many may have gone for ever. Others have come back. Old people are apt to decry long-haired youths, perhaps ignorant that their parents shocked their elders by and creating a fashion for short hair. (In fact, male hair styles over the centuries have traditionally been long.)

Nothing goes on forever – certainly not in business. But some things do come back again. These two statements come together in a theory known variously as the 'Product Life-Cycle' or the 'Demand Life-Cycle'. Sometimes the two terms are used interchangeably. At other times, the demand cycle is used to describe the role of an individual product or service within a total product group. To avoid confusion, the terms will be used in this chapter in the latter sense.

5.1 Life-cycles in business

Sitting at his desk, a managing director of a small company was congratulating himself on the straight-line increase in sales. A friend who was visiting him, mischievously decided to bring him down to earth, by pointing out that each step on a sales graph represents a smaller percentage gain than the preceding one. If there had been equal percentage gains, they would have been represented by a steadily rising rate of slope. While the straight-line graph will represent a 100 per cent increase from one unit to two, it will be only a five per cent gain from 20 to 21. By the time the slope represents an increase from 1999 to 2000, the percentage gain is only 0.05 per cent.

A study of large numbers of product histories shows that there is a general shape that sales histories take (Figure 9). However, what follows is a generalization: your industry, or your company within

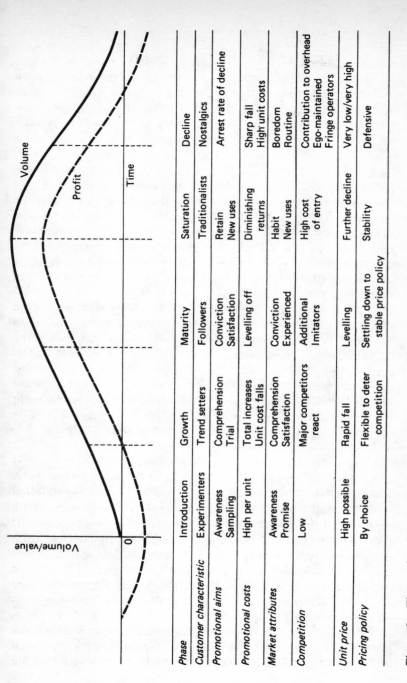

Phase	Introduction	Growth	Maturity	Saturation	Decline
Customer characteristic	Experimenters	Trend setters	Followers	Traditionalists	Nostalgics
Promotional aims	Awareness Sampling	Comprehension Trial	Conviction Satisfaction	Retain New uses	Arrest rate of decline
Promotional costs	High per unit	Total increases Unit cost falls	Levelling off	Diminishing returns	Sharp fall High unit costs
Market attributes	Awareness Promise	Comprehension Satisfaction	Conviction Experienced	Habit New uses	Boredom Routine
Competition	Low	Major competitors react	Additional Imitators	High cost of entry	Contribution to overhead Ego-maintained Fringe operators
Unit price	High possible	Rapid fall	Levelling	Further decline	Very low/very high
Pricing policy	By choice	Flexible to deter competition	Settling down to stable price policy	Stability	Defensive

Figure 9 *The product life-cycle concept*

85

it, will not necessarily follow the shape described. There is a high likelihood that it will, but the time period required for the general shape to be perceived may be quite short or very long indeed. Coal provides an example of a life-cycle which is extremely long, but which nevertheless exhibits all the classic signs as other sources of energy become more widely used. At the other end of the scale, certain transistorized components have been replaced by more efficient ones so quickly that the down-slope is almost vertical and the time-span often not much more than six months from launch to demise. Later in the chapter, we will look at some well-known departures from this general shape of life-cycle.

To start with, however, let us define the concept of the life-cycle. This describes: what will happen when the natural forces present in a market are allowed to have free play; that is, what will happen unless you do something to prevent it.

A well-documented rebuttal of the concept was presented by the marketing director of a leading confectionery company in the UK. One of his products had been in long-term decline, and therefore had been abandoned by the previous manager. The product was revamped, relaunched with suitable advertising and quickly moved into growth and profitability again.

Far from rebutting the concept, there were two elements in the story which actually confirmed it. First, his had been the only product which was declining within a whole sector, which was still growing. Second, he had done something about it, and had fought (successfully for the time being) the natural tendency of all products to mature, slow down and eventually die – unless rejuvenated by actions such as this manager's. (Of course, there is no guarantee that such actions will always be successful.)

Figure 9 represents both volume and value. The volume curve is fairly flat in the early stages, but rises quickly before flattening off. Often, this flat top can be very long. In other cases, there is a fairly sharp peak. Products such as tea and biscuits have had long plateau periods. Tea in the UK has gone beyond that plateau and into decline, but biscuits have not yet done so.

On the other hand, to take an example used in the first chapter, saturation for ceiling tiles occurs when every ceiling is fitted with tiles. Since that is unlikely to happen on one particular day, the combination of new houses being built, the last few old houses being converted and some replacements for old tiles will combine to maintain the flat top for a short while. That is why frequency of purchase becomes an important element in the life of a product.

Profit assumes the same general shape, but it is stepped in relation to the volume curve. No profit is made for quite a long time in the beginning, because until a business has customers, all it can have is costs. As sales increase, these costs will first be covered and then past investment will be recouped. This is known as 'the pay-back period'. Real net contributions come after that point, which is also known as the 'break-even point'. Note that profit starts to fall before volume declines. There are few businesses that can escape the ravages of the law of diminishing returns. It is usually possible to find more customers to service, but the unit cost of doing so almost inevitably rises. The only way to escape the law of diminishing returns on revenue is to make realistic differential charges for the service.

An illustration may make this clear. Consider Heinz tomato soup. The product is nationally known and has the same price throughout the country. Suppose that Heinz distribute their soup to 95 per cent of the grocery shops throughout the country – the missing 5 per cent being in the Scilly Isles, the Orkneys and the more remote hill country of Scotland and Wales. But even the 95 per cent that Heinz do reach are not equally easy to reach: some of the grocery shops will be within minutes of the factory; some within half an hour; some within an hour; some will take more than a day to get to – and that means different costs in getting the product to them, which means that some of the outlets are more profitable than others.

Another factor determining profitability is the volume sold by each particular outlet: those in large population centres, those which happen to be supermarkets, or those in particular parts of the country, may sell many times the volume of a smaller, more remote shop. Clearly, it will cost less per tin to take it to the larger outlet than it will to take it to the smaller one. There are further factors which complicate the relationship between sales volume and profit, but let us get back to the relationship between them so far as the life cycle is concerned.

5.2 The introductory phase

When a new service or product is introduced, the people most likely to become customers will be experimenters and fashion leaders. Even the most frivolous of consumer markets contain a large proportion of people who never buy new products until they have been on the market long enough to 'get the bugs out of the system'. On the other hand, there appears to be a certain proportion of householders who try all new domestic products as soon as they appear. This almost guarantees initial sales, but it also makes much more difficult any reliable estimates of the level of regular demand.

Promotion during the introductory phase will be aimed at creating awareness of the product and inducing trial. Promotional means, such as free or subsidized samples, may be one way of achieving this. However, whichever way it is done, the trial period involves high unit costs of promotion and these will last until sufficient volume has been created.

To make the potential market aware of the new product or service and induce the necessary trial, some indication has to be given of what the product will do and why it is right for them. This is called a customer proposition. In some cases, competition may be low and that will be an asset – unless the product is a pioneering one.

With a completely new product, the initiator has the opportunity to set their own pricing policy and they have the chance to choose their strategy much more freely: high initial price affords the opportunity of price reductions when competition appears, and low initial price may provide rapid penetration of the market.

Whether with a pioneering product or with a more established one, the launch is obviously a high-risk phase. The public may not respond to the product at all, or it may enjoy quite high levels of initial sale without reaching repeat levels that will enable even the investment to be recouped.

5.3 The growth phase

With the beginning of the growth phase, the trend-setters and pace-setters in the market become buyers. There may come a time when everybody seems to want your product. Shortages could then result, which make it easier for competition to enter. Even without shortages, major competitors are hardly likely to pass up an opportunity of getting into a significant new market.

In promotional terms, marketing has to be aimed during the growth stage not merely at awareness of the existence of a product, but at understanding of the benefits it offers. If advertising is appropriate, it will have to explain more than was necessary when the primary objective was to create awareness. Although actual budgets for promotional purposes may still be rising, unit costs should be coming down rapidly. Price could become a promotional tool at this stage, especially if the first company in has been able to accumulate a little 'fat' (or profit) to defend its position. The total product, including service aspects, training, etc, may well need to be examined with a view to maintaining an advantage over new competitors.

5.4 Maturity

When this stage arrives in the product life-cycle, the growth slope begins to become less steep, irrespective of the number of competitors. As a compensation, however, this is the period of real profit and one you will want to prolong. Buyers are, by now, pretty convinced about product performance and enjoying satisfaction from it. Each succeeding use of the product or service is likely to confirm that satisfaction, so that promotion can be held at a reasonable level. In this phase, the main task of advertising is to hold your customers against the counter-claims of competitors.

A new kind of competitor is also likely to appear at this stage – the imitator whose products are frequently referred to as 'me toos'. Often, they behave like parasites, living off the reputation and promotion of the leading companies and usually competing on different grounds, such as sheer availability, price, discounts and service. Clearly, several of these possible competitive *advantages* are simply *alternatives*: heavily discounted goods are not usually backed by an excellent quality of service. Where goods are in short supply, there is little point in providing them cheaply – often they may be more expensive, to make additional profit out of customer demand. Several firms have created and maintained a healthy profit record out of never being market leaders but always following, and taking advantage of, the maturity phase of a life-cycle.

Every aspect of this stage tends to be characterized by levelling-off. Promotion has to be watched carefully or higher unit costs will result. Prices settle down because customers should be aware, by now, of what the product is worth to them; any quick or sharp change of price will affect buying patterns.

In Figure 9, profit is shown declining just at the end of this third phase: it is possible to delay profit decline, but it has been plotted in at this point in the graph to emphasize that as sales level off, the temptation to pursue volume can easily lead to diminishing returns.

5.5 Saturation

This is the point where the product is being bought by all those who are likely to buy it. This is the point where profit decline is most likely to accelerate, not only because of reducing returns per unit sold, but also through the reluctance of existing customers to accept inevitable price increases. Customer boredom or the arrival of newer or improved products are other threats.

At the same time, however, manufacturers may be looking to promote new uses for the product: habit plays a very large part in sustaining saturation. The cost of entry for new competitors is likely to be prohibitive and the market is not as attractive as a growing one – though these are not, of course, necessarily sufficient to prevent competition.

What happens to price will largely depend on two things: the initial pricing strategy and the degree of freedom to act (either for competitive or government reasons). There is a general tendency for actual price to fall. Discounting often begins to take the place of other forms of promotion even though list prices do not change. In the case of service industries, additional service elements may be added. Pan Am had the interesting problem of what to do when their average aircraft occupancy had reached saturation point but, owing to the multiple pricing structure in existence, full-fare businesspeople were sitting alongside half-fare, advance booking tourists. Pan Am's answer was to designate certain areas of their aircraft as 'Executive Areas' where they provided extra services. In the same way, many American insurance companies have added counselling services so that bereaved beneficiaries can receive the help needed at such times.

5.6 Decline

The typical brief given to a marketing expert in this phase is:

> 'Hold the rate of decline to less than that of the market as a whole' *or possibly* '. . . at that of the market as a whole'.

Buyers at this stage of a product's life tend to be nostalgics. They may be older, but don't sniff at them, especially at a time when the number of older people in most industrialized countries is going up, both absolutely and as a proportion of the whole population. In fact, the 'grey' market is emerging as one in its own right, parallel to the emergence of the teenage market in the Sixties.

However, it may sometimes be necessary to retain a product even where the market size of a product doesn't justify it, in order to retain a complete range of products.

Promotion usually falls dramatically during this period and faces a constant battle because of the need to avoid increasing unit costs per sale. Price is frequently the prime weapon available and manufacturers look over their shoulder to see what the competition is charging. They may have to look hard also at what the competition is giving away each day: buyers' boredom may have set in and they often need a strong stimulus to rouse their interest. Giveaways, buying incentives and various types of incentive programmes, are frequently used at this time. Price itself could be very low or very high.

Where it is necessary to keep machinery turning or people gainfully employed, prices may be slashed to minimum contribution levels in order to achieve those objectives. (The minimum contribution level is, simply, that level where the product is producing the minimum acceptable rate of return – it is not necessary for the product to be producing an actual profit, as explained above, but there must come a point where it is making such a large loss that it is not worth keeping.) Wherever possible, companies will prefer to charge prices that reflect the true costs of providing the service to a minority market, on the assumption that anyone who wants it badly enough will pay for it.

Every company has overhead costs – certain expenses necessary to being in business – and these have to be paid whether anything is sold or not. The larger the company, the larger these overheads are likely to be. They become the first charge on the gross profits of an enterprise. Since these costs have to be met, many companies are prepared, in the short term at least, to continue selling goods and services so long as they produce something towards the costs of being in business. Products in decline often continue to be sold simply to provide a valuable contribution to total company overheads. So a product may be maintained on the market long after it appears to have served a useful life.

Of course, that is not the only reason why products may continue to exist long after their prime market has disappeared: sheer pride or unwillingness to give up may be the reason, especially if a product was the primary reason for the company's existence in the past. In fact, there are circumstances in which products may actually be launched into a declining market for the whole of that product category. Often, when a market is in decline, the intensity of competition slackens. Companies which would have been quick to respond to a new competitor earlier, may not only avoid retaliation, but also actually welcome an alternative source of supply which allows the now-declining brand to be withdrawn or reduced in scale, so that the older company's attention and energy can be redirected to more profitable areas. There is often a viable market on the fringe of any large one.

5.7 Cycles within cycles

In a situation where there is only one brand in the market, that brand's life-cycle is also the life-cycle of the product as a whole. However, where there is more than one brand available, that brand's life-cycle can differ enormously from that of the rest of the product.

Figure 10 illustrates the varying cycles which might exist within a market. Product A is first in and has kept going almost to the end. Product B was a follower but a very close one. Athough never quite matching A's sales, B's market share has grown even while the market as a whole has declined. C and D have both had shorter lives, D obviously deciding to launch only when C had withdrawn from the market.

If you try to divide the market profile into the five phases we have defined, you will find that only D reaches brand saturation at the same time as the market does. Indeed, it is quite possible for market saturation to be attained only after each individual product has reached its zenith. It is important to understand this. For all sorts of reasons, the products of different companies are not always equally acceptable as substitutes. There may be simple physical reasons like distributions, availability and service. There may be attitudinal reasons which bias certain people in favour of some companies and against others. Thus, early answers to the following questions must

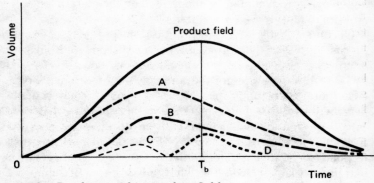

Figure 10 *Products within product field*

92

be obtained – what is happening in the market? What is happening to me? Why should I be any different? What can I do about it? And back you must go to the analysis of competitive strengths and weaknesses.

In looking at an individual life-cycle, it is essential that you compare it with the appropriate product or market life-cycle. When the UK tea business was pre-occupied with its own life-cycle, it was not able to understand its decline or what to do about it. When it started taking into account the life-cycle for other hot beverages, it took far more notice of the threat of instant coffee. From one of the strengths of instant coffee – convenience – came an attack in the form of tea bags, plus emotive appeals to the young who were being wooed by the modernity and convenience of instant coffee. The decline hasn't been halted, but it has been considerably slowed. Advertising appeals were discovered that could produce dramatic effects, but cost more than the industry was able to subscribe on a continuing basis. The increasing share of total trade taken by tea bags allowed the packers to improve their profits despite falling total tea volume.

A look at the tea life-cycle then showed a slight decline in total tea sales, a steep decline in packet teas, with varying degrees of decline according to price, and a contrasting and very steep increase for tea bags. Indeed, Figure 10 has elements of similarity with the UK tea market throughout the 1970s and 1980s with tea bags growing like product D but not yet at maturity.

The biscuit market is one which has undergone a terrific change in the same period. Biscuits have assumed the role of staple products in the UK home market. A section of the life-cycle from 1900 shows a smooth upward curve gradually flattening out in classic pattern and looking, in 1974, as though saturation may have been reached. Unusually, profit and total value had expanded because of a switch from lower-priced biscuits to more expensive ones. In particular, the proportion of chocolate biscuits in the total accounted for a considerable part of the growth of the market value. When times became hard and householders sought better value for money, the share of chocolate biscuits in the total declined rapidly. The householder replaced the more expensive chocolate-coated biscuits with less expensive, non-coated varieties; assorted biscuits with plain ones; sweet with dry. While the total market volume appeared static, the value curve had fallen.

This brings us to another useful lesson. Depending on the product field, one may have to take account of quite a number of different cycles. Banks and investment houses, mortgage brokers and insurance agents may have to take much more account of the normal economic trade cycle. (The word 'normal' doesn't mean that this is what always happens: although the frequency and relative regularity of the boom/slump cycle is well documented, the economy is always surprised by the cyclical changes every 22 months or so.) Investing in shares as against local authority loans, government bonds as against long-term bank deposits, current accounts as against building society shares – all these have cycles against which any particular schemes can be measured.

Examining these cycles may well show which is the most propitious moment to launch, and into which market. Lyons were very fortunate with Ready Brek, in that the consumers chose a market that was growing. Lyons themselves had chosen a market in the latter stages of decline – indeed, they had chosen the only sector of the breakfast cereal market that was declining at the time.

Figure 9 deliberately combines a summary of the characteristics of each stage with the generalized profile, but we always need to consider the two together. In the Ready Brek case, for example, entering a declining market should have meant high unit costs of promotion; encountering defensive pricing strategies from the competition; and overcoming the habits of ageing nostalgics in the porridge market. Compare that with the characteristics of a growth market which was the phase of the market Lyons actually found themselves. The marketing strategies required, and the chances of a long and successful life, are completely different.

5.8 Attacking the profit curve

One mistake that is often made is to believe that profit inevitably follows volume trends. It is quite possible to improve profits even though volume is in decline. This is where techniques of value analysis are so important. Basically, there are four things that a company might do:

1 Produce the same product at a lower cost (perhaps due to improved technology or larger runs) with no movement in price

2 Produce the same product at lower costs and pass some (or all) of the benefit to customers in the form of lower prices

3 Improve the product at no increase in cost – when there will be the option of keeping the price unchanged or of increasing the price by a sum lower than the extra value offered

94

4   Improve a product and be able to increase the price by quite a bit – regardless of whether costs per unit have gone up or down.

There is, of course, a relationship between quality, volume and price. One cannot be moved without affecting the others. The question is always that of the optimum mix of quality, volume and price at which the company maximizes its profit.

That is why it is unfortunate that so many companies divorce cost-cutting from marketing. Particular care must always be exercised to ensure that the customers' view of the outcome of cost-reduction agrees with those of the manufacturer. Many years ago, when Symbol Biscuits was independent, it decided to improve the quality of its biscuits by a system of central pumping of animal fats into all products. Moreover, this could be done at a significant saving over the older system for different fats of different products. Unfortunately for Symbol, consumers had grown to like vegetable fats, which was what the competition then offered, and the decline in sales of the more popular lines vastly offset the anticipated economies.

The moral ought to be clear – there are two roles for marketing departments in all cost-cutting exercises:

1   To ensure an understanding of the customer's perception of standards (ie, that the products continue to provide the same mix of satisfactions as they did formerly) and
2   To consider whether the changes offer new marketing strategies or tactics.

In other words, in the ideal situation, volume and profit trends should be considered together.

5.9   Alternative shapes

At the end of a day during a consultancy exercise with a leading UK company, which involved our six questions and the life-cycle, there was a consensus of opinion in the salesforce that four of their products were at such an advanced stage of decline that they ought to be abandoned (two of them were the company's biggest-selling lines).

The size and rapidity of the decline had convinced the salesforce that these products would not pick up again. In actual fact, what had happened was that wide knowledge of impending Customs and Excise Duty increases had resulted in enormous stocks being built up at the retail level, as well as the personal level. As soon as the product field was hit by the increases, orders fell away alarmingly. This was explained the next day, with the launch of a plan to boost demand – which was very successful. But what that example emphasizes is that conventional graphs smooth over short-term movements which can be misleading if one happens to sit at a peak or trough – unless the reasons for that peak or trough are taken into account.

5.10 Natural re-cycle

Figure 11 shows a product which seems to have been experiencing a conventional life-cycle and begun to show signs of tailing off when, suddenly and without any impetus from the manufacturer, sales take off again and repeat the early shape. Usually, the later phases are smaller versions of the first. Sometimes, they are much larger. The size of the re-cycle depends, in the first place, on how right the manufacturer was in positioning the product compared to the use for which customers want it. Re-cycles are characteristic of markets where future growth depends on finding new applications. Any market for systems is a good example. Computers were extensively used in the first instance for such tasks as payroll and invoicing. Then came sales records and analysis and it quickly became apparent that combining sales orders, records and invoices was leading to the need for a total information system. Carbonless papers have experienced a natural re-cycle growth curve as customers have discovered new uses, sometimes ahead of suppliers.

To guard against the danger of anticipating a longer or shorter decline than may really occur, close contact must be kept with

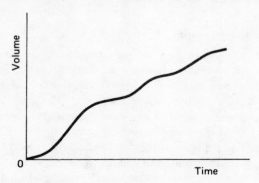

Figure 11 *Natural re-cycle*

customers and all new uses must be rapidly communicated back to head office so that they are assessed and promoted if thought to be worthwhile. Similarly, customer needs change all the time and their new needs should be analyzed to see whether available services or products are capable of meeting them. It may be the case that a new, or improved, product or service is required.

5.11   The humpback

The product which shows a humpback on its sales graph can be even more misleading, for it shows an actual decline before staging an apparently remarkable recovery (Figure 12). Most often this sort of graph is seen with new processes and materials in the case of industrial markets.

Why does this happen? Buyers often place trial orders, perhaps for a new material or process to be tried out in one section of a plant. They will not want enormous quantities of a product until they have thoroughly evaluated it. Their opinions, based on completed trials, will probably have to be confirmed by the Decision Making Unit. Until this has happened, few further orders will be placed. If everything works well, and the new product is approved, sales will take off. Some of the people who tried the product or process will decide against it, but they will be replaced by others.

There is a close parallel in consumer markets. We referred earlier to experimenters who try everything. In any successful new product launched in a high-frequency market, an average of 65 per cent of repeat sales will follow peak sales. The rest represent once-only buyers who experiment with a new product and then decide, for one of any number of reasons, not to take to it. Now, you might

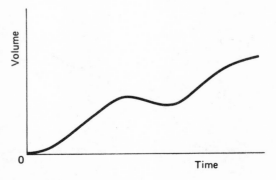

Figure 12   *'Humpback' cycle*

97

therefore expect that, after the initial peak, sales will plateau at 65 per cent. This is not so: the slope of the curve will be dictated by how frequently that 65 per cent decide to buy the product.

Clearly, one needs to maintain a very close relationship with customers while trials are in progress, to evaluate the severity and extent of the downturn in the hump, as well as to evaluate how large a recovery or upswing will result when orders start coming in after potential customers are satisfied with the performance of the product.

5.12   The plateau

This is self-explanatory, though the illustration in Figure 13 has a plateau which has a slight up-slope to it. In most markets, stability means growth in line with the economy. Actually, quite a sharp growth is needed annually to keep pace with inflation. And anything less than that means an actual loss of market position – and, possibly, profitability.

Products show a graph of this sort in situations where nothing better is available. The sales pattern for energy products (wood, coal, horse power) is due to this factor. This can mean a pleasant long life – until one is faced with the possibility of a quick demise of the product because of rapid replacement as soon as an acceptable substitute is found. Interestingly, when one is announced, it tends to have a humpbacked sales graph (for reasons which will now be evident to you). Demand for the new product will parallel a drop in demand for the product being replaced. Demand for such plateau products therefore tends to drop away very rapidly indeed, when it does drop. This can be particularly unpleasant for producers who

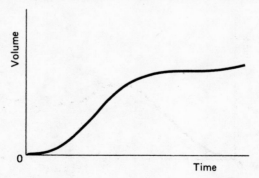

Figure 13   *Plateau cycle*

are unable to change their product – many plateau products are commodities and raw materials, and the majority of producing countries involved do not have resources to find and launch replacements.

5.13 The rampart

Figure 14 shows a life-cycle that seems to be halfway between a humpback and a plateau. It also appears to have something of the running level at which new consumer products might settle after dispensing with once-only buyers. The curve in Figure 14 could also represent the market for letterpress machinery, where it shows the effect of two life-cycles together: first, in relation to major markets, and second, in relation to subsidiary ones. The major markets will have moved on to more modern machinery, but there may still be a sufficient number of small-scale or specialist printers who confine their work to letterpress, which is still the best printing method for certain jobs under particular conditions.

Markets do not always die in one fell swoop. They often change their nature and scale. One can make use of this, by promoting new uses for a product which may enable a minority of users to increase their usage.

5.14 The generation cycle

It is possible to be sceptical about any of these cycles, and the generation cycle has attracted more scepticism than any of the others. Figure 15 (page 100) illustrates the cycle. The problem with this cycle is that it operates over such a long time-scale.

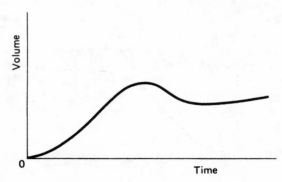

Figure 14 *'Rampart' cycle*

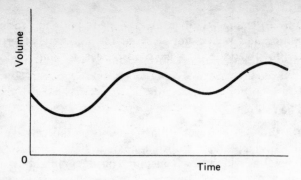

Figure 15 *Generation re-cycle*

The cycle relates to the sorts of fundamental changes in taste which arise, for example, across generations. The USA used to be a tea-drinking country (remember the Boston tea party?); it is now largely a coffee-drinking country, with tea occupying a special position because it is consumed mainly in iced form as a cold drink. Britain, on the other hand, used to be a coffee-drinking country; so much so, that the consumption of coffee in public places was banned at one time, because it was thought to cause too much interference in the nation's business.

Why have tastes changed so much? Principally because of changes of fashion among young people. By and large, in both countries, it was not the older people who changed habits. When out of the home, young people often express a preference for a different drink than that usually consumed at home. The different drink comes to be preferred in restaurants; gradually becomes the acceptable drink for the young among themselves; starts being served in each other's homes – and, inevitably, when these young people leave home and have families of their own, this becomes the drink of first choice.

Fashions come back too. Builders who once tore out fitted cupboards busily built them back in again later. Four-poster beds came back into fashion a few years ago; divans are for those furnishing deliberately in the 1930s style. Earrings have been through a phase when they were in for men, and granny prints for ladies' dresses.

All these are, of course, consumer items. The more considered the item, the less room there is for the dictates of fashion or for sheer rebellion. Where revolutions of style happen in non-consumer areas, it is because new uses have been found, new

100

reasons for use have been discovered (such as health and ecology) or simply because supplies of the replacement have run out or are temporarily in short supply. For example, there was a sudden upsurge in demand for 'old-fashioned' Kraft paper, for the outer protection of products during the petrol crisis of 1974. This was because the market had become dominated by shrink-wrapped plastic, which depends on oil.

5.15 Cycles: so what?

It will be clear that while such cycles can be seen by hindsight, it is difficult to know at any one dip or high, whether it is a temporary aberration or a more sustained phenomenon, and if so, which of the cycles it represents.

So the most useful questions to ask are: can these be identified correctly? Can they be anticipated? Can one do anything to speed them up? Do they offer us any clues on how to prolong the life of a product? How can one attempt to estimate the position of a market (or a product within a market) on a life-cycle curve?

5.16 Re-cycling products to prolong life

As we have already seen, one of the things that can be done in an attempt to prolong the life of a product is to re-cycle or re-launch it – though market forces are sometimes altogether too strong for any remedial action to be taken. Products like Lyons' individual fruit pies seem to have successfully withstood the ravages of time – though they have, in fact, changed dramatically over the years. The flavours have changed, the ingredients have been altered, and the shape has gone from round to square and back to round. Along with changes in packaging, and new advertising appeals, these efforts have all been aimed at giving a new impetus to sales so as to offset many of the characteristics (especially boredom) which afflict buyers when a product is in a mature market.

Liquid coffee, on the other hand, seems to be a classic example of the creation of a life-cycle in a reasonably short period. Before the Second World War, liquid coffee (or coffee essence) sold in bottles, represented by far the greatest volume of coffee consumed in the UK (measured in actual cups consumed). After the end of the war that situation continued for a few years and then the unmistakable signs began to appear: the younger householders were turning to the new instant coffees with flavours particularly appealing to those brought up on tea. Since then, hardly any significant quantity of new young buyers has come into that market. Liquid coffee is a case where taste and fashion appear to be too firmly against the product, because coffee essence lacks a modern image.

Planned re-cycling follows the example of Lyons' individual fruit pies. Figure 16 shows how such an attempt might appear, if successful. The natural growth curve of the first cycle is called the primary phase: this is what is expected to happen as a result of the initial positioning and marketing of the product. There are many ways in which a product can be re-cycled.

Changes in promotional appeals can do a remarkable amount for sales even without any change in the product – the perception of the product changes its value and appeal, and therefore the satisfaction it claims to offer. Sales of Oxo had plateaud for decades – the three most obvious 'bumps' in an otherwise flat sales graph correspond with the two World Wars and the Depression. At one stage, it appeared that only the start of another World War would move sales! A new advertising agency was commissioned to see what it could do, and it came up with two major strategies. One was a whole-hearted concentration on using Oxo for gravy-making instead of promoting it as a nutritious hot drink, and the other was to emphasize the role that Oxo could play in giving flavour to the cheaper cuts of meat. It was reasoned that in times of hardship sales had risen without any effort from the manufacturers, as far as could

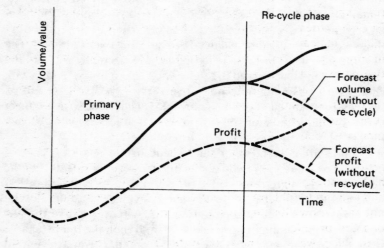

Figure 16 *Policy re-cycle*

102

be discovered because householders were using Oxo almost as a meat substitute.

So the only thing that was changed was the positioning of the product. Advertising set out to teach young householders how to make use of cheaper cuts of meat to make attractive, warming and healthy meals. The slogan 'Oxo gives a meal man appeal' became the theme of one of the most famous and longest-running television commercials in advertising history (the 'Katie' series). Subsequently, as that re-cycle seemed to lose steam, other means were used to jack up a falling sales curve. Flavoured Oxo ('Chicken' and 'Curry') were launched and an even meatier 'super' variety ('Golden Oxo') was added. Product variants provided a degree of excitement to a market in danger of becoming blasé, but they also provided the means of achieving new aspirations among those whose cooking habits had been changed by the message of the advertising. Eventually, even 'Katie' gave way to new advertising appeals.

Of course, you can find yourself in a re-cycle purely by chance. Often, it is by grace of a competitor who has made a mistake and left the field to you. Sometimes, especially in smaller markets, a new form of competition can add impetus to the older market. The heavy promotion behind lawnmowers which use the hover principle gave a big boost to all forms of lawnmower. Users of hand mowers wanted to look at the new machinery, and many found that the new mower was not suitable for their needs. Many found that the lack of roller did not give the familiar swathed pattern of the traditional English garden, so they turned to a petrol mower. An even larger number of people decided that it was time they bought a new mower in any case – even a hand one. And the phenomenon of the two-mower family came about.

A major attack by Qualcast on the hover market (using the advertising slogan 'It's a lot less bovver than a hover') created a reverse situation, with owners of hover mowers adding a cylinder mower to their stable.

Many companies have benefitted from another company's actions. Even more might have done so, or might have done better, had they been able to identify more rapidly what was happening, and had treated the preliminary stage of the re-cycle (even though not of their own making) just as they would the introductory stage of a new product.

In what ways are new products different from re-launched products? Re-cycled products change one or more of the following:

formula, price, distribution, availability, market position. They may involve moving into a completely new area of business, though it is always sound advice to stay close to businesses that you know well and understand. So one must always ask what can be done to regenerate profits from existing brands before moving into new fields where the company lacks experience. Often the two moves can go together, and the marginally improved profits of a revitalized product can be enough to offset the investment stages of completely new items and companies.

5.17 Finding out where you are

Success and failure in business are difficult to identify when they are happening. They are essentially comparative terms: business can be good compared with last year and lousy measured against the year before. Success is often like good health. You don't know you've got it until you lose it.

The biggest problem is the temptation to treat the life-cycle curve like any other sales graph and attempt to make conventional sales forecasts based on that. Sales forecasts rely on extrapolations from the past. The past is too heavily weighted to events that are not likely to recur. If more weight is given to recent events there is the danger that insufficient regard will be given to factors which might be capable of reversing the trend. What you need to understand is the reason for your sales, by analyzing customers according to relevant characteristics, by knowledge of their buying habits, and by the uses they make of the goods or services bought. You can then take intelligent action in response to the information.

This emphasizes the need for accurate and adequate customer records. The other thing to remember about sales forecasts and sales plans is that the competition is not going to sit back and allow you a clear run at the market. They too have know-how and guile; they too will be making their plans; they will counter-attack as soon as they see what you are up to.

In most markets, buyers enter at different times. That is why a market may give the appearance of growth when it has almost reached saturation – even if the buyers are all first-time buyers who are not coming back. So what do you need to do? You need to look at customers. Ask the six questions outlined earlier (who is buying, when, how often, where, for what are they using the product, why are they buying from you?). Then you are likely to stand a very much better chance of knowing where you are in a life-cycle and, more important, why you are in that position. It is only then that you can take action to change the situation.

The concept of the life-cycle gives you something to measure yourself against, something which helps you determine what kinds of battles you are fighting, or ought to be fighting. The concept of the life-cycle is an aid to making sense of your business, not a magical chart which tells you how you can work out what sales you are going to have.

Consider your life-cycle against the typical life-cycle in your industry, and against the life-cycle of your competitors. Think whether there is anything to be learned from the other life-cycle charts; ask yourself what has put you where you are, and whether any of these things can be changed to your advantage. From the welter of evidence and ideas that emerges as a result of this process, the prime task is to isolate the important ones from the unimportant ones. That, unfortunately, is a matter of experience, judgment, sensitivity, intuition and all the other things that go into the black box that is you!

The key area to consider is always buyer behaviour. Identify the changes that are taking place, and those that appear likely to take place. Ask yourself why the changes are happening. What will be the effect on your business? How can you change what you are doing in order to match the needs of the market more closely? Here are some other questions which may be of use:

1 Have any new competitors appeared on the market? Might environmental factors affect consumer habits in your market? Examples of these are legal changes, interest changes and cheaper or faster machinery.

2 Has the profile of consumers changed in any significant way? Is your market growing older, on average? Or younger? Are all your customers long-standing ones? Is there a sufficient number of newer users joining their ranks? Has the socio-economic structure of your market as a whole, or of your clientele, changed? Do customers still come from the same areas? If not, why not? What has happened to change things? Is this desirable or undesirable? Do you have to accept those changes as inevitable? Are there changes you want to accelerate; new changes you want to bring about?

3 Has the number of shops or distributors carrying your lines changed? Where and why? Have stock levels changed? Have the terms of business made it more difficult for customers to buy your products in their former quantities?

4   What has happened to the frequency of buying and the regularity of use? How has the size of the average order changed – from that of the final end-user, to that of intermediaries in the distribution network?

5   How have circumstances changed for your competitors, direct and indirect? Can anything be learned from them?

5.18   Summary

The concept of the life-cycle is a generalization that describes what happens to a market when no steps are taken to change direction. Familiarity with the possible shapes of life-cycles, and knowledge of those in your industry and product field, helps to understand what may be happening in your own case. Such an understanding will help you to overcome the influence of market forces which will otherwise drive you into the ground. A proper understanding of the market and of the life-cycle helps you control the destiny of your products and services. Deliberate re-cycling of a product can give new life to a flagging sales curve.

Re-cycling is accomplished by improvements to the basic satisfactions offered; by price changes; or by changes in market position. It is important not to confuse the life-cycle graph with a sales graph. The only thing which will help you to improve sales is an understanding of the underlying buying behaviour which has led to the present situation with your products and services. The six-question analysis is an invaluable aid to discovering where you are in the life-cycle and what you should do to reduce the threats and maximize the opportunities which confront you.

5.19   Checklist

1   Businesses are like people. They gestate, are born, grow rapidly at first, then more slowly, reach a state of maturity, go into decline and finally die. These stages describe the 'life-cycle' of a product or service.

2   There are two principal types of life-cycle:
    a. product life-cycle, which describes an individual product or brand, and
    b. demand life-cycle which describes a market.

3   The life-cycle has a generalized shape which describes what will happen, eventually, to any particular product or service, as well as to any sector or market, *unless steps are taken to change the situation.*

4   In the introductory stage, the buyers are probably the experimenters and the fashion leaders. Creating awareness of the new product or service will be the major aim, and resulting promotional costs will be high per unit sold. Depending upon market conditions, there may be a choice between launching at a high price to ensure rapid profitability, or at a low price to ensure rapid penetration and quicker pay-back of initial investment costs.

5   The growth stage attracts the trend-setters. Promotion must aim, therefore, at increasing understanding – of product qualities, uses, applications, and so on. Prices may be flexible, depending on the launch decision. If a high price was set, this may be lowered to deter or attack newcomers. If already low, promotional prices will be used rather than a further reduction in nominal price.

6   Maturity can be very short or very lengthy. In general, the longer it is, the more changes in the profit cycle are likely. Volume is usually easier to hold static than profits (because costs rise). By this phase, all likely 'followers' will have been attracted into the market. Promotional costs should be at their highest and advertising will concentrate on convincing users of the wisdom of their choice (and thus resisting the blandishments of competitive advertising and promotion). By now, too, a stable price policy (and the relation between list prices and promotional prices) should have been established.

7   Decline brings the options of holding the decline to that of the market as a whole; trying to out-pace the market by declining more slowly; or getting out. A policy of 'milking' is usually the most profitable. This is done by reducing the costs of selling to the minimum. The real 'nostalgics' will make efforts to continue to buy and this often maintains a low level of profitability for longer than anticipated when the strategy is set.

8   Products may be sold even though they are in marked decline, provided they continue to make a sufficient contribution to company overheads. This may be particularly significant when a more profitable product shares resources with one in decline.

9   Each product should be examined from the viewpoint of its own product life-cycle and the demand life-cycle for the market or product category in which it sells. Different products have different shares within the overall demand

life-cycle. It therefore becomes important to decide whether the demand cycle influences the individual product shapes or whether it is the other way round. Products that follow fashion or technological trends tend, as a rule, to be influenced by the demand cycle. However, even these can be influenced by a major, late introduction. It is possible that the entry of IBM into the personal computer market will become a classic example of this.

10　Five alternative shapes of demand cycles were identified (Figures 11 to 15). These occur more frequently, but not exclusively, in industrial markets. Perhaps the most dangerous, because of the possibility of complacence, is that described as the 'plateau'. It is safe to regard a plateau as a sign that customers cannot find anything better – but if they do they will quickly change to it.

11　Ideally, the decline stage will be prevented by recycling the product. That is, revamping it in such a way that new and additional customer benefits are perceived, and volume and profit increase as a result. However, this is not always possible, and a company should always be considering completely new products, so that it has growth phases for new products which offset the decline stages of older products.

12　The profit cycle can be considered separately from the demand curve and, if forced to choose between them, it is usually better to attack the profit curve rather than attempt to increase profits from volume efforts. There is usually a cost associated with attacking volume. However, it is dangerous to consider profit without thinking of what alternative marketing strategies and tactics might be appropriate.

13　It is particularly important carefully to measure whether customers view value changes in the same way you do.

14　It is not easy to recognize the shape of a life-cycle before you have passed a turning point. So it is better to examine the reasons why products in your field are going through a curve of that particular shape, and why your own particular products are where they are.

6

The marketing mix

It ain't what you do, it's the way that you do it.
That's what gets results.

(Popular song of the 1940s.)

In Chapter 2, we considered the marketing of different types of
businesses – industrial, consumer, service, etc. In this chapter, we
are going to look at a number of tools that are used in marketing.
What makes the difference in the marketplace is the number of
tools chosen, and the intelligence and thoroughness with which they
are used. The way these techniques are put together, and the
relative weight they are given, is called 'the marketing mix'.

6.1 Definitions

The simplest definition of the marketing mix is 'the Four Ps':
Product
Price
Place
Promotion
Each of these is reasonably self-explanatory, though 'Place' refers
not only to where the goods are made available, but also to the
channels through which they reach customers and intermediaries,
and the physical methods by which they are delivered.

It is sometimes thought that 'Selling' ought to be added to the
ingredients that go to make up the marketing mix. Proponents of
the Four Ps include selling under 'Promotion', because the Four Ps
provide a simple and easily remembered definition.

However, a less memorable and more accurate definition of the
marketing mix is:

Those elements which are capable of manipulation and variation
in order to improve the effectiveness of marketing programmes,
the way in which they are planned and combined, their relative
importance, and the proportion of each used to produce a desired
effect.

The elements of that definition are worth detailing:

1. *'Manipulation and variation'* You can change the order of importance, vary the money spent, make short-term tactical changes or long-term strategic ones.
2. *'To improve effectiveness'* Each company should strive to discover its optimum mix, which might be defined, simply, as the least amount of money and effort needed to achieve profit objectives.
3. *'Planned and combined'* Few of the items in the mix are complete substitutes, so the way they are used together is all-important.
4. *'Relative importance'* This can change from time to time.
5. *'Proportions . . . to produce a desired effect'* This is the area where the differences between competing companies really show. Otherwise, the major differences between marketing approaches are caused by the fact that certain elements of the marketing mix are not available, not appropriate, or simply don't work in that particular field or with that particular product.

6.2 The elements

Even the simplest list (eg, the Four Ps) is capable of enormous expansion. 'Price', for example, could include credit terms, cash discounts, prompt payment allowances, and so on. It is possible to look at the expanded list in terms of its direct, ancillary and indirect elements, as follows.

PRODUCT AND SERVICE PLANNING

The product or service itself is of course a 'direct' element, and it has various factors such as performance factors, target market sectors, and so on. 'Indirect' elements, such as market research and R&D, help specify the product performance and the appropriate target markets.

Key factors under this heading are identifying, anticipating and satisfying demand; the use of the six questions, portfolio analysis, the product's name; etc.

PRICING

This covers all such questions as: are you going after a premium market, for the middle of the market, for a low, stable or flexible market? Do you want one standard price or do you want price differentiation? What does 'price' include (terms, discounts, deals, etc.)? What are your trade margins going to be? And are they going to follow convention or break new ground?

SALES CHANNELS

Which ones are you going to use? Direct ones or indirect ones? How many levels do you want between yourself and the customer – you could have a single intermediary (for example, a distributor) or you could have several (eg, wholesaler, retailers). How are you going to select channel members – by qualifications, purchase or service levels; by offering an exclusive opening; by creating franchises; by being open to all?

PHYSICAL DISTRIBUTION

What methods are you going to use? What distribution schedules are most efficient? What sort of stock-holding policy are you going to have – in relation to how much you stock, as well as in relation to where you stock?

PERSONAL SELLING

What is the sales force to do (take orders, deliver, influence orders)? How many sales people should you have? In what form of management control ought you to invest? How will the salesforce be paid – salary only, commission only, salary plus commission?

ADVERTISING

How large a proportion of your overall budget will you devote to this? Who will you try to reach with this (the trade, customers or end-users)? What media do you intend to use? How often will you advertise? What sort of support would you like to offer to your dealers and distributors? Do you have objectives for your advertising budget which are clearly specified? What relationship will advertising have to other promotional methods and to personal selling?

PROMOTIONS

What role will promotions have in your mix? What will be its relation to advertising and personal selling? Will you aim your promotions at your customers, your end-users or the trade? Have you thought through and specified the objectives of your promotions clearly (eg, loyalty, trial, stocking, etc.)? How frequently will you use promotions – continuously, regularly, spasmodically, as the

111

occasion demands? Will you use promotions primarily as offence or as defence?

PACKING AND DISPLAY

This has practical aspects, such as adequate protection, convenience and identification. So you have to think carefully about materials and design. Do you have to package separately for the trade and the end-user? How important a role will be played by packaging and display?

SERVICE LEVELS

To whom do you want to emphasize service – dealer or customer? By whom? Where (at customer locations, factory, service depot)? How important is service going to be? (The more similar the product, the more important service is likely to be, and it is more important with technically complex products – though the Japanese seem to get away with practically no service.) How prompt do you propose to make your service – before sales, during installation, after sales? Who do you propose should pay for service and spares – and should it be on a full-cost basis, free or subsidized?

PUBLIC RELATIONS

How important a role is this going to play? Have you defined the various sectors of the public who will need to be serviced in different ways – customers, trade, shareholders, City institutions, workforce? What sorts of PR activities are appropriate for you to undertake, and at what level? Will they be related to particular times or events in any way?

One may well question the separation of advertising, promotion and public relations, and some people prefer 'Publicity' to 'Promotion' as the fourth 'P'. It may also seem questionable to leave public relations to the end. Advertising, promotion and public relations are separated here because they are treated that way by perhaps the majority of companies. Vast numbers of companies find media advertising inappropriate or still rely heavily on press releases to influence customers, and trade promotions to influence stockists. As for public relations, one ought to distinguish between product PR and corporate PR. The first is clearly a form of promotional publicity which has a 'direct' element. Corporate PR has more in common with the 'indirect' elements. We have put PR last because it is the one area where product and corporate aims are frequently confused, usually to the detriment of the needs of the product.

112

6.3 Why mixes vary

Different businesses and different companies enjoy different marketing mixes for three reasons: market, company and personal. Ideally, mix decisions are:

- *defined* by market reasons (who buys; where; how often; through which channels; direct and indirect competition?) and
- *conditioned* by company reasons (strengths and weaknesses; resources; traditions and conventions; attitudes).

Unfortunately, the mix is often determined on the basis of personal reasons, such as:

- Managerial background (for example, a manager with a financial background may distrust advertising because of the difficulties of quantifying results)
- Beliefs about the effectiveness of mix ingredients (salespeople often prefer to reduce prices or offer give-aways rather than use follow-up media advertising)
- Attitudes to change and risk (often revealed in statements like 'In an old-established business like ours . . .', 'That hasn't been done in this industry for the last . . .', 'It might work for soap powders . . .').

6.4 Typical mixes

Figure 17 (page 114) shows typical marketing mixes for six different types of business. For each of them, it considers whether the possible elements are of high, medium or low importance. You will notice that the diagram doesn't quite tie up with the list of 'direct' elements in Section 6.2: an extra item, 'Merchandising', has been added. Strictly speaking, this is an 'ancillary' item (ancillary to personal selling) but it is such an important element in the mix of fast-moving consumer goods (FMCG) that the diagram would be quite misleading without it. 'Personal selling' is not highly important in the FMCG category but 'Merchandising' is, and that explains why companies in that sector often employ a very large number of salespeople. The diagram is largely self-explanatory, though some explanation may be helpful.

Sales channels are of high importance only in the FMCG category. They are of medium importance to consumer durables only because that heading covers a wide range of goods (including those for which sales channel decisions are of prime importance) as

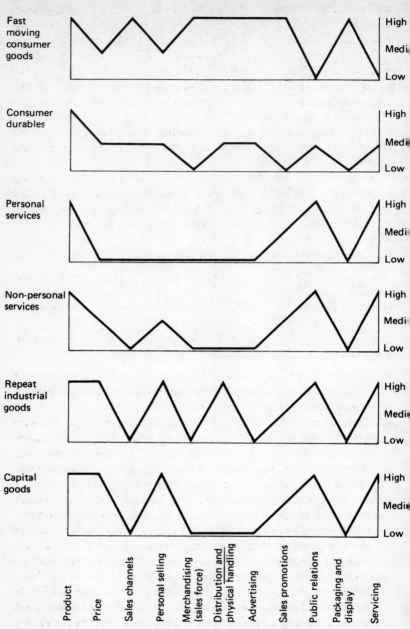

Figure 17 *Typical marketing mix patterns by industry type*

well as to those who are supplied direct to end-users. Although sales channels are shown as 'low' in importance for personal services, many such services are, of course, provided in retail outlets.

Personal selling is used most where sales are made directly by manufacturers to customers. Again, personal services are the exception. Suppliers of those services cannot create the *need*; the customer normally seeks out the provider of the service when he or she needs it.

The importance of physical distribution increases with frequency of purchase and the number of sales channels through which it has to pass.

Although packaging and display are of high importance only for FMCGs, this is an area where many industrial companies have been able to produce significant benefits by packaging and clever identification (such as colour coding for drugs in hospitals).

6.5 Manipulating the mix

A company's skill at determining the right marketing mix and varying it in the best way as time progresses, is crucial to competitive success. Ways in which the mix might be manipulated are shown for different categories of product in Figure 17.

To gain competitive advantage on the basis of the marketing mix, you can:

- Choose a radically different mix from your competitors. In long-established markets with traditional patterns, it may be better to stick with convention.

- Keep to the same mix but do better. Again, the improvements must be in areas your customers rate highly. This usually means that you have to try to improve in an area where your competitors already do well. If you are behind your competitors in this aspect, here is where you *must* improve.

- Keep to the traditional mix but make changes to specific elements. If sales channels are of great importance, are there new ways of getting your products to your prospects? Think of the way you buy things now compared with ten and 20 years ago and you will realize how even strongly-entrenched conventions can be attacked. A very simple example is the way in which the quantities customers buy has changed: the popularity of freezers and cars means that where people used to buy, say, one 1-kilo pack of washing powder a few years ago, they now buy a 5-kilo pack.

6.6 Summary

The marketing mix concept is the key to the profitable employment of the technique-related areas of marketing. The mix accounts for differences in marketing tactics employed in different industries as well as those adopted by competitors in the same market. However, varying the mix will only be valuable if it results in significant customer benefits; improves the cost-effectiveness of supplying those benefits; or reduces or eliminates expenditure on activities that do not produce rewarding benefits.

6.7 Checklist

1   The simplest description of the 'marketing mix' is that it consists of the Four Ps: product, price, place and promotion.
2   Controllable variables can be combined in different ways to produce desired results.
3   Opinions vary as to what elements should be included in 'marketing mix'. It helps to classify them as:
    Direct: the controllable, variable elements.
    Ancillary: those that represent extensions of the first category (for example, discounting can be regarded as ancillary to pricing).
    Indirect: elements which are not really items in the marketing mix but the use of which leads to a decision about the way the mix is assembled or varied. (Think, for example, of the effect of corporate PR on a company's products.)
4   Mixes vary for reasons relating to one or more of the following:
    The market
    The company
    Personal factors
5   In an ideal world, personal reasons would be unimportant.
6   The marketing mix should be selected for market reasons, but may have to be conditioned by company reasons (for example, strengths, weaknesses, abilities, resources).
7   Typical marketing mixes for a range of industries are shown in Figure 17. In each industry, a company's market mix may be manipulated by:
    ● Choosing a different mix from competition.
    ● Using a similar mix but performing better in one or more areas.
    ● Maintaining a similar mix but changing one or more elements.

8 Although we have considered only the relevant elements of the marketing mix, the amount of money which can be put behind particular elements, or the manpower devoted, can be decisive factors in selecting a successful marketing mix.

7

Where shall we go next?

'Would you tell me, please, which way I ought to go from here?'
'That depends a good deal on where you want to get to,' said the
Cat.
'I don't much care where . . .' said Alice.
'Then it doesn't matter which way you go', said the Cat.

Lewis Carroll

After completing the six questions, an exploration of life-cycle
issues, and the marketing mix, the next step which you can take
usefully is to compare a description of opportunities before you with
an analysis of actual results and profitability.

One of several conclusions could emerge from such a study.
Perhaps the results are out of line with the potential? If so, you need
to consider whether the day-to-day figures have concealed the real
movements in the market or whether the results of the self-analysis
have been altogether too pessimistic. It is not unknown, as an
earlier example showed, for short-term events to cast too long a
shadow on estimates of the future. The kinds of analysis that have
been suggested so far will highlight what kind of company you have
now and suggest what kind of company it could become.

7.1 Straightforward products

Nothing in business is ever all that straightforward. Nevertheless,
some areas are simpler to examine and deal with than others. The
first two of the five headings to be considered under the general
heading of 'straightforward products' are specifically related to the
life-cycle; the third may well be, although there could be other
explanations; the other two are quite unrelated.

PRESENT PROFITMAKERS
These are the lines which, however they are measured, are current
profit contributors. More than that, they have some clear and
continuous history of profit behind them and they are short of the

saturation point on their life-cycle. In all probability, candidates for this position will be towards the top of the growth phase and into maturity. It is difficult to be absolutely precise about the position on the cycle: in short-life products, a present profitmaker may only come about in the maturity phase; with a very long-life one, it could happen when it is fairly well advanced along the growth phase. In any case, one feels that these products are safe: efforts can be made to maximize profits and market share for as long as possible.

FUTURE PROFITMAKERS

These are products that have earned their spurs, as it were, but do not have a sufficient track record as profit-earners to justify the highest ranking. Again, the length of the life-cycle will determine the actual stage on the curve where this phase begins and ends. To qualify for this second group of profit-earners, a brand must have a sufficiently strong growth in volume to instil confidence that the product will continue to grow – and bring profits.

PROFITABLE SPECIALS

Few companies can resist the temptation to move at least marginally away from their main stream of activity. Frequently, the use of common resources (and especially where common plant is used) can fool the company into thinking that it is still sticking to its knitting.

Examples of such departures from the straight and narrow might be life assurance offices which provide cover for ballet dancers' injuries; or, for an industrial manufacturer, bolts in odd sizes and non-metric threads. No doubt, they were accepted as worth doing because they were perceived as low-risk by-products of main-stream activities.

Such marginal products are accepted because of the impression that no special or additional efforts will need to be put behind these lines. In fact it is almost certain that there will be. Look at it this way: someone's enthusiasm put the product into the range in the first place, and when that person is a senior manager, others may assume (and often rightly) that these lines are not to be deprived of attention. The actual time taken selling them can be much more than was ever anticipated and, thus, the real profit is much less than it might have been if the time could have been used for more central, higher-profit products.

Oil companies are good examples of firms that have found profitable 'specials' taking up more and more of representatives' time. They started by providing items like stationery and overalls as an additional service to their site-owners. Over the years, the time spent on those items has grown to take up the greater proportion of many an oil representative's call-time. When such products are being considered for inclusion, it is a good idea to err on the side of caution in estimating the resources employed, the 'nuisance value' entailed, and the danger that resources (which are always in short supply) will be allocated to products which produce less than the best return.

PRIORITY DEVELOPMENT PRODUCTS

By the time a business has examined itself in the ways suggested, it may well begin to feel that it has been going in directions that are not as good as others it might have chosen, and that its plans for future development have been on the wrong lines. If so, it should look very closely at products it may have in the pipeline. On the one hand, there is the danger of wasting investments of time, resources and money. On the other hand is the possibility that continuing the developments may lead to new problems later.

Between these is the possibility that the profits of present products will not be able to cover the turn-round time required to convert the present company into the 'new' company it wants to become. The latter is a good case for pushing ahead with priority projects. This may be the time to upgrade some development items which line up with the new directions which are emerging from the marketing re-examination.

FAILURES

If a company is unable to identify a product line as a failure right up to the time that it actually fails in the market, then immediate action ought to be taken to discover the cause, and do what is necessary to prevent this ever happening in the future.

Businesspeople fear failure. So much so that they are often reluctant to admit failure even to themselves. Yet business history is full of failures that have been compounded by this very fear. History also shows that success can be due to the rapid excision of failures. Tesco Supermarkets provides an example of very good practice in this matter: any of their stores that doesn't come up to target within a short and clearly-defined trading period is mercilessly closed.

Associated with the fear of failure is a worry about loss of face. Yet the fact is that courageous action never loses face; what can be disastrous is when your customer recognizes that your line is a failure before you do. This is never more true than with items selling through retailers, wholesalers and distributors. Nothing disturbs them more (for they live by stock-turn) than 'sleepers' – that is, lines that just sit on their shelves and never move. Rapid action often earns the opportunity of going back to the same store or depot with an improved version and getting a fair chance on the shelves again. Companies with such a reputation find the launching of new products easier.

Good money can easily be poured in after bad, and there is a strong case for withdrawing unprofitable lines as early as possible – as soon as one is certain that nothing can be done effectively to save them. However, as we have noted earlier, there may be circumstances where it can make some sense to maintain an unprofitable line for a while. The only real safeguard is to have sufficient sources of profit at various stages of development and life-cycle to enable swift excisions of failed or poor products whenever necessary.

Products can fail for one of innumerable reasons. Even within an otherwise healthy growth curve, a product can sink because of inherent lack of profitability, wrong pricing strategy, high cost of sales, bad management, and so on. All these things can easily happen quite early in the life-cycle and it may be necessary to take the decision to withdraw even though the sales curve holds out promise of further growth.

It is all too easy to arrive at a position where good volume can be achieved, but the prices continue to be uneconomic. Many businesspeople refer to this as the 'plastic pipe syndrome': it was discovered that plastic piping for the building trade could only achieve sales at prices that did not justify making the pipes.

7.2   Problem products

The dividing line between straightforward and problem products is a thin one. The bottom of the 'straightforward' list begins to merge with the top of the 'problem products' category: a failure is obviously a problem that has been allowed to go too far. Specials can so easily become problems if they are not watched very closely.

In any case, the following four categories of product represent some of the more difficult areas of business. It is in these areas that effective marketing can really come into its own.

YESTERDAY'S PROFITMAKERS/TODAY'S LOSERS
A marketing manager at Lyons once had to face the problem of a

high-volume brand which showed a 'net contribution loss' of £9,000 – after contributing £600,000 towards the cost of a £1,000,000 salesforce. That brand made by far the largest single contribution to sales revenue and could not have been replaced by other brands.

Such a problem product usually becomes a problem at the top of its life-cycle, when it is hit by diminishing profit returns even though sales volume may continue to increase. Often the problems can be made more severe precisely by the efforts to improve the situation. In theory, sales can be pushed until the extra cost of generating them is exactly equal to the extra revenue gained (that is, where marginal cost equals marginal revenue). Unfortunately, theories regarding marginal elements in business are exceptionally difficult to use.

Because of the enormous difficulty of accurately forecasting the turning point of a sales curve, managers are reluctant to reduce, let alone abandon, effort 'too early '. Even when decline sets in, the immediate reaction is likely to be that of putting extra effort behind the line so as to remove what everyone feels is a temporary problem.

It is not easy to overcome this human tendency. And the correct action to be taken does rather depend on whether it is the beginning of long-term decline or simply the result of over-reaching in the market. There is normally a strong case for regarding it as the latter, at least initially. Deliberate pruning of low-volume and low-frequency customers is often the way to reduce cost and achieve a higher profit per unit, albeit from lower total sales. If promotional costs are too high, they will contribute to the problem. Dropping back to a previously acceptable level, probably associated with a lower, but more profitable, level of sale may solve this difficulty.

In many cases, however, the only real answer is to have products in each stage of the life-cycle (including products under development) so that each decline is replaced by the rise of a new profit-maker.

PATCHWORK PRODUCTS

Marketers are always looking for opportunities, not problems. A 'patchwork product' is one with so many problems that solving one problem is followed immediately by another. It is natural to worry about a problem. Yet, so often, there is nothing that can be done about it. (Or something can be done about it, but the cost is out of all proportion to the benefits.)

Patchwork products can be likened to a tyre which insists on getting deflated. Some problems can be solved by one clear solution, such as the replacement of the valve rubber. Other problems seem more like a series of punctures resulting from a perished inner tube.

At one time, in the field of ladies' hairdressing, there were two problems: inflation had made hairdressers realize that what they were really selling was time; and their price levels meant that they were inadequately rewarded for that scarce commodity. At the same time, their clientele was steadily getting older: the trade had a classic life-cycle problem, with profits having started to fall well before peak volume, but sales now beginning to decline as well.

The fundamental problem related to age. The older women were used to low prices for skilled services. The traditional wisdom among hairdressers was that the basic cut-and-set had to be low in price or women would not come into the salon – once they had come in, of course, there might be the opportunity to sell them other services that were more profitable.

However, young people were not going into salons, because they wanted long straight natural styles that were totally foreign to the styles with which their parents came home from the salons. The problem seemed insoluble, till it was sorted out by a change in fashion. A few hairdressers began to offer precision cutting and blow-styling at what seemed to be outrageous prices. The fashion magazines took up the styles. Young people went to salons to ask for these new-style haircuts and, to their surprise, were often turned away: many hairdressers had convinced themselves that they could not afford to offer blow-styling which was a time-consuming operation and for which they didn't have the staff.

Blow-styling now accounts for the biggest single part of most hairdressers' trade, and almost 50 per cent of total profits. Not only did the young come in, they came in with the realization that what they wanted took time and cost money. Young people have entirely different attitudes from their parents to paying for time. If you can remember a £1 haircut, it comes hard to pay £3 for one. But if the first price you ever paid for a haircut was £3 it isn't so difficult to pay £5. Almost by accident, ladies' hairdressing had found the opportunity that sprang from its biggest problem.

There were even significant spin-off benefits. For example, the answer to the question, 'Who will do it?', turned out to be some of the senior apprentices – or even those apprentices whose skill with the scissors wasn't what the hairdressers had hoped. However, the young people having their hair styled in this way *wanted* to believe that this was a highly skilled operation. The regard in which they held the local hairdresser, or a particular stylist or the promoted junior, went up by leaps and bounds when they could get what they wanted at prices they expected to pay.

There are several considerations that can be used as checks to ensure that, in trying to improve a problem situation, good money isn't thrown after bad. The problem product should have:

- An existing and sizeable volume of sales
- A high probability of exceptional benefits if the measures succeed
- Substantial growth and/or profit opportunities
- A clearly defined problem

Whenever there is a temptation to put extra resources behind sales in a poor area, one should always ask whether there is not potential in better areas that deserves backing first. That is the way to allocate scarce resources in business. If this principle was followed, there would be fewer patchwork products around.

UNNECESSARY, UNPROFITABLE PRODUCTS

There are cases where it is necessary, if only in the short run, to be unprofitable in certain areas. When Gillette first gave away razors in order to sell the blades which would obviously be their big long-term market, they were doing what was unprofitable in the short term, but which would lead to long-term profits.

When a pharmaceutical company sells one item in a range of treatments at a loss, it is doing so to hold customers. Pharmaceuticals is a field where it is frequently necessary to provide a whole range of treatment or equipment, and to view the profitability of the range as a whole, even where some items may be unprofitable. Service industries, too, often find it necessary to provide 'extras' in order to both obtain and retain customers.

This is fine, so long as the situation is watched continuously and carefully. There is a tendency for the eye to be taken off the ball – and then the loss escalates beyond what is reasonable. One must continuously question whether it is necessary to supply an unprofitable product.

Products which are both unnecessary and unprofitable often arise from the selling stage of a company's development, when the salesforce starts saying things like: 'We already call on builders' merchants with nuts, bolts and screws; they also buy hammers, why don't we supply those too?' So the range develops, until you have a range of products, some of which may be a long way from your basic concept of business and outside your real strengths and competence. Salespeople are frequently convinced that products A, B and C will not sell unless you carry X, Y and Z. Events seldom bear this out (the exceptions to this being of the type outlined at the beginning of this sub-section).

There is a danger that another company will start at the other end of the scale and end up selling a similar range of products to your own. Now buyers may look at the total range available from each of you and the price and service they get from each. They may conclude that, although your nuts and bolts are superior to the other party's, there isn't enough in it to justify losing the lower prices and higher discount across the range that your competitor offers.

Might this happen in any case, even if you didn't compete across the whole range? It might, but it actually doesn't happen all that often without provocation. There are two acts of provocation in that example. The first is against the other supplier, whose domain you attacked by extending your range to his or her specialist area. The second, and more important, is the provocation you offered to the buyer: if your range hadn't matched so closely with your competitor's, the buyer might never have made the comparison that has now been made.

Many companies have been staggered at the ease with which they have been able to take unprofitable products off the market when necessity has forced them to practise range-reduction. So it makes considerable sense to question whether any line should ever be allowed to grow without careful consideration.

INVESTMENTS IN MANAGEMENT EGO

Perhaps the most important single reason for 'specials' appearing in a range is the whim of an individual manager. Many successful products have been created out of such whims. Indeed, most companies grew up out of conviction on the part of single individuals that there was profit to be made out of something that they enjoyed doing. So such whims are certainly to be encouraged and nourished, but they need to be encouraged in a way that is disciplined and demanding.

How can this delicate balance be achieved between an environment that nourishes individual hunches and a discipline which ensures that money isn't merely wasted? Well, some money is always going to be wasted, because some hunches are bound to be wrong – or at least they are going to be incapable of exploitation at that particular time, or by that particular company. The sensible thing is to have some commonly-shared understanding in the company about the amount or proportion of money that can be spent on these things.

One of the best ways of doing this is to have an annual 'fund' for this purpose, with all such projects fighting for a possible share of it – though of course it may be that, from time to time, one such project takes up the whole of the 'money available'. In this way, all investments or losses as a result of the accepted hunches are quantified against their potential, and a rational eye can be kept on each of them, with a view to deciding when the time is ripe for more money to be put into one of them, or for the plug to be pulled.

Some of the examples quoted earlier in this book were very much the result of management ego, with an individual's ideas or instinct being allowed to override all objections and independent analysis. The magazine that failed was launched against very strong evidence from the market. The new form of roof insulation should never have been developed if the manufacturers had analyzed market requirements.

Many life-cycle problems are compounded by the refusal of managers to believe the evidence before them. It is never easy for a company which has been highly successful in Business A to come to terms with the fact that its future may really lie in Business B. This is particularly difficult for the founder of a business; and it may be difficult for a business to take such a decision while he or she is around, even if no longer involved with the business actively.

Few managers are ready to admit that they, too, are guilty of such investments in their ego. Although most managers are not in a position to launch products against the evidence of the marketplace, they are frequently guilty of showing favouritism to products or customers, and giving disproportionate amounts of time and resources to those sectors. Practically every salesperson has a favourite product – we all enjoy certain aspects of our business more than others. Left to ourselves, we try harder on products of which we are fond.

7.3 The Boston Grid

With the results of the six questions and the range analysis, combined with estimating the positions of your products on their life-cycles, it will be possible to examine what type of company you are, and to begin to make decisions about the kind of company you would like to become. The Boston Grid was originally formulated by the Boston Consulting Group. It is sometimes called portfolio analysis, and has certain similarities with the ideas we have already discussed, but it presents another way of looking at where a company is now, and what it might appropriately do next.

Figure 18 illustrates the Grid. The four categories relate market share to the rate of market growth, both categories being further divided into high and low – though in real life, of course, one would find a continuum rather than a division.

Each of the four categories in the Grid is given a nickname – for example, Category 1 combines high market share in a market which is growing slowly. Products which are in this sector are called 'cash cows' because they can provide vital funds for the development of new products and essential support for growing ones. 'Stars' are products which have a high market share in a growing market. Categories 3 and 4 represent the problem areas – Category 3 is, in fact, called 'problem children'. The difficulty with products in this sector is that the market enjoys a high rate of growth but the brand or product has only a low share of that market. Finally, Category 4 is called 'dogs' – low share of a market that is not growing too quickly.

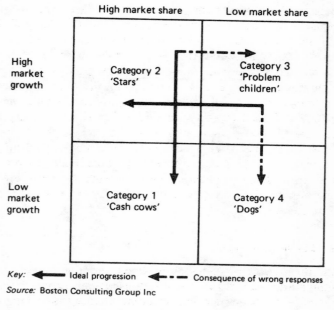

Figure 18 *The cash quadrants*

127

Comparing these ideas with our earlier analysis, we could put the ideas together in this way:

'Cash cows' = today's profitmakers
'Stars' = tomorrow's profitmakers
'Problem children' = products that could become tomorrow's profitmakers, but could easily become yesterday's lossmakers too.

The lines on Figure 18 show both the ideal progression and the consequences of getting things wrong. A 'problem child' ought to be made to grow into a 'star' and ultimately develop into a 'cash cow'. However, if not given development time and funds, or if promoted wrongly, it could easily fall back to become a 'dog'. The ultimate destiny of a 'dog' is failure and withdrawal – unless re-cycled.

A 'cash cow' is hardly likely to revert to being a 'star', unless there is substantial change in the demand life-cycle caused, for example, by users finding new uses for the product. It is all too easy, however, for a 'star' to fall back and, by losing share, to become a problem again.

The Boston Grid reformulates an older principle for examining market position by a simple combination of sales growth, market share and the important aspect of profitablity. This is set out in Table 3.

Table 3   *Product ratings by sales growth, market share and profit level*

Reference No.	Sales growth	Profit level	Market share
1	High	High	High
2	High	High	Low
3	High	Low	Low
4	Low	Low	Low
5	Low	High	High
6	Low	High	Low
7	Low	Low	High
8	High	Low	High

Reference No. 1 A happy position but one likely to attract competition, specially if there is room to enter at lower prices or if competitors are prepared to take lower profit rates. Sales will not grow for ever, so the important thing is to maintain both the high market share and satisfactory profits.

Reference No. 2 Failure to secure a high share in a period of rapid sales growth, combined with high profits, means one of two things: either the low share is consistent with marketing strategy or the company is greedy and could make its position safer by investing more resources in ensuring share growth. Moreover, the present position is likely to be attractive to competition.

Reference No. 3 Good growth, everything else is low. The danger here is of building a high share at too low a rate of profit. This could be a market that will never generate good levels of profit. Investment in this situation requires careful watch over all three elements to prevent any one advancing at the expense of the other.

Reference No. 4 Everything is wrong with this one! Milk it or get out fast.

Reference No. 5 Profits are good and share is OK but there appears to be little or no market growth. Looks like a life-cycle plateau. Use the profit to protect share, for life becomes tough and highly competitive under these circumstances, especially if there is over-capacity in the industry. Look for opportunities to segment the market, or to produce different products for different market segments. The long-run answer is new products ready to take the place of the present one.

Reference No. 6 Examine the reasons why profits are high despite low sales growth and low share. If it is a developing market, it would make sense to employ the profits to build share and push sales higher than they are at the moment. It may be that the product has found a small but highly profitable market niche.

Reference No. 7 With no sales growth, any fall in market share will further reduce profits. Share must, therefore, be maintained. Mature products often come into this category.

Reference No. 8 An almost certain indication of a product that has 'bought' its way into a market. Because there is apparently good market growth, any fall in share need not lead to a fall in sales (the product will simply not be growing quite as fast as the competition). It has a high share which normally indicates reasonable buyer loyalty and that should make it less risky to build profits, which must be the major aim for a product of this kind.

129

7.4 Summary

We have looked at three different but overlapping types of analysis that can help a company plot its way forward. Which of these methods you use does not matter greatly, provided you use at least one of them regularly.

A contribution test, looking at the various ways in which products might contribute to the welfare of the company, will impose a useful and necessary discipline on the answers to the six questions, and link up with life-cycle analysis to provide the basis for categorizing a product range. Products can be listed as:

- Present profitmakers
- Future profitmakers
- Profitable specials
- Priority development products
- Failures
- Contributors to overheads
- Patchwork products
- Unnecessary, unprofitable products
- Investments in management ego

Now you can describe what type of company you have and, taking this into account as well as the environment as a whole, you can choose a direction for the company's future. There are two fundamental areas of choice: horizontal or vertical integration, and marketing- or technology-centred organization.

7.5 Checklist

1 After any form of largely verbal analysis, it makes sense to examine the figures carefully to see if they are in line with the opportunities identified. If they are not in line, there are two possibilities: either the analysis is faulty, or past marketing efforts have not maximized opportunities. If the latter, re-examine both the fundamental strategy and the way the marketing mix has been developed and applied.
2 One way of looking at opportunities and classifying products within a total mix is to divide them into 'straightforward' and 'problem children'. At the top come those products which are clearly making enough profit to provide dividends for share-holders and fund the development of new products and the growth of younger ones. At the other extreme come those

products that perhaps should never have been launched, and those that have had their day and now absorb undue amounts of time, effort and money.

3 From time to time, it may be necessary to continue to market a product that might otherwise be withdrawn. The best justification for continuing a product is when it provides necessary support to other lines in the range or otherwise contributes significantly to company overheads. However, such a policy could indicate that the company has fallen a long way behind with the development of new products. Support cannot be given to declining products indefinitely.

4 When tackling problem products, it must be clear that there is sufficient potential in the market to turn the product into a winner.

5 The Boston Grid shows how easy it is for a product to fall back from a more successful category to a far less successful one. 'Cash cows' are necessary to the success of any company: always remember that it is today's successful products that pay for tomorrow's successes. Unless sufficient attention is given to those, there won't be any new products tomorrow.

6 Alternatively, analyzing a product range by a combination of sales growth, market share and profit levels produces eight categories, each with its own appropriate action.

7 Which model you use makes relatively little difference. The model which is likely to work best is a matter of management style. With sophisticated management, the Boston Grid is capable of far more development than its treatment here suggests. With companies relatively new to marketing analysis, the 'straightforward'/'problem children' analysis usually works best and easily develops into the format explained in Table 3.

8 What is important is that every company adopts some systematic method for continually analyzing its position and assessing the relevance of its marketing strategies and activities to the positions revealed.

8

Plans are nothing, planning is everything

> This very remarkable man
> Commends a most remarkable plan:
> You can do what you want
> If you don't think you can't,
> So don't think you can't think you can.
>
> Charles Inge

Anyone who has actually achieved something forecasted has either had luck on his or her side or cheated. The odds against precise achievement of a plan are far too high. Soon after joining one of the companies I have worked for, I became involved in a detailed investigation of every part of the business to attempt to track down the reasons for profits failing to meet the target by just over £1 million.

We were near the end of searching through all the records and had only found some £30,000 of the deficit when we were about to leave the office of one of the chief executives.

'I know where the missing million is,' he said. A year earlier, the chief executive of his group had rejected the first forecast of the division and asked for another £1 million. The sum was built into the budget. But the division achieved only its original forecast, and the difference between the two was about £1 million.

Organizational plans often suffer this sort of fate: if the target figure produced isn't considered good enough, it is changed for a higher one even though nothing else in the original plan is changed.

The emphasis of this chapter will be on the process of planning – get that right and your plan will look after itself. Of the making of plans there is no end. Some plans might be achievable in an ideal world and with ideal people. Others are designed really to achieve predetermined objectives. Sound planning produces plans that have the following features:

- They are flexible
- They are as practical and realistic as possible
- They take account of likely situations which could arise and which might necessitate changing the plan radically
- They are the result of a continuous process of appraisal, consideration, monitoring and re-appraisal

8.1 The ideal plan

The way in which plans are drawn up differs from organization to organization. It would make sense to have only one set of processes by which every company's plans were drawn up if every company was similar to its neighbour. Nevertheless, there are certain things that all plans have in common. In particular, senior managers want firm recommendations – not a set of alternatives which leaves them with the hard work of having to make a choice between them. They may not necessarily agree with the recommendation presented to them, but it is still helpful to have a set of reasons why one is preferred to another. In addition, they want to know how much profit will result from a plan, over what period and with what degree of certainty or risk.

The key factors, to ensure that you have the right planning process, and therefore get the right sorts of plans, are:

- The extent to which the past is examined
- How far plans are projected into the future
- How much detail is included
- What emphasis is placed on strategy, tactics and execution
- The number of alternatives to be considered
- The degree of flexibility permitted during the plan's life.

Some years ago, a charter airline decided to carry out an analysis of its timekeeping record. It discovered that on the flight between Luton and Athens it had a remarkable record of being within, plus or minus, two minutes of 'estimated time of arrival' on 94 per cent of occasions. The managing director thought it would be interesting to examine the flight plans and see how often the captain had followed them in full. In 92 per cent of cases where the flight had arrived within the plus or minus two minutes bracket, the pilot had made significant variations from his registered flight plan. Yet he achieved his objective.

All sorts of events had intervened: wind speed changed, wind direction altered, heavy traffic meant diversions, and so on. Yet, by trimming his rudder, changing his speed and re-routing in mid-air, he could still achieve his plan. A business is like an aircraft in this way: adjustments have to be made according to circumstances if the plan is to be achieved. Prices may have to be changed, different product lines may have to be pushed, new service packages may have to replace planned ones, and so on. All these should be given first priority rather than, as too often happens, reducing the target or changing the strategy.

Thus, achieving the ideal plan is a matter of:

- Careful pre-planning
- The right sequence
- Producing a plan that has a reasonable chance of success
- Controlling performance during the plan's life.

8.2 Pre-planning for success

Objectives, strategy and tactics – these words are often used in many different ways. So it may be useful to be clear about the exact sense in which these three are being used in this book.

Objectives are the numerical targets set by the corporate centre. They should always be set out in ways that are measurable, for only then can performance be monitored properly. Objectives can be broken down in various ways for each profit centre.

Stragegy is the position the enterprise will adopt in striving to achieve the defined objectives. (This is what we were particularly concerned with in Chapters 4 and 7.)

Tactics are the means by which the strategy will be achieved and these may need to change in the light of circumstances if the strategy is to be maintained and the objectives achieved.

A simple example will show how the three relate. The objective of Ubique Limited is to achieve profits of £500,000 in year one and increase by 15 per cent per annum thereafter. The strategy will be to appeal to premium markets for hand-produced furniture with traditional designs. Tactics will include direct representation to leading department stores; participation in the Ideal Home exhibition; special shows in local furniture stores dealing in high quality goods; and higher than average profit margins for stockists.

Some kinds of objective are better suited for use at corporate levels; others are more appropriate for profit centres. There are three main types of objective, although they may also be used in combination.

Perhaps the most popular is a simple comparative statement of intent, for example, to improve profits by five per cent on last year. Its very simplicity hides its virtues. The statement invites the question 'How?' Answers might include: increase sales volume by ten per cent; raise brand share to 30 per cent of the market; increase effective sterling-weighted distribution by another 15 per cent; increase calling ratio; require each advertisement to generate ten more sales leads: increase the conversion ratio for leads from 30 to 35 per cent – and so on. The deeper you consider the question, the more likely it is to begin to dictate the necessary tactics and the higher the degree of measurability over a wider area of business planning.

In all planning, it is a good idea to take each aspect one at a time and consider how the plan could be achieved if that were the only avenue open to you. Here is an example relating to a grocery product.

For achieving the target solely by increasing sales, the problem would be that the required high level of sales per outlet would be unlikely without an increase in distribution. The problem with increasing distribution is that sterling-weighted distribution is already 78 per cent (without taking Co-operatives into consideration). The only profitable way to expand distribution is to find a way of getting the Co-ops (who have their own brand) to stock our product. Alternatively, we could try placing an increased reliance on advertising – that is, on improving its effectiveness and increasing spending on it. It is not clear that this would produce the necessary result – perhaps it may be worth commissioning research to see what results we might expect.

The exercise resulted in the conclusion that this brand had gone almost as far as it could without the participation of the Co-operative outlets.

The comparative method is sometimes regarded as unsophisticated. However, in hard times, even the most sophisticated companies fall back to it. In times of rampant inflation, when standing still means absorbing heavily increased costs, the comparative statements are often amended to something like 'five per cent better than the level necessary to simply absorb higher costs'.

The comparative method can be used to define survival limits. However, the boom years of the late 1960s showed the real deficiencies of simpler methods at the corporate level of large companies (even though they remain an effective way of stating the targets for a small- to medium-sized profit unit or business). Many companies who appeared to be doing well were merely matching up to the performances of other similar companies. In particular, it was clear that their money could earn bigger rewards if used in other ways. Thus, companies with cash in the business, or under-utilized or under-valued assets, quickly became the prey of those better able to recognize more rewarding uses of cash.

Business ratios were already quite well-known as a method of inter-firm comparison. Now they became increasingly used as a means of setting objectives. One in particular was rapidly incorporated into many companies: the concept of return on capital employed (or return on investment – ROI). In other words, the concept is that money invested in any one business ought to earn at least what could be obtained from a reasonably safe investment; otherwise, why take all the risks of business? In any case, if shareholders are to be attracted to the shares of your firm, they must feel that they can earn a reasonable rate of return for their savings.

The formula is simple:

$$\frac{\text{Operating profits}}{\text{Operating assets}} \times 100$$

Although the idea is splendid, in practice the method can lead to difficulties. An easy way of improving the ratio when profits are static is to reduce investment. Many sections of British industry (the motor industry was a classic example) are heavily under-invested, a situation which has largely passed unnoticed by the investors who have their eye on a good ratio between profits and assets. There are many other manifestations of this phenomenon, such as sale and lease-back of property (whereby the vendor receives cash for an asset but pays a long-term rental); hiring company vehicles; leasing furniture; and so on.

They all have one common characteristic: they substitute a cash drain for an asset that has alrady been paid for! Although profit ratios may look good when the deal is done, the cash receipts can easily evaporate and profits have to increase to pay for the cash drain. The inability to finance high interest rates on cash borrowing was the major characteristic of many financial crashes during 1974/5.

136

There are two fairly simple defences against these excesses. One is to make sure that the ROI is calculated on *total assets*, including cash. The other, which has additional benefits aside from the safety factor, is to use more than one ratio. Various companies recognize between 18 and 21 business ratios. Three will actually be enough to make sure you aren't just deceiving yourself. In addition to relating profits to capital employed, use some break-downs that measure some of the fundamentals of your business. Relate operating profits (in the same way as in the formula above) to:

- Real assets (plant, property, etc.)
- Stocks (raw materials, finished goods in store and in transit)
- Net debtors/creditors (the difference between what you owe and what you are owed).

So now you have measures which consider how your investment relates to other uses of money; how the real assets in that sum relate; a measure related to all the raw materials of your trade plus the finished goods that no one else has yet paid for; and, finally, a measure that tells you whether you can expect enough to come in to pay your outgoings. If you have played any of the tricks mentioned earlier, the results will show up somewhere else. For example, a sale and lease-back deal will improve your profit ratio, but show up as an adverse factor on cash flow; if something hasn't been done to increase the sums owed to you, the net debtor/creditor figure will become unfavourable.

The additional advantage of examining three ratios is that it forces attention on each of the major components of the business: the factory (or office, branch or outlet), the stocks and the cash. (For those engaged in service businesses or other labour-intensive industries, with no factory or stock worth talking about, a ratio could compare instead the profits generated against the amount paid for the staff – including salaries, PAYE, pensions, rents, rates and office and other outgoings. This is called Return on Labour Employed in the place of real assets.)*

CASH SUMS

All objectives have to be converted into cash sums at some time or other. In many cases a cash sum is all that is required. They have the advantage of tangibility and easy monitoring without creating

* For a fuller exposition of business ratios and their use and abuse in business, see 'Profit and Cash Control', in *Directing the Marketing Effort* by Ray L. Willsmer, Pan Management Series (1975).

special tools and systems, and managers generally understand money better than ratios and percentages. Something that relates cash to volume has always been the simplest and most effective form of incentive to salespeople and managers alike.

It has been said several times already in this book that no costing system can be entirely fair to all brands and items within it, and we saw from the contribution test how misleading costing figures can be if looked at only in one light. Where a company has many products on the same costing system, and especially when it uses a number of common resources, there are several potential dangers.

One is that developing and struggling brands can so easily be 'penalized', while others that appear to generate higher-than target profit rates are actually not worth support (which is often the reason why they appear to do so well – they do not absorb the same costing load that developing brands do). Where it is necessary for the long-term good of a company to 'excuse' some brands from full cost recovery, while requiring others to produce more than their allotted target profit rate, there is a great deal to be said for giving the managers of individual profit centres cash sums as their target.

On the whole, this is better than giving new brands 'free rides', especially where combined with a steadily increasing cash sum.

A dangerous justification for new lines is that they take no extra resources, therefore they should be excused some elements of cost. The argument holds good only so long as someone else effects full recovery for them.

COMBINATIONS

It is seldom possible to calculate the actual assets employed in the production of one particular product line. In many cases, it cannot even be done for a division. Ratios are usually reserved for the central organization and need to be broken down into profit centres. This is usually done as a cash share of the required central objective. Normally it takes some account of past performance, of reasonable expectations for the future and of fairness to all parts of a business.

Thus the most frequent combination is a target improvement over the previous year, consistent with the required rate of profit, which will enable the company to meet its objectives.

RESOURCE ANALYSIS

Once the objectives are set, the real work of pre-planning begins. The annual marketing plan has as its major (many say only) justification the opportunity to stand back from the trees and look at the wood. This is a question of going through the six questions; examining any changes in life-cycle position; re-thinking your product category; and deciding if you are still on course for your planned strategy or if a change is necessary.

It is extremely important that you do not get into the habit of change for change's sake. Many young marketing executives believe that they are failing in their duty if they do not change something every 12 months. If they can't change the strategy, they want to change the advertising, which is the vehicle through which the strategy is communicated. It usually requires a major upheaval in a market to justify a change in strategy and one should be careful about changes in component parts, which both reflect and communicate that strategy. If the hardest thing in marketing is discovering the right strategy, the second most difficult is convincing managers to stay with it.

The guiding principle of resource analysis should be the 'SWOT' sequence:

- Strengths
- Weaknesses
- Opportunities
- Threats

The order is important. Proceed from strength before eliminating weaknesses; maximize opportunities before tackling threats. The time to tackle weaknesses is when they reduce your strength in the market-place; threats become problems when they limit or reduce your opportunities.

Remember that the basis of all resource planning is identifying profitable opportunities. Remember, too, that real resources only exist outside the business – until you have created customers, all you have is cost.

CO-ORDINATION

One of the principal jobs of marketing is internal co-ordination. Nowhere is this role more vital than in the preliminary stages of planning. A plan which is not fully discussed with all those critically involved, and which is not fully communicated to each active participant is not going to work. Clashes must be avoided and priorities assigned where necessary. An agreed strategy can easily be nullified by people accepting the plan in theory, but not committing themselves to work out all the implications of it. 'We'll

139

have the strategy and we love the plan but we can't afford to increase the salesforce' is a typical woolly response – and then people wonder why such a good plan failed.

Planning also means acceptance of one basic reality: the best plan for a company as a whole means the second- or even the third-best plan for some elements of it.

Particular attention needs to be paid to time-lags. Marketing people are always keen to know the actual moment of purchase and the time of use. There is a danger of assuming that some sort of mystical process is going to deliver the precise item needed at the right time. The lag between production and distribution needs a different set of targets from those required for the salesforce – which are themselves different from forecast customer sales (using 'customer' in the widest possible sense), while the money will come in even later.

Production usually finds it helpful to have warning of peaks and troughs; of the possible range of production requirements; of the exact time when promotional stock needs to be available; of special packs and deals; and so on. In many cases, labour recruitment is a limiting factor while legislation makes it difficult to lay employees off for even a month at a time – assuming that one had the hardness of heart to be able to do so without any qualms in the first place.

The timing of production requirements affects the amount of raw materials held – and this can have dramatic effects on a company's profits. The finance department needs to know the timing of cash flows, what money is fully committed but not yet spent, and so on. A break-down in communication in any one of these areas can seriously damage the effectiveness of any business plan.

8.3   The sequence by which effective plans are made

Most companies have an annual operating plan, and there are an infinite number of different ways of arriving at such plans. No particular method of planning may be better than any other. Each has its merits. If someone asks which planning method is best, the answer is: that method which best fits the ethos and organization systems of the company.

It is possible, sometimes, to suggest the inclusion of items that help understanding and speed communications, but these do not alter any planning method. However, improvements in the system by which plans are drawn up can often be suggested, and have a more fundamental impact. Since properly-developed plans save time and money, it is worth attending to this question.

One of the most irritating things in the area of planning – which you too may have experienced – is when a manager or group of managers spend long hours for several weeks preparing a plan, and then agonizing over the best way to present it, only to have it rejected on the basis of facts that were always known to some other manager but simply not communicated. The most usual problem, for one reason or another, is that of how much money might be available.

The sequence outlined in the following paragraphs has been developed on the basis of considerable experience. It is the simplest, least complicated and quickest sequence which will deliver a plan that will work for your company.

The essence of the method consists in firing-off a number of 'warning shots' which require a response and an authority to proceed before moving on to the next stage. Similarly, ideas can be tried out to see how they appear to fit with organizational and managerial temperature. In this way, managers avoid damaging rebuffs, while senior managers 'grow with' the plan through these warning shots, so that ugly surprises are avoided.

The sequence works for any kind of company. Here it is described for the benefit of a fairly complex organization. If your organization is a relatively simple one by comparison, you don't need to do an enormous amount of work in adapting the sequence to yourself: all you need do is cross out the stages which do not apply to you.

PRODUCT STRATEGY

The first step in an organizational plan should be the development of a strategy for each product. This strategy should be written by each of the line managers responsible for the products. Preferably, the line managers concerned should write the strategy on their own. In any case, the participation of other people ought to be kept to the minimum at this point: they should check their assumptions, but no more ('Am I right in assuming that we cannot produce any more on the present line, and that you need a four-month lead time for a new plant?').

In many companies, a brand manager's request has the sanctity of an order and people will go and beaver away for hours and weeks. This tendency must be discouraged: all that is needed at this stage is one-word answers. A line manager who has been living with a product line every day of his or her working life for some time, will usually be able to write a strategy document in a few hours, without any help.

141

The strategy paper needs to be kept simple. All that is needed is an outline of ideas, hopes, expectations. (Remember the poor managers above you who are going to have to read strategy reports regarding each of the products and lines under them.) The following headings indicate the sorts of things which are needed – though you may find that not all the headings are relevant to your operation, or that you need a few others.

Objectives: short- and long-term. This needs to be expressed in the simplest possible way: for example, 'to have 15 per cent of the market and a profit of £50,000 next year – and to have 35 per cent of the market with £350,000 in five years'. This gives an important indication to the reviewing manager, who needs to juggle the pretensions of all the brands (and the resources required by them!).

Consumer proposition. Having assumed or ascertained a customer need, you suggest how the product or service fulfils the need, and you assess (perhaps on the basis of research, the results of which you have) how customers respond to it.

Strategy. The strategy should be carefully chosen for its relevance and impact. It should reflect the benefits sought by the customer and the position selected by the company as the best way to present those benefits to the chosen market sector. Of course, it is important that the strategy should define prime prospects, but it is equally important that the strategy should eliminate unwanted or unimportant customers as well. In other words, who would you like to concentrate on attracting as customers and why?

Tactics. An indication of the main avenues of attack: how do you propose to implement your strategy, out-shout the competition, attract the particular kind of customer you want?

Promotional messages and media. What is the message you want to put over (not necessarily the exact words) and the media you propose to use – this doesn't relate to radio and television alone, it could easily be handbills or a loud-hailer at the streetcorner? Why would you choose that medium? In the case of a combination of media, why do you choose those media and why in those proportions?

Special promotions and schemes. It is important for the reviewing manager to be aware of these in order to consider the impact on the company's profile, and to eliminate any possible clashes or overload on the support staff due to other factors.

New resources. Do you need more salespeople, secretaries, computers, software, vans, etc. Remember that other people will also be arguing for resources to be put into their departments, and that there probably won't be enough money to support all departments as much as they would like. (You can discover your department's comparative worth in the company by comparing what proportion of your requested resources you succeed in getting, as against what proportion of their requested resources other departments succeed in getting.)

The final document doesn't need to be much longer than the explanatory paragraphs for each heading given above (that is, about two typewritten pages). As time goes on, familiarity will reduce the need for detail even further.

DIVISIONAL STRATEGY

The essence of the 'warning shot' method is that the product manager's immediate boss is aware of each phase of planning and endorses and supports what is proposed before enormous amounts of time and money are spent on developing anything in detail. The product manager's boss must now look through all the product strategy papers from the various product managers under him or her, to consider whether, and how, the papers fit together, as well as how they fit into the strategy of the whole division which the boss manages. (This may well be the whole company in the case of a small enterprise.)

Let's take an example. A senior manager might have two marketing managers under him or her, two sales managers and an account manager. They meet to consider each of the brand strategies, asking how the suggestions fit with the company's abilities and resources, making notes as they go about the areas where they doubt the ability of their resources to cope with the demands made on them. They also need to consider how these suggestions tie in with the division's profit objective, so that any improvements necessary or desirable can be thought about. Then, each brand manager in turn comes along to argue for their strategy and receive the divisional response, going away either with authority to proceed to the next step, or to produce an amended strategy taking into account the resources that can actually be allocated. Invariably, the biggest area of conflict is the size of the salesforce available, particularly in relation to special sales drives.

If such conflicts are apparent early in the process, then product managers can re-examine their strategy and planned outcomes in the light of the sorts of resources they know are likely to be available. Of course, it is possible that senior managers are so impressed with the product manager's strategy that they take on the work of trying to re-negotiate the division's objectives and resources with superiors.

Anyway, the principal advantages of including these steps in your planning process is that product managers go forward sure in the knowledge that they are treading the right road.

CORPORATE STRATEGY

Depending on the size and complexity of the company, it may be necessary to repeat the divisional strategy procedure at corporate level with exactly the same objectives. The sooner the centre is aware of possible discrepancies from agreed objectives, the earlier it is that remedial action can be taken.

From the company's point of view, the major function of this continual testing for fit with overall objectives is to recognize those parts which can make best returns with the support provided.

PLANNED SALES

Let us assume that clearance has filtered back to whoever produced the original brand strategy. Attention now moves to the sales forecast which is the outcome of the strategy. Fully detailed sales forecasts can now be prepared in such a way that other departments can make the appropriate adjustments to allow for their timing.

All detailed planning starts only at this point, but it can now begin with the assurance that only a major and unexpected upheaval will cause the planning to be wasted. Production and distribution planning can begin. Feasibility studies can be mounted, costings prepared and, possibly, adjustments and reconciliations proposed.

It is very important at this stage to have close co-ordination between the different departments of the company, particularly sales and production – or, in the case of service industries, the credit department, or the bookings and reservations section or service engineers – whichever happens to be the 'powerhouse' of your operation. By co-ordination we mean exactly what was meant earlier: presenting to the 'powerhouse' department several alternative ranges of probable sales targets.

This is done in order to discourage an incredulous response when it is too late, or a subservient response which doesn't point out some major disadvantage. Instead, it encourages a dialogue between the 'powerhouse' and sales departments, allows them to make 'best' and 'worst' forecasts, recommend changes in timing, or take other steps which will enable a maximization of overall profit. There is no point in a plan which produces high profit from the sales department if this is going to be offset by a disproportionate increase in factory costs: the figures for the brand may look good, but those for the company will not.

The aim of this phase is to end up with 'agreed planned sales' which is, in effect, a considered verdict on feasibility. It is the most practical means of bringing all the other departments into the act of detailed planning. The outcome is all the figures necessary for the final stage of the plan.

ANNUAL OPERATING PLAN

Sometimes called 'the marketing plan', this includes all those elements of cost that make up the necessary input into the plan. The format is variable, although some suggested headings will come later. This is the final request for funds, with the justification for them; the details of the strategy; the outline of the tactics (the details are usually approved separately, later); and the control figure for the duration of the plan.

Under the sequential system described up to this stage, there should be careful and frequent communication between departments as well as with superiors so that there is time to take everyone's concerns and suggestions into account, and to consider the ramifications of any reduction in resources available or desired; enforced increases in targets; and so on.

PLAN AND COMMITMENT SUMMARY

This can be part of, or appended to, the annual operating plan: alternatively, it can be a separate document. The reason for drawing this up is that the final operating plan is a confidential document, and it cannot be worked without the willing co-operation of a number of people who will never see the plan and who will never be aware fully of the inter-relationships involved.

The Plan and Commitment Summary (also called just The Plan Summary) makes it possible for them to have sufficient awareness of the overall plan to motivate them and to enable co-ordination, without divulging the confidential aspects of the plan. The Plan

Summary needs only three headings:
- Activity
- Manager responsible
- Completion date

This ensures that everyone concerned understands, and has agreed to, the key points involved. If the marketing people have exercised their responsibility for co-ordination, there will be no problem at this stage. So why go to the bother of putting down this summary at all? The reason is to double-check the crucial elements for the progress (or perhaps for the survival) of the firm. Moreover, the Summary Plan enables senior management to see clearly that the marketing department has done its work (if it has!) and assured everyone that all concerned have agreed to do what is required of them. It also clarifies for everyone that the co-ordination responsibilities have been thought through.

The major problem with plans is not that of drawing them up, but of seeing that they are adhered to and that they produce the results for which they were designed. The single largest cause for failure or underachievement is that one of the parties concerned in an aspect of the plan is able to deny categorically any knowledge of being required to do a specific task, or at least to do so by a particular time. A Plan and Commitment Summary, circulated to every individual by name, is a simple safeguard. If a plan is to succeed, it must ensure that every factor which might cause it to fail has been thoroughly considered.

8.4 Give your plan a chance

The stages already discussed should provide a good foundation for the success of a plan. What needs to be added are careful control procedures to ensure that new situations are recognized, so that alternative tactics to implement the same fundamental strategy are considered – indeed, if necessary, that the strategy itself is re-examined and, where necessary, changed plans are put into effect.

Three other important areas can seriously affect the chances of success, and these should be taken into account by everyone involved before agreeing the plan:
- Realistic forecasting
- Taking account of factors outside the business
- The realism of the plan

In the final analysis, a plan is only as good as the forecast of circumstances and outcomes. Some of the important aspects of forecasting will be considered in the next chapter. At this point, it is only necessary to emphasize that forecasts must be objective and consistent with reality. 'Hope' is a completely inappropriate word to find in a forecast: it betrays a wrong attitude of mind to the forecast. We all have hopes, and there is a place for them in life of course, but the whole point of planning is to eliminate the need to depend on chance occurrences. What we are trying to do is to identify all that might occur, and prepare plans for each contingency.

Most companies are quite good at forecasting sales. However, we need to forecast far more than sales in a realistic plan.

REALISTIC PLANS

Too many plans are merely numerical. Often the actions required to achieve the figures are not even considered. This is especially true of some of the so-called 'Go-go' companies, whose obsession with figures can be seen to have been excessive and damaging. Nevertheless, skilled managers learn a great deal from the figures. One very useful device is to examine the figures in a plan for any divorce from realism. Tables 4 & 5 (page 148) present an actual case from a financially 'independent' subsidiary of a large company. Table 4 appears to be realistic, sad though it may be that the market share is going to slip a little.

However, when the sales record of the company was examined (it had never been asked for earlier), the figures were clearly unrealistic (Table 5). Here was a company that had been increasing sales at six per cent, suddenly anticipating a nine per cent increase. How were they going to achieve this additional increase? In fact, they were planning nothing new at all. Worse, an examination of the plans drawn up in previous years revealed that they had always forecast a nine per cent increase in sales – but always achieved six per cent. Why were they achieving six per cent and not more? (Actually, they would have been achieving less if they had depended entirely on what they were doing to market themselves: they were achieving six per cent only because the market sector as a whole was growing quickly – and they were losing total market share at a much faster speed than their plan acknowledged.)

So the plan appeared reasonable, but was totally unrealistic: in fact, what they had produced was not a plan at all, merely a piece of bureaucratic paper; it had not been produced as a result of anything resembling the planning process outlined earlier in this chapter.

There is a lesson to be learnt from this example. The realism of

147

Table 4 *First plan, Company SK, £000s*

	Year 0	Year +1
Total market	3100	3410
Market growth	—	+10%
SK sales	1147	1250
Sales growth	—	+9%
Share of market	37%	36.7%

Table 5 *Revised plan, Company SK, £000s*

	Year −2	Year −1	Year 0	Year +1
Total market	2562	2818	3100	3410
Market growth	+10%	+10%	+10%	+10%
SK sales	1021	1082	1147	1250
Sales growth		+6%	+6%	+9%
Market share	39.9%	38.4%	37.0%	36.7%

any plan is vastly improved when the past history and experience of the enterprise is taken into account. This enables you to ensure that current and future plans match the experience, the historically-proved ability of the company, and past and current trends and results. Examining past history also affords the opportunity of examining the rationale in any changes from the past that are attempted; of considering how feasible such changes are; and working out the practical steps that will be necessary to bring such changes about.

How far back do you look, and how far forward? This is sometimes called a 'planning horizon'. What sort of planning horizon should your company use? That is a difficult question to answer simply. Most businesses will look this September at next January, within a context of three years of history and three years of future plans.

But there are exceptions to this. The travel business, for instance, operates so far ahead, because of the need to book beds, airplanes or airplane seats, hotel leases, and so on, that the earliest year they can actually do anything about may be three years away. So the plan they produce for two or three years ahead is the equivalent of the one most companies produce for the next quarter. Since year one is, in effect, two years away for such companies, they adopt a planning cycle of five years ahead at any given time.

Some of them take the simpler view that a large number of leases (of hotels as well as aircraft) are based on seven years. In any case, these factors indicate the sorts of factors you might keep in mind when deciding what sort of planning horizon is appropriate for your company: you need to look at the critical factors and decide the effective lead time. That will begin to define the horizon for your business. Projecting plans some way beyond the year under consideration helps prevent too frequent changes of direction and is a considerable aid to both understanding and involvement by all levels of management.

What about detail? How much detail should be included? If the emphasis is placed on strategy, detail becomes much less important and, rather than tackle each topic too thinly, it is usually better for full details to be supplied with an individual plan for each tactical exercise – and these can be added below the body of the main text, as appendices.

Finally, while a large number of possible alternatives could be considered, if the emphasis is on a strategic solution, fewer alternatives will suggest themselves. Moreover, it makes life easier for everyone if only two alternatives are presented – the recommended course of action and one other course of action that will achieve pre-determined financial objectives if the first does not. Each of these will be treated in greater detail in its appropriate context.

A realistic plan is one which demonstrates a match with the internal character of the company for which the plan is made. That alone will not make it work, of course: account must also be taken of external factors.

OUTSIDE FACTORS

This section could equally well be titled, 'Taking account of the unexpected'. Of course, this sounds impossible – and it is of course impossible to do so perfectly or completely. Nevertheless, all so-called unexpected events have happened before. They are going to happen again, and their occurrence can be anticipated to a greater or lesser extent.

What, practically, can be done to take account of the unexpected? The first step is to clarify the picture you have of your market. Are any of your competitors likely to change their price? Improve their product? Enlarge their sales force? Increase their advertising? Change their total package? Provide better levels of service? Will the government intervene in any area, producing new laws and regulations affecting your business?

A plan can only consider those variables which are thought – or known – to be significant. Therefore, the most important questions to ask are: how good is your intelligence-gathering system? Will you be able to pick up quickly every hint of an increase or decrease in the importance of these variables? Are you likely to spot any new variables equally quickly?

Each of those questions has the word 'quickly' in it, and that is of course a very imprecise word. *How* quick do you need to be? There is a simple, practical answer to that: you must be able to get hold of such information at least as early as (and preferably before) your competitors.

If your intelligence-gathering system is not up to these tasks, then its improvement should be the first thing you do. How can you improve your intelligence-gathering system? Ask yourself if you belong to any of the trade associations and bodies in your market sector? If you don't, you may wish to consider joining one or more of them. If you already belong to one, consider if that is the one that is most useful from the viewpoint of gathering information relating to trends and new influences in your market sector. On the basis of this evaluation, you may wish to change or add to the organization(s) to which you belong. You may even wish to consider helping to start a new organization, if necessary – though you must be careful to define the limits of the new organization in such a way that you benefit as few as possible of your competitors.

Next, do you keep up with the general daily news? It is easy to look at page one, and then to skip to the centre pages, and any other favourite page. Think also whether you subscribe to a sufficient number of trade journals, both in your market sector, and in the general business press. Do you scan them regularly, or do you have others who have been assigned to help with this work: if so, you must ensure that any important findings are brought to you as a matter of urgency, and that you have a regular meeting with such people to ensure that you are aware of all important developments, and potential developments.

Once you are confident that you are in a position to keep up with any new threats and opportunities, the next step is to quantify these if possible. Such quantification will lead to some understanding of the probability of success; of degrees of risk; and of the key assumptions on which the success of your planning depends.

These assumptions should always be spelt out in your plan document itself. Then you have a readily available list of significant factors, to which you can turn when trying to account for any variation from the plan.

Figure 19 (page 152) shows a form of tabulation which is appropriate to any kind of business. In large companies, it is useful for key assumptions to be handed down to operating units. The Thomson Organization, for example, used to tell its operating companies what rate of inflation should be assumed unless they knew something different in relation to their operation. If the head office, for example, instructed their subsidiaries to calculate inflation in wages at 15 per cent, but Thomson Regional Newspapers had signed an agreement with their unions for 14 per cent (or 16 per cent), then the figure they knew to be correct for their own business was what they were to take into account. Figure 19 does concentrate on product line factors but you can see how easily it can be modified to start with those assumptions which have been handed down from head office.

Another step which will help you with taking account of the unexpected, is to list all the things that have ever influenced it and those that might do so. The 'Six Day War' and its effects on oil supplies during the 1970s caught out many companies from a wide range of businesses; Black Monday had profound effects on share values and the amounts of money available; the new Finance Bill each year can change the amount of discretionary income available to the consumer – let us call this List A.

Figure 20 (page 153) shows a way of considering the possibilities in List A and what you might do about them. Into the first of the three blocks, you put those factors from List A which would *certainly* affect the plan. Here is an example of what such a list might contain for a firm in central heating:

- Increase in initial deposits for hire purchase
- Reduction in periods of payment
- Increases in interest rates
- Changes in ratio of costs between oil, electricity and gas

This block is the first place we examine for explanations of any deviations from the plan. One of the most instructive things that you can do next, is to look back and see how often and how significantly each of these factors has changed in the last five years. Then cast your mind further back, and discuss with colleagues, any occasion which sticks in the memory when one of these factors was changed significantly. Keep a log of all these points. (Some companies keep this in a bound volume called, 'When the world changed'. A rather inflated title, true, but it reminds us of the fact that assumptions are the ground on which we build.)

Plan element	Economic environment	Customer behaviour	Competitive behaviour	Own position	Raw materials
Product line					
Prices					
Direct sales					
Delivery					
Advertising					
Packaging					
Credit policy					

Fig. 10. *Planning ...*

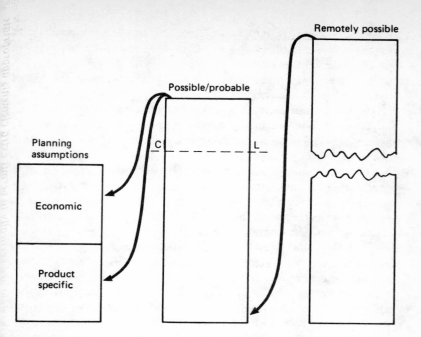

Figure 20   *Expecting the unexpected*

When assumptions change it is like an earthquake – though it is surprising how quickly people forget events that were quite significant at the time. The smaller the business, the smaller the events which can be significant – changes of staff, for example. In one striking case, a company's new employee started operating the account according to the procedure employed in his previous job. The result was an apparently steep drop in sales: he was registering sales only when they were invoiced, as against previous practice, when a sale was logged at the time of delivery. Until this problem was identified and sorted out, the company concerned had divergent information in its Invoices files as well as in its Payments files.

Into the second block in Figure 20, we put all those factors from List A which *could* influence the plan. These may be things which your version of 'When the world changed' shows have happened before but are fairly unlikely. For example, most British businesses were affected by the three-day working week of 1974: it could happen again. Not an item for block one at the moment, perhaps, but it may well deserve a place in block two or three, depending on your judgment of the possibility and its effect on your business.

153

One other sort of happening goes into the second block – any events which may affect you at one or two removes. Examples are strikes, and purchases of related items: ie, sales of whisky are going to be more responsive to changes in their price relative to the cost of living, rather than changes in price by itself.

The third block contains the remoter possibilities.

Taking each of the three blocks by turn, you need to look at each assumption and work out what you are going to do if the assumption changes.

There are really very few so-called crises that do not contain some predictable elements. Many more have fairly regular cycles. If a company starts with a sound strategy, the chances of a crisis seriously affecting anything other than its tactics are substantially reduced; no amount of tactical maneuvering will correct a basically unsound strategy. Many marketing experts work to what they call the earthquake theory. Although seismologists cannot predict the exact time of an earthquake, they can plot those areas of the earth's crust where fissures are most likely to occur. With that knowledge, the inhabitants of those places can be better prepared, while the experts look for tell-tale signs of an impending disaster.

If you are sailing, it is far easier to take evasive action if you can estimate the arrival of a storm. You may not get all the way back to harbour safely, but you can reduce the time you are at risk. This is what this system is designed to do. The line 'CL' in Figure 20 is the contingency line. For all the items in block one, and any that rise above CL in block two, prepare a contingency plan. Keep your eye on the events below CL: as soon as one rises above the line (by becoming a more imminent threat), produce a contingency plan for it.

Contingency plans are often called 'What if' plans. This term has been adopted by software producers for micro (or personal) computers. The widespread availability of spreadsheet programmes provides tremendous opportunities for marketing planners. The advantage of these programmes is that they make their calculations at almost unbelievable speed. At the touch of a single key, you can have worked out for you the consequences of changing a single variable, or of changing several variables simultaneously – even in opposing directions. Everyone interested in marketing needs to acquire familiarity with computer spreadsheets.

All this emphasizes the need for flexibility in a plan. A rigid plan is fairly pointless: it is one of the basic reasons for the high failure rate of business forecasts. A good plan is based on a carefully evolved strategy, one which will last for many years. The outcome of the plan is a profit figure. From strategy to profit consists of a series of carefully planned tactical actions with their timings and costs. Many are actions that would have been taken in any case, even without a plan, while others are entirely original. Flexibility will be necessary if the plan is to be achieved, for it is extremely unlikely that all the events will turn out exactly as planned.

8.5 The content of the plan

Here are some suggestions for those who may not have produced an annual operating plan before or who may be considering change. Not all these elements will be relevant to everyone reading this book; and do bear in mind that the process is more important than the plan itself.

Background Write down any important developments in the market or in product development since the last plan, showing the way these affect the current situation and the plans.

Current situation Examine actual performance against forecast performance to point up any lessons that have been learned, and any new strengths and/or weaknesses which have emerged.

Marketing objectives and strategy Ask yourself what are your major objectives for the coming year in particular, and the longer term in general. Ask yourself if your objectives are SMART – that is, do they **S**tretch you, are they **M**easurable, **A**chievable, **R**ealistic and defined by some **T**ime boundary? Clearly define strategic positioning.

Profit Compare bottom line figures with past performance and current objectives, noting any significant variances and reasons for them.

Product line Note all new products introduced and all products withdrawn, phased out or modified. Clarify which lines are to be pushed in present markets. Identify which products are going to be pushed for new markets or for new applications.

Pricing What needs to be noted under this heading are any changes in your charging structure, your terms of business, your credit arrangements if any, and all uncharged or subsidized services.

Sales activity Changes in size and organization of salesforce, sales conferences and seminars, remuneration, commission, recruitment, training, etc.

Advertising and sales promotion At this stage, you do not need to answer the question of how the advertising and promotions are going to happen, you only need to write down why any advertising or promotions are recommended – and what sort they are. You will need to mention what funds you require and how that figure compares with your allocation of funds last year. If you use an advertising agency, you might include their recommendations on creative, media and promotional strategies, and then go on to review the effectiveness of last year's PR and promotions, giving a broad picture of the kinds of promotion and PR which might be appropriate, with their objectives.

Technical service This should cover:

- pre-sales testing, advice, assistance and applications research
- after-sales service, advice and training
- any spares organization, claims departments or personal counsellor
- size and scope of technical forces
- charging policy.

Physical distribution Think about delivery time objectives, stock levels, seasonal changes, location of stocks and depots, transportation methods.

Distributors and factors What is going to be your policy on discounts, payment structure, co-operation, communication, training, motivation, assistance, etc.?

Market research What new information do you require? What action is planned to obtain it? At what cost? To what use will it be put?

Product development The material under this heading should relate to re-cycling and developent of existing products rather than completely new ones.

Packaging Do you need new packaging or materials? Why? What is that going to cost the company? What is it going to cost the customer? What will be its anticipated effect on sales and profit?

Marketing organization and staff A cost item which ideally should not be on this plan. As a business overhead, it should not be a direct charge on a revenue-generating budget, but should be put with other overheads budgets. This is frequently included in industrial budgets where it is often a first charge on promotional budgets.

There may well be other items which are appropriate to include in a plan for your business. In particular, the chief executive, or possibly the finance director, may want to see key business ratios included – or, possibly, capital budgets related to the revenue-generating plans.

However, there is one general format that suits any content, and makes it simpler for senior management to digest:

1 Start with a one-page summary
2 Keep the content as concise and as factual as possible (with any necessary masses of figures confined to appendices).

Certain appendices should be common to all plans produced by a particular company; what these are will be a matter of discussion within each company. The first will almost certainly be some sort of look forward at the climate and future of the company, and the second will be some sort of look back at the company's history.

Next (if these have not already been included in one of the first two) will certainly be detailed profit figures. There is a good case for keeping next year's figures next to the current ones, while the longer-term view probably needs fewer details so that volumes and values are more clearly highlighted. Consumer product companies may well find that the next most important appendix is advertising and sales promotion; industrial companies may put the salesforce next: it is a question of what is the next most important factor in *your* business.

The overall idea is that busy chief executives can extract the essential sense from a plan by reading the summary and three or four key appendices. If the summary doesn't indicate the reasons for any apparent logical discrepancies, then they will know immediately which plan they need to scrutinize in greatest detail first.

8.6 Controlling the working of the plan

It is not enough to produce a plan that is splendidly written and presented. It has to be monitored constantly. Some of the areas in which it needs to be monitored have greater space devoted to them later in the book, but here are the main headings, with a few explanatory notes where applicable.

THE PRODUCT

Many marketing managers use the systems suggested here, but then forget to check that the quality of their product is what they believe it should be. The very first place in which you should look for any deviation in sales is in the area of the quality of the product or service you are providing. Business history is littered with cases where managers have changed an ingredient or component without testing the reaction of the end-user. Though they themselves could discern no material difference, customers felt dissatisfied. Regular users know a great deal about the goods and services they buy and can often recognize fine nuances that their suppliers have never recognized or may even be incapable of recognizing – because customers actually pay to buy the product with a particular use in mind. Continual testing and quality awareness is vital, specially with services – devices such as 'test shopping' may be necessary to discover how customers are actually treated.

SALES

Everyone checks sales. But are the records of past sales kept for purely historical purposes, or are they collected and analyzed in such a way that action that is remedial or enhancing can be taken as soon as possible? The ideal is daily reporting of sales by the lowest possible unit of purchase. If the next stage up in sales management has figures with that frequency, there is every opportunity of a rapid call-back on a previously unsuccessful visit.

The lowest unit of call and the frequency of calls will of course vary by industry, but all figures should be kept in a form that allows rapid inspection and remedial action. Only after that should the figures be aggregated into the monthly management control figures.

The basic areas which need to be checked are volume, profit from sales, share of market, repeat sales and sales by area or unit.

PROFIT

Sales figures tend to be under the microscope all the time. Profit forecasts, on the other hand, are not attended to with such alacrity. Changes in prices of raw materials and wages take place so frequently and make such a difference to overall costs that they warrant more attention. Marketing is undertaken for profit. So it is absolutely essential that the marketing executive should watch not only the sales figures, but also the overall profitability of his or her operation. Profits need to be calculated realistically and variances noted and notified to superiors promptly.

158

For adequate control, and in order to modify plans where necessary, the original objectives, overhead and materials budgets should be subjected to exactly the same disciplines as sales budgets. Some companies do not divulge such 'sensitive' information to marketing executives, on the grounds that it is confidential. If marketing managers cannot be trusted to use this information to improve the long-term profits of the business, they should be replaced. On the other hand, if senior managers can't bring themselves to trust these figures to marketing managers, then it is the senior managers who deserve to be replaced.

COMPETITIVE REACTIONS

We have already discussed how important it is to keep an ear to your competitors' methods and activities. Adequate and rapid reporting systems must be established if the information is to be of any practical use to the business.

Competitive advertising, promotional programmes and other promotional activities, changes in pricing policy, terms, discounts, training and servicing facilities – these are examples of the sorts of things which need to be watched. Indeed, any item you consider important is likely to be considered important by your competitors too, and is therefore likely to figure in their plans.

BUDGETS

Actual results, in all areas, need to be compared to budgets continuously, but how is this to be done? Some sort of management information system is needed, and there are many on the market nowadays, especially in the form of computer software. Here are some questions to ask about any system of management information, whether computerized, mechanical or manual:

- Does it really help managers, or is it just a mass of figures? If you want a fair indication of its usefulness, ask – not how often people *should* use the information, but – how often people *are* likely to use the system.
- Does it show at a glance the discrepancies between budget and performance? You need immediately to be able to see any areas in which current performance isn't matching what is expected.
- Does it avoid 'information indigestion'? In other words, if you are on budget, do you need to know more? You will need to know more from time to time, so the system should be able to provide the information to you when you need it, and in relation to your questions about it.

- Does it 'weight' the information it presents? Does it take note of the 80:20 rule and the concept of sterling weighted sales and distribution?

Clearly, the system that these questions implicitly recommend is one that is based on 'exception reporting'. That is, figures are only reported when they deviate from budget by a predetermined amount.

There are other areas which may need the same degree of continual monitoring. People who use advertising regularly, for example, will no doubt work out at least some crude system for checking the effectiveness of their advertising – if nothing else, of whether the sales generated by the advertisement pay for it. Similarly, the effectiveness of the salesforce will be under continual review by the sales director.

8.7 Conclusion

A company's past helps us to establish its 'character'. This is an inestimable guide to forecasting its future. The past is implicit in all planning, so there is no reason why it shouldn't be reviewed by all companies more fully and openly. In a parallel way, every plan acquires meaning and direction only from its view of the future. Some indication and quantification of that future is therefore necessary, however inaccurate it may turn out to be. It is interesting that people never complain about plans and targets which are reached or exceeded, only about those which are not reached. This is acceptable from uninstructed or lay people; it is not the attitude that intelligent and thoughtful people should take. If a plan is reached or exceeded, they should ask rather whether the plan represented all that they might have been capable of achieving, and whether the planning procedure is adequate.

8.8 Summary

General (later President) Eisenhower had a sign behind his desk when he commanded the Allied Forces in Europe. It read:

Plans are nothing
Planning is everything

This emphasizes that if the process of planning has been done properly, then the plan will be enacted. The best set of outcomes will be produced by careful consultation before any plans are drawn up, examining all alternatives; anticipating possible reactions from competitors; anticipating your own reactions to any moves on the part of the competition; 'giving a plan a chance'; and the preparation of plans to cover every foreseeable contingency.

Although difficult, the aim should be to produce the best fit between resources and results so that any change in one will result, at least, in a need to reconsider the other. Using a sequence like the one outlined gives the best chance of an efficient and productive match between the results expected and the resources supplied.

8.9   Checklist

1   After considering all reasonable alternatives, any plan must produce firm recommendations. The recommended course of action is chosen, normally, on the basis of what will provide the best long-term result.

2   The best plan for the company will almost never be the sum total of all the best plans for individual products, units or subsidiary companies within it. Since all the plans cannot be fully resourced, some plans will have to be amended.

3   Before the plan is written down, the techniques described in earlier chapters (the six questions, portfolio analysis, etc.) should be combined in the resource analysis stage. If this has already been done, the findings are reviewed and form the basis for the SWOT analysis.

4   The objectives of the marketing plan may be comparative, or they may be based on cash sums or the use of business ratios. Objectives are usually drawn up in some combination of these. In large corporations, where assets and human resources may be shared, it becomes more difficult to apply relevant ratios to any individual part of the business.

5   Some probing questions to ask of any marketing plan are: will the design of the plan achieve the company's objectives? Have the plans been formulated after due consideration of the company's history and character? Are they realistic? Are they communicated to all responsible for achieving them?

6   All resulting aspects of the possible plan must then be communicated to ensure that everybody will be able to pull in the agreed direction, and is prepared to do so at the right time. Care should be taken not to commit departments to undue or unnecessary action before the plan has been agreed, at least in outline.

7   A sequence that begins with a series of 'warning shots' is

161

recommended as the best and safest way of maximizing the match of available resources and desirable results.

8 'Product strategies' are reviewed and combined to form 'Divisional' and/or 'Corporate' strategies, as necessary.

9 The aim of the strategy documents is to check the fit of individual plans within corporate objectives and to receive authority to proceed to detailed planning. Once detailed planning begins, money is often irrevocably committed, as are the early stages of the plan.

10 Since the people responsible for implementing the plan do not always see the documents, a 'Plan and Commitment Summary' is a good idea.

11 The most basic question to ask yourself regarding any plan is: 'How realistic is it?' That is, how matched to probable outside events, and to the internal character of the organization.

12 Few things are totally unexpected, though their timing is often unpredictable. The suggested three-block system enables one to consider contingency plans for those events which are most likely to occur or change. This imposes a discipline which encourages all managers to look for events which represent, or are the result of, opportunities or threats. They can therefore be dealt with well before they become problems – or missed opportunities.

13 The plan is controlled by continual examination of the product or service, sales, costs and profits. All elements within the plan, or all elements which could affect its outcomes and achievements must be subject to the same discipline, reviews and timing.

14 The complex relationships and interactions within a plan, and especially the response to competitive reactions (which may trigger a further response from other competitors) are most easily assessed by the use of a spreadsheet ('What if . . .') programme. Such programmes are now available even for micro-computers.

15 Tactics are highly flexible, and they serve the strategy, which can be regarded as the company's masterplan for success. You may sometimes need to change the masterplan as well, but this should be undertaken only after much consultation.

9

Foretelling the future

This chapter is about the techniques and methods of forecasting, discussed here in relation to sales.

Forecasts shape plans, but plans also shape forecasts. We have seen how plans are derived from consideration of possible alternatives involving forecasts of the results of possible actions. Like so much in marketing, forecasting is half art and half science. Sensible managers use the half that is 'science' wherever possible, though all reliable forecasts are likely to contain at least an input from those people in the business most closely connected with the market and therefore likely to understand it best.

However, it is more than likely that circumstances will arise where total reliance has to be placed on personal opinions and intuition. Mathematical or numerical method alone is often inadequate.

In the majority of companies, far too little forecasting is used. Sales forecasts are often the only ones attempted, for it is univerally recognized that the sales forecast is the bedrock from which all other things stem. However, it is essential to try to forecast other things too: profits, for example. These necessarily arise only from sales, though the two are not necessarily directly proportionate, as we have seen. Forecasts of labour requirements may relate directly to own-company sales, to possible alternative plans, and to demands for labour from neighbouring companies. Forecasts of investment may need to consider what level of demand there is going to be for products or services from other companies and countries. Consideration of such forecasts often prompts actions which cannot even be considered unless the inter-relationships between variables have been understood and noted.

9.1 Selecting the method

No method of forecasting applies to all circumstances and companies. Unfortunately, most managers rely on the moving average projected forward. This is a perfectly valid way of forecasting in certain circumstances, but it is in any case only one ingredient in forecasting.

Different factors affect markets at different times. Factors which may be terribly important for a forecast three months ahead could well be totally insignificant for a forecast for the next 12 months. For a five-year forecast, completely new factors may need to be taken into account. So the same forecaster, working with the same facts, in relation to the same products and services, may need to use several different methods and compare the results, especially when looking at different time-horizons.

The type of business you are in will help you to determine the best method(s) to use. Consumer products, and the majority of services, usually have under their own control more of the factors which are significant in business. Even if they do not own the actual means of distribution, many of the key factors involve decisions which they themselves can take: price, promotional special deals, distribution channels, delivery times, and so on.

On the other hand, industrial companies (which meet a derived demand) tend to have far fewer areas of direct influence. Moreover, it may be impossible to obtain information about what is happening further along the total system of which the product is only a part. Obviously, this kind of forecast is going to be more difficult and involve totally different techniques from a forecast which concerns a product which has fewer factors outside the influence of the company.

Derived demand occurs because the product is necessary to the manufacture of another. So, to ensure the necessary supplies, the manufacturer of that other product needs to come to the supplier with forecasts of likely needs. These need to be accepted for what they are, without total reliance being placed on them: every forecast views the world from the viewpoint of the company producing it, and you need to develop a view of the plans of all the companies which you supply, and develop your own forecast.

The position on the demand cycle also helps choose which forecasting techniques are most appropriate for you. Specially important is the amount and precise nature of the information, and other assistance needed for forecasting in the different stages.

In the very early stage of a product life-cycle, for example, one needs to know if orders are coming via repeat purchase or from first-time purchases. The total sales curve can look exactly the same, but the forecast from it will be entirely different on the basis of this fact. Halfway up the curve of a life-cycle, the proportion of repeat versus first-time orders may not matter so much. What one may need more are accurate estimates of steady demand, so that production, raw materials and labour resources can be planned accordingly.

Since there is a trade-off between cost and accuracy, another matter of concern is the likely benefit of the results of the forecast. For example, if a forecast costs £10,000 to prepare, but the profit on the resulting sales is only £8,000 then it doesn't appear worth doing – unless the longer-term ramifications can provide sufficient pay-back.

The purpose of the forecast will also determine the method. If you are considering entering a business for the first time, it may be sufficient to have a fairly rough estimate of market size. It comes as a surprise to many managers that a rough and ready estimate of the size of market ought to be enough: a decision which has to be taken on results accurate to the last £100 is clearly a very risky decision. One that will still work, even if the estimated size of the market has a £100,000 error in it, is far less risky.

However, if the purpose of the forecast is a budget, or a target for performance, then much greater accuracy is needed. When the purpose is to set quality standards, you will need totally different measures. If you want to forecast how growth will be affected by changes in strategy or tactics you will need highly sophisticated techniques. These are now available on spreadsheet computer programmes and are therefore accessible to people who think of themselves as not particularly clever at mathematics.

There are many other factors that help determine the method, including:

- The context in which the forecast has to be made
- How much historical data is available
- How relevant that data is
- How many changes from past events are anticipated
- How much time is available for making the forecasts
- The margins of error that are permissible.

Finally, when one forecast (almost certainly the sales forecast) is used as the basis for all the others, four questions need to be asked which can help determine whether the same method is trustworthy for any different purpose; in many cases, new factors may have to be taken into account, such as:

- What methods and techniques were used for the forecast you are using as a base?
- What economic assumptions were included?
- What assumptions have been made about the behaviour and possible reactions of competitors?
- Were standard costs used or are likely price or cost changes incorporated?

9.2 The stages of forecasting

The following method will work for total markets, industry sectors, or individual customers, although the weighting you give to different elements may change quite markedly. This is true also of most other techniques of forecasting.

Good forecasting procedure employs the following sequence, or as much of it as is necessary:

1 Clarify background assumptions (for example, will Britain join the European Community's Exchange Rate Mechanism? When will the laws and regulations be harmonized?)
2 Define planning assumptions (as set out in Chapter 8)
3 Identify trends
4 Set the time-horizon of the forecast (but remember that there is a relationship between time-span and methods used)
5 Convert projections into predictions of market behaviour (this will be explained in a moment)
6 Take into account additional evidence of which you may be aware – such as the closure of certain customer companies, changes in ownership, changes in attitudes to quality, service, etc.
7 Apply business judgment, relevant experience and the intuition of those who have proved to be the 'best guessers'
8 Integrate results of human experience and intuition
9 Draw up your forecast.

9.3 Projections

Most forecasting methods attempt to discern a pattern in past behaviour which can be carried forward into the future. At one extreme is the computer-based, highly sophisticated technique, while at another is the laying of a plastic ruler across a set of figures, or the drawing of a freehand curve as a continuation of an existing shape.

Actually, the two extremes are not so far apart as they may seem. If you have a good eye for putting an equal number of space on either side of an imaginary line, the plastic ruler (which allows you to see what would otherwise be covered) may be satisfactory. If you have both a good eye and a steady hand then the freehand curve will work for you. What the computer does is essentially the same. It simply uses complex operations to ensure the greatest possible accuracy, and its principal advantage is in those cases where the figures jump up and down all over the place and no human eye can discern a pattern.

Between the more obviously 'do-it-yourself' methods and the use of the complex computer programmes, comes a range of techniques which will be discussed next. Such techniques include trend analysis and simple moving averages and totals – matters where the computer can make an enormous contribution to speeding up the calculations.

First, however, a word of warning. The problem with projection is that it assumes a future just like the past. In the very short term, this may be accurate, but its accuracy lessens dramatically as the time-span is increased. In fact, even in quite short periods, things that were considered unthinkable become accepted. New products, new uses and new usage patterns come into play, reducing the similarity between past and future. Nevertheless, there is often considerable value in projections based on the past. A simple projection is normally the first mathematical stage of any eventual forecast. This enables us to see, if everything else continues as it has done, whether the future looks good enough to be satisfactory. If it does not look satisfactory, we can consider what actions we might need to take and what we might do to make it better. Most good planners make such a projection before starting detailed planning.

9.4 Predictions

Predictions are different from mere projections, and need far more information. To make a prediction, it is necessary to try to discover what events seem to go with others (that is, if there are any correlations) and if there seem to be any factors to account for consequent changes (causal relationships). The more we learn about such events, the greater will be the accuracy both of our plans and of our forecasts. For example, the accuracy with which the sales of a company can be predicted depends on the accuracy with which movements in the relevant factors can be predicted. Long-term trend fitting and projection can be of great assistance in determining such relationships, especially where they are lagged in time.

An example of this may help. A child's birth produces certain events, after a suitable length of time – assuming that everything continues normally. What sorts of things? Baby clothes, starting school, school uniform, changing schools, opening savings accounts, bank accounts, houses, baby clothes again (as they have their own families), and so on. The age of a population is often a significant lagged indicator.

Purchase of plant presages entry into an industry and may generate a lagged demand for packaging material, banking services, insurance, advertising and many others. Those are fairly simple causal indicators. The search for other indicators may be far more complex. It is very useful to simulate ('what would happen if . . .') not only the causal events which are known, but also much less likely ones.

The three-day week which resulted from the miners' strike in 1974 might have been less damaging if more businesses had simulated the effect of a dramatic reduction in fuel and power supplies. Different levels of unemployment, changes in interest rates, raising the school-leaving age, new housing starts, volume of advertising – these are all examples of the sorts of event which may have a causal effect in the future.

Any business should search for its own significant 'leading indicator' – the sort of event which sets off a chain of purchasing events. Not every business will find one. Some may find several – and not always pulling in the same direction. However, predictions can be assisted by statistical methods.

9.5 Statistical methods

These can be used wherever several years' data exist in continuous form. They depend on clear trends and stable relationships between relevant factors: new or changing relationships can entirely invalidate the results of statistical methods. An understanding of time series and trend fitting is essential to the appreciation of statistical methods.

TIME SERIES ANALYSIS
A time series is a set of raw numbers in date order. Submitting them to analysis helps to identify, and perhaps explain, several important

factors, such as:

- any regular variation from a norm
- any kind of feature which repeats itself
- the direction of trends
- the rate of growth or decline of those trends.

The techniques work best for short-term forecasting, but they can be used for longer periods where an industry has very stable relationships between factors and availability of detailed data. Time series analysis is unable to be predictive: it does not indicate turning points which may be ahead in sales and profit curves.

EXTRAPOLATION

Frequently used in time series analysis, this simply means that the method has been used not only to understand the patterns of the past, but also to project that into the future – that is, beyond the range of supporting data. In other words, one takes the facts of the past and uses them to estimate what is going to happen in the future. We have no evidence of what is going to happen, only guidance from past experience.

Extrapolation is reasonable at some times, but not at others. For example, on the basis of an enormous amount of experience, one can extrapolate that the sun is going to 'rise' tomorrow; even predict the time at which it is going to appear. On the other hand, because your market sector has been growing at a steady two per cent over the rate of inflation for the last ten years, that does not necessarily mean it will continue to do so for the next ten years: it might do so, or its rate of growth could vary quite dramatically – for better or for worse.

TREND FITTING

Sales trends are much more clearly apparent from a long series of data than from a few, and often no great amount of work is needed to unearth them. The patterns are often easily discernible. One of the three basic shapes (which we will explain in a moment), for example, might be apparent without the need for any 'smoothing' technique.

Where such shapes are not obvious, 'trend fitting' is of greatest help. In Figure 21 (page 170) there is a fairly simple upward trend visible. If one looked only at the most recent date, one might feel that the sales were growing satisfactorily and needed no special attention. Trend fitting indicates however, that the correct forecast will be in a downward direction (on the basis of past experience) – unless something is done about it.

169

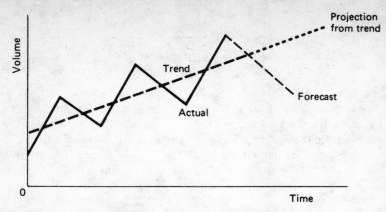

Figure 21 *Projections from trend and short-term data*

One objection to trend fitting is that the future is highly unlikely to be like the past. However, all experience shows that the vast majority of well-formed patterns hold their shape for at least half a year. There are of course exceptions, such as natural disasters, economic disasters, wars, and so on. However, most projections last long enough to justify the course of action proposed and can stand being changed half-way through the year, especially if everyone concerned is well briefed about the possibility in advance. Simulation of possible alternatives is necessary to help prepare for different eventualities.

Before looking at the way in which trends are fitted, let us take a look at the three basic shapes:

1 *Linear trends* These are straight lines which increase by the same, or nearly the same amounts each year. Table 6 shows a company which is growing at 20 units a year. A properly-drawn graph would show a perfectly straight line inclining upwards. Equations for various slopes are easy to derive and thus projection can be very accurate indeed, even in cases which are not as straightforward.

2 *Exponential trends* These increase by the same percentage each year and would normally appear as a curve (unless plotted on semi-log paper, where they would appear as straight lines). In Table 6, there is a simple increase of 20 per cent each year on the base figure of Year 1.

170

Table 6

Year	Linear trend	Exponential trend
1	50	50.00
2	70	60.00
3	90	72.00
4	110	86.40
5	130	103.68
6	150	124.42
7	170	149.30
8	190	179.16
9	210	214.99
10	230	257.99

3   *S-shaped curve* This is a very familiar pattern in marketing. You will recollect that the growth stage of a life-cycle can conform to this general shape. There are several descriptions and corresponding equations of various complexity to describe the shape and to provide the means of projection. Figure 22 shows just two of the more common shapes. The dotted line is fairly typical of new launches – a slow build-up, rapid growth as the product catches on, and then maturity. The solid line illustrates the 'penetration' launch in which everything possible is done to obtain rapid results: high levels of promotion, low prices, trade deals, etc. ('Penetration' pricing is discussed in Chapter 11.)

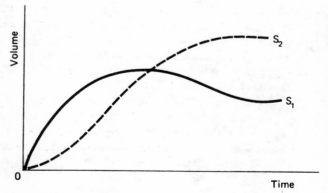

Figure 22   *Typical S-shaped curves*

171

SMOOTHING THE TREND

Sales histories are rarely as neat or clear as the linear, exponential or Sigma shapes. Figure 23 illustrates a more typical, and difficult, sales history. It seems difficult to discern any clear shape in it, though if you look hard, you can discern at least two shapes. Although each year seems to have two peaks and two troughs, corresponding peaks and troughs seem to have varied widely year by year. In such a case, one single act of smoothing may not be enough, and it may need smoothing several times before a shape begins to appear. The trouble is that the more the figures are smoothed, the further from reality they are. If the final smoothing were to come out like the dotted line in Figure 23, you might well have serious doubts about any projection from a line which varies so much from most recent points on the sales curve.

You need to analyze more than the mere figures available here in order to understand why the figures vary so much, examining your company's own internal history and ability to perform over these periods, but looking also at the performance of the market sector, and at the underlying economic conditions. You need to take into account also the difference between demand and sales. If demand has not been fully satisfied at any of the periods under discussion, the sales trend will not be a true indicator of the future possibilities if you are able to increase supply.

One other thing: do ensure that none of the conventions or systems by which the figures have been logged have actually been changed in the period under discussion. Figures for the US tea and

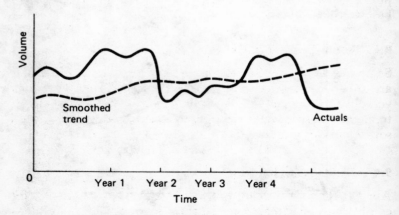

Figure 23 *Problems of projecting from seasonal data*

172

coffee market were totally confused at one point because of a change in the ratio of leaf tea and bean coffee in instant products: the tea market showed one trend by sale of packages but another by leaf tea equivalent – hardly surprising when instant tea mixes can contain as little as three per cent leaf tea by volume!

However, the simplest and most used method of smoothing is the moving average. Decide on a suitable period – say, 12 months. Add up the sales for the chosen period and divide by 12. When the next monthly sales return comes, add it to the previous total but deduct from that the sales figure for the first of the original 12 months. Divide the new total by 12. The formula can be shown as follows:

$$\frac{\text{Period 1 to 12}}{12} \qquad \frac{\text{Period 2 to 13}}{12} \qquad \frac{\text{Period 3 to 14}}{12}$$

Another way of smoothing is that of working, not on the basis of the averages, but on the basis of the 12-monthly totals. (Salespeople are sometimes happier with the larger figures!) Either method will give a smoother curve.

The need for taking the underlying factors into account cannot be ignored, but there are one or two things which can help improve accuracy even on a purely mathematical basis. For example, the most recent events can be given greater weight. Indeed, figures from different periods can all be assigned different weights. For example, in Figure 23 one might want to ignore Year 3 on the grounds that it was exceptional and unlikely to recur. How one weights each of these periods, or any one of them is always a problem. There is no easy solution, except that one discovers the best weightage by trial and error.

9.6 Putting back the kinks

Smoothing helps one to see shapes and trends, but smoothed figures are usually too flat to provide forecasts of any reliability – for that you need to compare them with the raw figures. In other words, trends and seasonal variations need to be seen together to provide a sound basis for forecasting.

9.7 Qualitative techniques

Any situation where data is scarce presents an opportunity for considering one of these non-statistical methods (though these can provide a useful check or means of understanding even where

173

statistical data are available). There is also an increasing number of occasions in the modern world where, due to rapid changes in market conditions, the past is not a reliable indicator for the future. Qualitative methods can, therefore, be used by themselves or in combination with quantitative methods.

Qualitative methods attempt to make use of human judgment in a systematic way, by employing various rating schemes to put numerical values on expert opinions. For the method to be useful, all the possible variables in the system being investigated, as well as all the judgments about them, need to be brought together in the most logical way possible. The great danger is bias, so adequate safeguards against this must be built in. One of the best ways of doing this is to ensure a dialogue between the various 'expert' views.

PROBABILITY ANALYSIS

This is best illustrated by a group of managers who may be equally divided between those who rate a new product as a likely success and those who rate it a probable failure. With a 50:50 split, the decision is usually taken by the most senior manager. However, if senior managers wish, they can get much more information out of their apparently divided colleagues, on which to base their own decision.

When asked to assign probabilities to their views in mathematical terms, those arguing for success might feel that they are 65 per cent certain, while those who think the product will fail are only 55 per cent certain of their view. If we add the two favourable probabilities (65 & 45) and the two unfavourable ones (35 & 55) and divide both figures by two (because we have only two sets of opinions) we get:

$$\frac{(65 \, \& 45) \; : \; (35 \, \& \, 55)}{2}$$

which works out to 55:45.

Because one group of managers is more positive in its opinions about success than the other is about failure, the balance of probabilities comes down firmly on the side of success.

Clearly, the outcome is obvious in this example. If a dozen managers have very different probabilities of success and failure, the balance of opinion may not be so clear. But the basic point is that a 50:50 split in numbers expressing a view for and against a product does not mean a 50:50 probability.

The best known and probably the most universally applicable of the qualitative methods is known as the 'Delphi technique' – another way of saying, literally, 'consulting the oracle'. It works by means of a questionnaire. Say you devise one about the likelihood of success with a new product, submit it to a wide cross-section of managers who are likely to have valid views to express, based on experience of that sort of field. The various opinions on each sub-section of the questionnaire are collated and passed back, anonymously, for comment.

Each original participant is asked to review the feedback and comment on it, giving the reasons for their own views as well as why they reject any other views. This goes on until either a clear consensus emerges or until it becomes clear that there is going to be no more movement in the views. The reporting stage summarizes two things: what might be termed the 'average' of the opinions, and the spread of viewpoints.

There are variations around this basic method. Many practitioners prefer to conduct personal interviews at the feedback stage, especially when it is the first use of the method in a company. Personal contact allows one to feed opinions back in a way that guarantees comment: 'Some people have expressed a view that the market will be at least double the size you suggested, for the following reasons. . . . What comment do you have on this opinion?'

Figure 24 (page 176) shows how outcomes are typically expressed and is an actual example of the method in use. A company manufacturing expensive heavy plant had a problem: it had to rely on sales forecasts by its salesforce, which turned out to be 95 per cent correct in terms of *who* would buy, but 80 per cent wrong on *when* they would buy. As a result, the company had to adopt the practice of beginning production only when firm orders came in, which of course produced long lead times and sometimes uneconomic production runs.

The solution was to encourage the salesforce not only to assign probabilities to the actual order (they were already pretty good at that) but also to: the earliest time that an order might be placed, the latest it could be expected, and the most probable time of ordering.

This provided three points which bounded the probabilities:

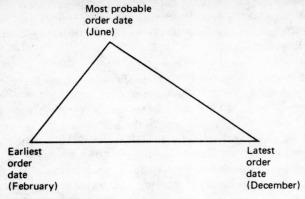

Figure 24 *Delphi expression of order dates*

Within three months of adopting this method, production costs were reduced by 40 per cent, lead times from 12 months to four, and profits improved dramatically. The combination of 'earliest' and 'latest' dates allowed the firm to commence manufacture in high anticipation of firm orders. Within six months, the company reported that the 'most probable' date had reached 70 per cent accuracy and was improving.

9.8 Econometric methods

These methods often strike terror into the hearts of managers, but are not as complicated as they appear. They attempt to improve the accuracy of forecasts by including economic factors in their considerations. They are based on the existence in many industries of 'leading' economic factors – for example, changes in hire purchase terms and interest rates frequently lead to changes in sales of a large range of commodities.

Such changes are themselves often preceded by other changes in economic activity, such as in the balance of payments, in the general state of trade, and so on. The search is for causal factors in the economy, that is, those factors which change before related events in specified industries.

Adequate data is a basic necessity. The systematic search for relationships involves complex statistical methods, which are greatly increased and speeded up nowadays by the widespread use of computers. Many industries have found such models valuable. Others have found that they themselves may lead the very events they are examining. The Thomson Organization found that significant indicators of the future of advertisement revenue – that is, income from the sale of advertising space – were the rate of sale of second-hand cars and the number of job vacancies advertised in their own publications!

Clearly, the econometric model needed to be made more sophisticated, and to look at wider economic factors which influenced the rate of sale of second-hand cars and the number of job advertisements. In actual fact, in this case, government statisticians worked without much progress on this question for some time, and ended up using figures from the Thomson Organization, because Thomson had discovered variables which seemed to presage changes in the level of the economy.

9.9 Testing as an aid to forecasting

If you need to know what the effect of change might be on your forecast, it will often make sense to try that change out in a sector of a market. Such tests can include the trial of a new product in an area of the country chosen for its similarity to overall market characteristics, and the possibility that results can be scaled up in some way to national equivalents on a realistic basis.

Area tests may be used for changes in price; packaging; service levels; distribution; advertising weight or effectiveness; new promotional messages and schemes; and many other things. In every case, an attempt is being made to provide more accurate and numerate opinions about the effect of future activities upon forecasts.

However, there are many slips possible in the choice of an area and results can easily be invalidated by a less than objective test that gets past the scrutiny of everyone concerned. Many companies find that they unconsciously bias tests towards success – for example, by not measuring whether the effort they are able to put into a small area of the country can possibly be replicated on a larger scale. Nevertheless, such tests can be extremely useful for indicating the viability of a product and particularly for indicating the effectiveness of alternative products or alternative ways of doing things.

You won't go far wrong if you think of such a test as an attempt to limit risk – a sort of insurance policy. Instead of the full-scale plant, you are using pilot plants. Instead of heavy expenditure on advertising, you make a relatively low investment in research. Instead of using the whole salesforce, the time of only a small proportion of the salesforce is taken up. Even where there may be doubt about the results in other matters, one advantage of such tests is that they reveal the 'bugs' that there might be in a product or service, including the proposals for its marketing. This is why tests of this kind tend to be used specially in product development.

Certain guidelines apply to all such tests, whatever the uses to which their findings are put:

1 Test only one variable at a time
2 Don't change your mind about what to test half-way through the exercise (this happens more often than you might think)
3 Stick to the purpose for which the test was designed
4 Allow sufficient time. Few tests reveal anything in much less than a year
5 Design appropriate measuring tools and understand the margins of error that are possible with those measures: for example, most market research is conducted to a margin of error of plus or minus five per cent. If a two per cent movement will enable you to decide to go ahead, you need measures that are more accurate – and therefore more expensive
6 Make sure that the chosen area contains a population that is representative of the population to which you eventually want to market the product or service
7 Remember you are not interested in the national population profile – unless every individual in the country is a potential customer. From the viewpoint of the test, you are interested in a population representative of those people who use your type of product or service.

9.10   The uses of forecasts

There is a vast number of uses to which forecasts can be put, but a few of the more usual uses (and the problems associated with them) are as follows:

SIZE OF MARKET

When thinking of a possible new market, or entry into an existing one, two of the first questions to ask are: how big is that market and where is it going? But do consider carefully whether you need to forecast market size and growth: there are published estimates of these available, and you would be well-advised to look at these first, with a view to evaluating whether you feel they are valid. Certainly, for what is often called 'first order scanning', that sort of analysis will be enough to decide on questions of basic interest. You can then undertake a more precise measurement of the market until it is possible to do so in the context of a finished and tested new product or service for that market.

Markets are made up of different and competing products or brands. Care is needed to ensure that a forecast of the total market is consistent with the likely progress of brands within it. In Figure 25, for instance, the market has been growing steadily. Any of the techniques of projection would have that line going upwards. But if one examines the predicted performance of the two brands within the market, this shows that something is wrong. Either Brand B will not lose market as expected, or Brand A will make faster progress – or, conceivably, the market as a whole will decline to the new projection for A & B.

Another phenomenon which ought to be noted is the different rates of progress for segments within a market. Markets are not only made up of different brands but of very different kinds of buyer. Figure 26 (page 180) represents a segmentation analysis of a market – say, the market for hi-fi equipment for domestic use. Initially, price was very high and the appeal would be more likely to be greater to the upper-income groups. The spread of knowledge about hi-fi, the growth in distribution of models and the gradual

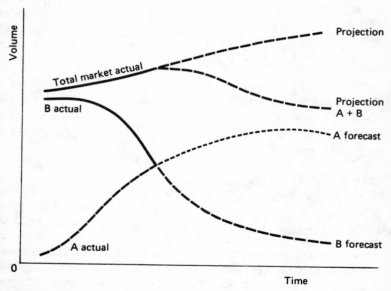

Figure 25 *Projecting market size*

179

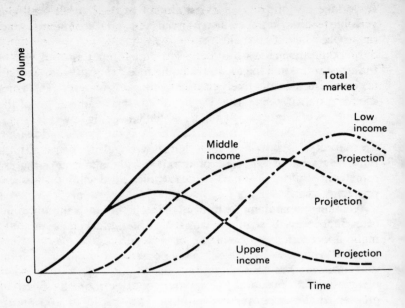

Figure 26 *Segmentation of a market*

reductions in price would bring in those groups with lower disposable income so that, by the time the market is well-developed, saturation of the first buyers means that only a small amount of replacement buying is taking place.

In the example shown, all three groups have passed their peak and the market forecast has now to be derived from estimates of replacement buying, trading-up and adding extra items to a system. There are close parallels in all types of business. Instead of socio-economic groups, they may be types of firm, size of business, adventurous and cautious investors, and many others. To sum up, the forecast of a market may be either or all of the following:

- The growth rate of the total market
- The total of the individual products
- The addition of the growth rates of different segments of buyers
- The amalgamation of different reasons for buying.

Some estimates of market size run into another problem: a situation where trade-ins feature largely (such as private cars, office type-writers, commercial aircraft, bicycles, etc.). For example, if you were to count the total number of sales of aircraft in any one year and add this to the figures for previous years, the result would be very misleading, because some aircraft would be counted several times (they have been sold by one owner to another several times during their flying life). In other words, the forecast for the market for new aircraft must allow for trade-ins and write-offs. The demand for new aircraft would be better estimated by doing the following calculation:

Opening stock of aircraft minus write-offs plus growth factor = demand for new aircraft.

Even that, of course, assumes that the total stock has been carefully calculated not to include all the second-hand sales during the preceding year.

What has been said so far indicates clearly that simple application of even the most sophisticated statistical techniques is likely to be highly misleading as a forecast of market size and growth unless combined with sound common sense, market research, segmentation analysis and a thorough knowledge of the way the market behaves. Some businesses will require more of these steps than others, while some may need to get involved in test situations before they can really estimate a market including themselves, as distinct from the one in which they have not been involved.

Services, consumer businesses and durables generally find that analysis of market segments and their different buying rates and behaviour is crucial. As we saw when discussing the identification of your position on the product life-cycle, prediction of market turning points is much easier from analysis of buyer behaviour than solely from projection techniques.

For some industrial companies, the use of input-output analysis could be valuable. This technique, pioneered in the USA by Liontieff, analyzes how each part of industry draws raw materials and components from others and to what extent its products are, in turn, taken up by others. In theory, inputs and outputs in the total must be equal. If there is complete information about a total system, then it is possible to trace changes in any one sector back to the original suppliers, thus easing the task of prediction about the resultant changes in demand for the intermediary products of other sectors.

Unfortunately, the UK does not collect figures in this form (the United States does) so that methods other than government statistics have to be used. Nevertheless, even incomplete analysis can be better than none at all, and using the theoretical concept –

that every input has an output – can enable the industrial company to build a total system picture which must improve its knowledge of the background to its forecasts and, consequently, the market predictions it makes.

Obviously, too, the value of predictions about its own products will be improved.

COMPANY SALES

Forecasting total company sales is much like predicting total market sales. Total company sales will only reach forecast levels if each of the company's products behaves as predicted. Something like Figure 2 will show what gaps have to be met either by new products or by re-cycled ones. This use of that sort of graph is thought, by many people, to be of greater use in long-term forecasts of a company's future than in forecasts of the sales of present products. In any case, it is generally better to arrive at total company sales by adding up the performance of all component brands.

This has the advantage of biasing you towards considering the performance of brands within markets – and markets tend to move much more slowly than individual products or services within them. Clearly, stability will be more characteristic of larger markets than of smaller ones. In smaller markets, a marked change in the sales of one company's products can upset the momentum of the market as a whole. In larger markets, growth and shrinkage tends to be in relation to other brands rather than affecting the market as a whole.

Predicting the sales of an individual company in those circumstances means predicting share of market. Although many models have been built, and although some of them have been quite useful as predictors of behaviour in individual markets, there is no universal tool which is capable of predicting brand share under all circumstances in all markets.

Having said that, most of what has been included under the discussion of statistical techniques and market size will apply to sales forecasts for individual brands.

NEW PRODUCT FORECASTS

There are many occasions when a really new product emerges and it is difficult to know where to start when attempting to forecast. In such cases, it is worth asking how necessary a forecast really is: all that the company may need to know is whether there is a potentially growing market which will support, at present, the minimum level of sales necessary. Simple break-even analysis may suffice;

historical market trends may provide enough information; input-output analysis could give the answer; expert market opinion about the possibility of reaching levels of viable sale may be all that is necessary. The degree of risk inherent in a mistake will depend on the sophistication of the market and the complexity of the decisions to be taken.

Generally, where the risk is high, the questions requiring accurate forecasts are of a longer-term nature, such as:

- Should we enter the market at all?
- With what involvement?
- In which sector(s)?
- With what investment?
- What strategy?
- What tactics?
- What alternatives should be considered?

Naturally, the longer the period covered by the forecast, the higher the likelihood of error. Nevertheless, as was emphasized in Chapter 8, making these forecasts does at least indicate the risks inherent in different courses of action and what kinds of measures will have to be taken if those risks are to be contained to an affordable level.

The main tools of this type of forecast are sometimes not considered to be forecasting methods at all. These tools are: market research; market tests; measures of buying intention and likely penetration; the differential rates of that penetration among different types and groups of buyers; how quickly old products are likely to be replaced by new ones, and so on.

Predictions are then made on the basis of the most relevant of those factors and the best estimates of the likely effects of the launch strategy and follow-up tactics.

There is, however, a difference between forecasting sales of a new product into a *known* market and into one in which the company has no experience at all. In a market you already know, the planned production can be compared with competitive products and with any known or expected development in that market. The relevance and effectiveness of market research is increased and so is any comparative market testing. One additional method that might be applied to any kind of business is 'Product Difference Analysis'. Known qualities of importance to buyers are compared to markedly inferior ones with, perhaps, five points in between, to give a comparative numerical score. The opinions, when collated, provide an indication of the likelihood of success, provided that you can communicate those qualities successfully to the potential market (customers can't be expected to know what you know unless there is some means of telling them).

A more formalized method, much favoured in the United States for industrial and consumer durable products, is 'Disaggregated Market Analysis'. This simply means breaking a market down into its component parts and segments (by use, buyers, income groups, etc.) and, from these, attempting to identify the factors most likely to influence growth. Thus, a company may be able to say that no successful markets for its product will exist unless certain key areas of business buy first. A simple and very obvious example would be synthetic fibres that have to be made up into garments, carpets, curtains, furniture covers, etc, before people can be persuaded to buy products made of synthetic fibres.

Quite often, that method is combined with a much more universally applicable one: a comparison with a similar product in a market with a well-documented history. The first television manufacturers looked hard at the early history of radio and how sales grew and spread through communities – correctly reasoning that there would be very close parallels. For colour television, they looked at the growth of black and white television: who bought first, and so on. They also looked at the disaggregated data since a supply of valves and tubes was a prime necessity for the growth of the market. So a very useful forecasting tool is the question, 'Which existing market are we most likely to resemble?'

There are several markets where the best judge of a potential new entrant may be an experienced and closely involved individual. Two very different examples of this can be found in perfumery and hair cosmetics, at one extreme, and crockery and pottery, at another. If individual knowledge and experience is combined with careful pre-testing of product performance to check that the individual is still in tune with the market, one probably has the best of all possible worlds in business.

However, specially in industrial markets, nothing may be known about the market to be entered and there may be no readily available (or sufficiently well-chronicled) product or market from which to learn. History may not help either where new technology is involved. Input-output analysis can be extremely helpful in this context, although the paucity of information about industry as a whole is a limitation at present. Input-output analysis can also help define possible new areas for services by revealing gaps and areas where interchange can be eased. Nevertheless, constructing a

184

diagram of all the flows within the total system of an industry, from raw materials to end-use, can be of great value.

In many of these cases, there is no real option to using the Delphi method, perhaps with some measure of probability analysis to assist quantification and indicate margins of error, as well as the confidence of management. Once again, it is careful marketing analysis, backed up by independent research where applicable, that provides the data from which forecasts can be constructed.

9.11   Accuracy and cost

It is always necessary to have some comparison of costs and benefits in mind. Is the cost of the method and the time involved going to prove worthwhile? There are many qualitative and computer-based techniques which could improve the accuracy of a forecast enormously, but would be of little value if the cost exceeded the returns from the sales, or if it took so long that the company lost its sales opportunities while waiting for the results.

In Figure 27, a model of the decisions involved is shown in simplified form. Not surprisingly, the highest accuracy goes with the

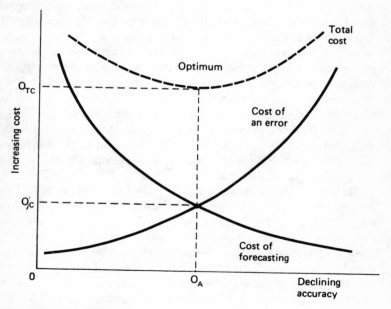

Figure 27   *Cost and accuracy*

185

highest cost. The cost of an error rises from left to right: declining accuracy is associated with increasing cost of mistakes. If the two cost elements are now added together, they produce a curve that reaches its optimum low-cost point immediately above the intersection of the individual curves. Every manager should strive for the ideal reconciliation between cost and accuracy in forecasting.

Complex computer programmes and extensive market research are often applied to questions where common sense will provide a sufficiently correct answer in minutes.

Finally, forecasts should not merely be amended – they must be *updated*. Recording a variance from a forecast is one thing; taking account of that variance and predicting how that will affect various periods of business is quite another. Waiting another 12 months for another formal cycle of planning and forecasting could easily be disastrous.

9.12 Summary

Forecasting is the child of knowledge and intuition. Knowledge can do little more than project past events forward in time, but it is unlikely that past circumstances (which past figures reflect) will ever come again. This problem is not overcome even by the more sophisticated methods of weighting different periods to change the level of importance of different sets of figures from the past. Human judgment and evaluation are essential to convert a projection into a prediction and a prediction into a forecast. Though over-emphasis on human judgment can lead to bias, common sense and experience need to be utilized if statistical projections and market research are to produce results that are usable in marketing and sales.

The methods used will vary according to circumstances, but the aim must always be: greatest possible accuracy at the lowest risk of loss through a bad decision – that is, at the lowest absolute cost in money, and the shortest time-span in preparing forecasts.

The principal difference between projection and prediction on the one hand, and a final forecast on the other, is simply that the first two provide logical and numerical data. The forecast, however, is a quantified statement of what you intend to make happen. So it includes plans and desires, though one makes these as realistic as possible by relating them to market tests and customer trials.

Forecasts need to be constantly updated and amended, and their implications digested, worked through in current and future plans, and then implemented in the business.

9.13 Checklist

1 'Forecasts shape plans and plans shape forecasts'. Consideration of sales trends helps to identify the limits on future plans. The outcome of recommended plans produces sales forecasts which trigger departmental budgets and profit projections.
2 The method(s) selected for forecasting will depend on:

- the type of business and the degree of control it has over key factors
- the position of the product on the demand life-cycle, and on the product life-cycle
- the purpose of the forecast
- its context
- the quantity of relevant past data available
- how much time is available
- the acceptable margins of error.

3 The full sequence of forecasting begins with setting background and planning assumptions; identifying trends; projecting these trends forward in time; amending them by reference to leading indicators and all known facts about the market; and, finally and most importantly, using as much human experience, intuition and judgment as is available for interpreting, understanding and acting on the data produced.
4 Projections assume that the future will be like the past, although it is possible to select which bits of the past will be allowed to influence that future.
5 Predictions rely on the use of indicators, correlations, facts and opinions to condition projections.
6 The forecast spells what the firm intends to do about the possibilities revealed by the earlier stages.
7 Statistical methods relate to projections and extrapolations. Mathematically accurate (in that they project by formula), they are often wrong because markets do not conform to formulae. On average, depending on how long the relevant business period is, statistical methods have their uses up to six periods ahead.
8 Qualitative techniques rely on quantified opinions. They provide a safeguard against undue influence on the part of one view. Probabilities can be assigned to events, times or opinions to measure possible outcomes.
9 Nowadays, econometric methods are more accessible than they used to be via personal computer. However, no model is

187

universally applicable. Few are accurate for long periods, even for individual products. Their main use is in simulation of the possible outcomes of changes in inter-related variables.

10 Market tests may also be used for forecasting purposes, but special care is necessary in the selection of the factors which are tested and from which predictions will be made.

11 One must make sure that every element of such tests can be replicated on a wider scale. Preferably, such tests should: run for 12 months; test only one thing at a time; and be very carefully monitored and measured.

12 Possible influences on market size may be:

- the growth rate of the market as a whole
- the sum of the individual products within the market
- the growth rate of market segments
- all the different reasons for buying added together.

13 Where replacements, trade-ins and the like are important, demand equals the opening stock minus write-offs, plus a growth factor. The figure regarding opening stock must exclude second-hand sales.

14 Company sales forecasts are very similar to market forecasts except that markets generally move less rapidly than products, because products compete for shares of that market.

15 New products in new markets require specialized techniques of input-output analysis, disaggregated demand analysis and the Delphi technique, though some products may have to make do with examining the case of the most-similar example from business history.

16 It may not be necessary to forecast the total market accurately if all that is needed is to decide whether company sales can break-even or if a market of sufficient size exists to absorb total or profitable capacity.

17 Cost and accuracy must go together. If the cost (which may be time as well as money) exceeds the profit, it will not be worth doing. However, the less time and money spent on forecasting, the greater the risk of error.

18 Forecasts should not simply be amended (such as when variance to data is simply added or subtracted from the original forecast). Every change should signal the need for a complete review.

10

The vital difference

'It is a socialist idea that making profits is a vice. I consider the real vice is making losses.'

Winston Churchill

A company's life and death are determined by profit: this is what makes profit the vital difference. Profit is the reward for taking commercial risk. In the vast majority of cases, the practical alternatives are along a spectrum, with low profit rates but high turnover at one end, and high profit but low turnover at the other. Not surprisingly, there are remarkably few cases where opportunities exist of making very high profits at high turnover levels.

If such situations existed, they would naturally encourage competition from firms prepared to work for lower prices and profits. There are a few exceptions, where market opportunities are limited, such as with the independent television companies in Britain at present, where only a few licences were available, and those lucky enough to acquire them acquired also what came to be called a 'licence to print money'.

Marketing is an uncomfortable area in which to operate. There are situations where consumers do not value a product or service except at a price that affords an 'abnormal' level of profit. Such cases exist far more often than is generally accepted. It is always easy to see when you are charging too much, because people stop buying. Unless you actually try it out in some way, it is impossible to foretell how much more they might buy if the price was higher. There are literally thousands of examples of products and services where this has been proved beyond any reasonable doubt – from precision engineering to cake mixes, hotels to holidays, houses to furnishings.

Profit can also be examined from the viewpoint of finance, but that is not our perspective: we will confine our attention to profit as it affects the activities of the marketing executive.

10.1 What is profit?

Next time you feel like having some fun at a management meeting, ask each of the people there for their definition of profit. You are likely to get answers like this:

> (from a factory manager) 'The value added in production'
>
> (from a sales manager) 'What is left after company expenses have been deducted from sales revenue'
>
> (from a brand manager) 'The brand contribution after deduction of all fixed and variable costs and divisional overheads from sales revenue'
>
> (from a finance director) 'The final operating profit after deduction of all costs, expenses, charges and taxes, so representing the sum available for distribution to shareholders and retention as reserves in the company'.

Profit means different things to different people for two fundamental reasons. First, because they have been allowed to let their role affect their view of total company performance. Second, because the concept of company profit is a set of conventions which varies considerably from company to company. So each of those definitions perceives some valid aspect of profit and we need to look at each of them in turn.

The factory manager's view given above is very much the classical economist's view. True, many of the dramatic business collapses of the mid-1970s may have been avoided if the companies themselves, as well as the individuals and institutions who invested in them, had remembered that there is a world of difference between real value added, in either production or marketing, and purely numerical changes in valuation, which reflect mere changes in attitude. To be fair, however, it is quite difficult to distinguish addition to value affecting intangible items.

If a travel company puts together a package of ticket booking, hotel reservation, transport from door to door and an adequate supply of food and entertainment at the resort, it is adding value in the buyer's mind; this addition is comparable with the act of, say, harvesting peas, grading them, processing, packaging and supplying them refrigerated to retail outlets.

On the other hand, most people find it very difficult to appreciate how any value can possibly be added to an unoccupied building that is deliberately being kept empty for a long period. Added value is not profit, as such, but it is a vital ingredient in both profit and consumer satisfaction. And since no business can have profits until it has customers, it is appropriate in every company to monitor carefully the degree of value that it adds in whatever might be called its 'production process'. It is also important to ensure that you have the same idea of what constitutes value as the customer has.

All too often, salespeople discover the concept of 'working capital' with a shock. Their whole training, induction and reward system emphasizes selling and sales policy, which usually militates against understanding that sales actually need to be financed. Most salespeople think that it is the sum the company takes away from the cash produced by the sales team. In times when the sales volume and revenue go up but profits go down – a common feature during inflationary times – it is easy to blame the unseen hands in head office for the company's ills.

In fact, as everyone who has ever started their own business knows only too well, a business starts with costs. That is why capital is needed to fund the setting-up costs until revenue begins to flow in. Most businesses find, too, that there are significant operating plateaux which have to be financed. A piece of machinery may not become efficient and economic until it is producing at 80 per cent capacity. If one salesperson can handle 20 customers, the 21st means that the company has to employ a new salesperson. Not only will the extra customer not be profitable, he or she will reduce the average profitability of the other 20. So any company is continually having to find cash to cover not only existing business but planned future expansion. For this it usually needs three things:

1 Satisfactory profit levels from existing business
2 Access to cash due to it, as rapidly as possible
3 Sources of new finance for all needs that it cannot immediately finance itself.

Your salesforce needs a proper appreciation of the way in which sales are financed if it is to understand and complete its task – which ends only with the collection of the cash that is due for orders obtained.

Marketing specialists, too, tend to work within a narrow and special concept of profit, influenced by the concept of profit contribution. This is usually asked of subsidiary businesses by the head office or holding group, though it may be applied in very much smaller businesses where it may be impossible to allocate fixed investment with an acceptable degree of correctness to individual products or services.

Simply put, profit contribution is what is left for the company after all the specifically allocated costs, charges and expenses have been deducted from sales revenue; the final net profit of the company is of course not produced until all other charges have been met.

Finally, there is the finance director's definition of profit. It isn't surprising that this comes closest to a commonly accepted definition of corporate net profit. Although a high proportion of corporate accountants might agree with most of that definition, they could disagree violently about the figures that such a definition might actually produce: neither accountancy convention nor company law lays down any common standard. So it is possible for companies in exactly the same kind of business to have the same amount of turnover with the same costs and expenses, with the same sorts of charges from banks, and yet produce different profit levels.

They may value their stocks differently, for example. They may take different attitudes to writing-off development expenditure on new products launched during the current year. They may have different depreciation policies. Just read the different views of different financial commentators on the same set of published results, and you will see clearly not only how conventions can vary but how very differently the same convention can be interpreted under varying conditions by different people.

Similar differences in attitudes and evaluation become evident when a new acquisition is included in a set of accounts for the first time. It is often found that the use of the new owner's conventions reduces the profits of the acquired company for earlier years. When GEC acquired AEI in late 1967, it took over a company with forecast profits of £10 million.

When the accounts were amalgamated, GEC showed that AEI had produced a loss of £4.5 million for 1967. In the swing of £14.5 million, only £5 million could be attributed to any differences regarding tangible things; £9.5 million was due to differences between conventions of accounting procedure!

Where does all this leave us? Obviously, profit is largely an individual concept based upon a few generally accepted conventions (some rather stronger ones are laid down by the Inland Revenue) and there is a very large area of discretion. Only one fact is inescapable – cash. Companies fail when they can no longer finance their sales or when they are no longer able to convince their backers of their ability to service their debts – that is, to pay interest charges on borrowed money and to repay in full on the due date. So marketing is about the generation of cash. This is a basic truth, whatever the circumstances, but it is never more vital than in times of inflation.

An understanding of this may lead to a policy of deliberately concentrating on good payers and ensuring that you are not subsidizing bad customers. It will certainly encourage a realistic look at customers and the realization that the customer who never pays until the final demand is hardly a customer at all. It also encourages very careful consideration of the ways in which profits arise and the methods by which they can be increased.

10.2 Increasing profits

Time has always been the enemy of the businessperson – it was businesspeople who invented the expression, 'Time is money'. However, there is some small comfort available in the fact that most of the basic arts of business can be reduced to fairly simple lists. Just as there are really only six basic questions about business, so there are only four ways in which you can improve your profits:

- Raise prices
- Reduce costs
- Sell more
- Improve the profit mix.

Three of these can be illustrated easily in the same table; the last is more complicated.

In the second column of Table 7 (page 194), prices have been raised by five per cent. If we were all in the happy position where that was both possible and permissible, and if the price could be increased without any increase in costs, then the whole of the increase would go through to the bottom line as extra profit. Because nothing else has changed, a five per cent increase in price becomes a 45 per cent increase in profit.

In the third column, costs have been reduced by five per cent. Each of the three cost lines has been reduced by the same amount. Clearly, it is unrealistic to believe that many companies can reduce all three simultaneously, though the overall effect might well be achieved by concentrating on just one area; even labour costs can be reduced in times of inflation by redundancy, natural wastage and improved productivity. However, a five per cent reduction in costs, though it does not produce a rise in profit equal to that provided by a five per cent increase in prices, does provide a 40 per cent increase in profits.

Table 7 *Improving profit by single steps, £s*

	Current figures	After 5% price increase	After 5% cost decrease	After 5% sales increase	After 15% sales increase
Sales turnover	720	756	720	756	828
Material costs	300	300	285	315	345
Wages & salaries	180	180	171	189	207
General overheads	160	160	152	160	160
Net contribution	80	116	112	92	116
Increase in net contribution		+45%	+40%	+15%	+45%

Now look what happens when price remains unchanged but sales revenue goes up by five per cent. This time, the increase does not come through to the bottom line. Some of it is dissipated in increased costs of financing the sales (working at material costs of 42 per cent of revenue and wages and salaries at 25 per cent, rounded up). So this provides only a 15 per cent increase in profit. In fact, if we want to produce a profit increase of 45 per cent, which we get from a five per cent increase in price, we will have to increase sales by 15 per cent.

And how realistic is that? And, if it can be done now, why wasn't it done earlier? Yet isn't that just what most managers ask for when profits must be raised? The natural tendency is to push the sales force to sell more, yet it is by far the most difficult way of increasing profits, simply because of the need to finance sales. Different sets of figures will produce different results, but you will find the order is always the same: sales increases are the hardest way of increasing profits.

Service industries, which need to invest far less in raw materials, may find that the relationship between cost, selling price and sales revenue is different, yet the principle remains the same for them too: sales increases are harder and will add less to profit than, say, cost reduction or price increase.

Table 8 shows what happens when the three things are combined. It naturally makes sense to start, always, by paying attention to cutting costs, then to raising price, and only then to seeing how it is possible to sell more. What is essential is to make sure that products or services of the best possible quality from the customer's point of

194

Table 8 *Improving profit by combined steps, £s*

	Current figures	After 5% cost decrease	Plus 5% price increase	Plus 5% sales increase	Plus 15% sales increase*
Sales turnover	720	720	756	794	869
Material costs	300	285	285	299	330
Wages & salaries	180	171	171	179	200
General overheads	160	152	152	152	152
Net contribution	80	112	148	164	187
Increase in net contribution		+40%	+85%	+105%	+134%

*15% increase on 5% price increase column

view, are provided at the most economic cost, without undue wastage of people or materials, and without unnecessary frills. Then ensure that the price is right – which is the price at which the product or service is rated by the customers you wish to attract. Only then does it make sense to exhort the salesforce to greater effort.

However, we need to take the analysis another step. Many companies will find that there is an item we have not dicussed yet which provides greatest benefit. Getting business priorities right means selling more of the higher-profit lines wherever feasible – even at the expense of lower-value lines where necessary. This fact is a little more difficult to illustrate through a table of the sort we have used with the earlier cases in this chapter, but Table 9 uses figures relevant to the company on which Tables 7 and 8 are based.

From the summary of contributions per case, it is clear that – all

Table 9 *Contributions summary, £s*

	Contributions per case	Contributions per unit of machine time
Product A	6	6.00
Product B	11	2.75
Product C	6	3.00
Product D	2	0.70
Product E	-3	Negative

other things being equal – it will require about two cases of products A and C and six of D to equal the contribution of B. If this was all that had to be taken into account, then B would be the line to push at the expense of the others, and specially of the unrewarding product E.

If, however, the situation is that all the products use the same resources and one product can only be made at the expense of another product, then it is necessary to look at contribution per unit of machine time before arriving at a conclusion about the ideal product mix to yield maximum profits. Naturally, the picture changes. A becomes the best line to promote, because the contribution from A is now seen to be worth two of C and more than double the contribution of B.

10.3 Profit and sales

If the salesforce is to enter into a true profit partnership in a company, there are two areas of importance. First, the snobbery that puts cash collection and invoice-chasing as menial tasks not befitting a sales executive must be removed from the salesforce, if necessary by dismissing salespeople who do not, or will not, understand and accept the idiocy of this. It cannot be emphasized too strongly, particularly in times of rampant inflation or recession, that a salesperson's task is not complete until the cash has been received. Many companies now believe that securing prompt payment should count towards bonus payments.

Traditionally, however, salesforces are given volume targets. All forms of bonus and other incentives are calculated in such a way that they are geared to the pursuit of volume. Yet, as has been seen, this can be highly unprofitable.

It isn't necessary to reveal all the company's secrets to a salesforce, but it can be helpful to encourage them to consider some simple indicators of the company's profit priorities. One device is to measure all sales in some sort of standard unit. For example, give each product a weight according to its profit contribution. In the case of Table 9, it might work out like this:

Product A	3 standard units
Product B	6 standard units
Product C	3 standard units
Product D	1 standard unit

In this example, D is taken as the base product and the others are calculated accordingly. If bonus payments are based on the standard units, then the salesforce will quickly see where their own – and their company's – priorities and interests lie.

Standard units present a very practical way of relating sales efforts to profitability without divulging confidential information. Moreover, they can be used to vary the emphasis in sales effort, if and when that is needed. In periods of production difficulty, when machine-time contributions become a crucial consideration, or during special promotions and slack sales, a company could say, for example, that Products A and B are going to change places for the next three months – that is, A will be worth 6 standard units and B worth only 3. The only caution that needs to be given is: don't change the values too often, or they will become debased.

There are many other ways in which profitability and sales effort may be more closely related, such as break-even charts to decide on any new cost elements (new salespeople, new vehicles, new offices, *et al*). But, in a book on marketing rather than on sales, it is probably enough to say that a salesforce needs guidance on where to concentrate effort so that its work is of maximum possible benefit to the company.

10.4 Profit and the marketer

There are still many companies which do not allow their marketing people to have full profit information. This is rather like sending players onto the field with one hand tied behind their back. Marketing is inescapably linked with profit and all the ways in which that might be raised. As the co-ordinator of the various departments, the marketing executive should be ideally placed to identify opportunities for profitable action. If marketing executives know that the factory has difficulty re-engaging labour laid-off during the summer months, they may be able to devise schemes that prevent the lay-off. At least it will be possible to calculate which is cheaper: to allow the labour to be laid-off or to try to have a special promotion at that time to increase sales.

Where the marketing executive is reduced to seeing only the figures relating to sales, then possible opportunities will be lost in other areas. There is also a danger of over-emphasis on one area of business, with the remaining staff regarded as somewhat unnecessary and certainly incompetent people who use up too many company resources.

Not only should marketing executives have all profit-related information, they should also be informed instantly of any changes which affect profitability. It is a strange fact of business that sales budgets are amended frequently, while other changes which are known to have a much more important long-range effect, are not used to amend predictions, forecasts and plans. Most companies report such differences as 'prime cost variances' or even 'unexplained differences'.

A famous tea and coffee company reported prime cost variances against a standard set in 1938 for a full 30 years. A printing company which normally enters its financial year with agreed wage rates negotiated with its trade union, but nevertheless calls these 'unexplained differences' at the year-end.

There is a well-known case of a marketing executive who, with his brand managers, sweated through a year trying to make a particular profit target. They got to within £30,000 of the target and thought they had done a pretty good job in a very difficult year, though they wished they hadn't had to do so much surgery to get there. However, when the final figures were published, the profits were £1.2 million higher than the marketing folk had thought they had achieved. The company had been keeping close to its chest 'prime cost differences' which produced that final result. Senior management had reasoned that if these young marketing people got to hear about the money that wasn't being spent, they would want to use it for advertising or some other wild promotion scheme. Had they known the facts, the young managers might have avoided some of the drastic surgery they undertook, which eventually led to the demise of three of the largest brands in the company – the very ones, in fact, which produced 80 per cent of the favourable difference.

An enterprise is in business to make a profit. The more people there are in the enterprise who know what their part is in that objective, the better the chance of achieving it. They do not all need to know every shred of information. Coded and weighted information (such as standard units) can be enough. But they do need to know – and know quickly – when things change. Moreover, they should be invited to suggest how adverse changes might be overcome and positive developments utilized to the full.

10.5 Inflation

During times of rapidly increasing costs and prices, there are two particular things that businesspeople can do. The first is to concentrate on getting the right profit mix – which may change more quickly than you would like, but then social and business attitudes seem to accept rapid change more easily in inflationary times.

It may pay you to hasten the decline of a life-cycle, unless you can find a profitable way of re-cycling a product. Re-cycling presents an attractive alternative to falling profits. If you can revamp products or services to give additional customer benefits, those additional benefits can reflect current costs. The more the benefits that the re-cycled product can be seen to provide, the greater can be its saleability in spite of its higher cost. Where government controls exist, re-cycled products may present a legitimate way of avoiding restraint orders on existing products.

Re-cycled and new products are essential to surviving inflation. New products have two great advantages: they lack historic cost and they are launched into updated price-expectation patterns. Historic cost is the enemy of profit in times of inflation. If new production methods and new ingredients cannot be found, then new products with new cost and price structures may well provide the answer.

10.6 Marketing in hard times

If you are to make the best of hard times, there are three fundamental things that need to be understood:

1 Hard times are periods of slow growth – or even no apparent growth at all.
2 Your growth will only be possible at the expense of others.
3 Technology will continue to improve.

This may seem too simple to need to be said, yet many disasters in hard times happen because of a refusal or disinclination to accept these three truths. Companies respond far too late to the implications of slower growth, turnover and profit. When volume is short, competition gets tougher: failure to control costs will be disastrous.

Nevertheless, there are things you can do. It is rare for the whole of a market to be in equal decline. In fact, there is usually at least one sector which is growing even in the most difficult times. If you can find it, you can produce differentiated products for it. If your planning process includes careful market analysis, then such a sector will be of no surprise to you. Assessment of the vulnerability of different segments of a market should be second nature and may lead to decisions about maintaining contact with sectors that offer better long-term security than others.

In hard times, your customers are probably having hard times too. This is the time to search for better cost-benefits for them. It is often the case that higher prices will be paid for items producing better cost-benefits than can be reflected in costs of production. Now, more than ever, is the time to emphasize product quality, not to drop it – which is what seems to be the reaction of many companies to hard times, often as a justification for lower prices.

Innovations in technology provide the opportunity to produce innovation and improvement, specially if they can be combined with customer cost-benefits.

Particular attention should be paid to the efficiency of your marketing mix. All your marketing activities will need to be sharper and more clearly cost-effective. Wherever possible, concentrate on the more measurable activities and think twice about those that are uncertain or immeasurable. It usually pays to look hard at stockholding, distribution methods and efficiency. If volume falls, the suitability of old delivery and stockholding standards must be questioned. Are the salesforce's call rates still appropriate? Are their tasks still relevant? Should there be some change?

In short, hard times call for creative analysis of sales opportunities, for frequent questioning of why things are done that way, and for asking whether the old standards are still relevant. Above all else, one needs to be poised and ready to take advantage of any upswing as soon as it happens, and not to have become so lean that the company has no energy to attack new opportunities.

10.7 Summary

Marketing people are particularly prone to confuse high sales revenue with high profit. Their company's systems of communication and reward often actively encourage this delusion. Profit consists of what remains after expenses, and the expenses of operating capital, have been met.

There are four major methods by which profit can be increased:

1 Selling more
2 Raising prices
3 Cutting costs
4 Improving the profit mix.

These are best marshalled in the following order of priority: get costs right; align prices correctly in line with customers' ideas of acceptable range and risk; emphasize the most profitable items in the range; and give incentives to the salesforce to sell more according to the new priority. The greater the amount and quality of profit information disseminated, in appropriate forms, the more chance there is of changes in cost areas being offset by positive marketing action. Not only should this information be provided to responsible executives, but it should be updated and amended at least as frequently as sales budgets.

10.8 Checklist

1   We quickly discover when prices are pitched too high, but it is far more difficult to establish the point at which sales – or at least profits – might be higher if prices were raised.
2   In most companies, the marketing function works with the concept of profit contributions. True, final net profit does not arise until all shared costs, general overheads and company charges have been deducted. But focusing on this fact distorts the perception and motivation of the marketing function. It is far better for them to understand what profit actually is – including all the factors that go towards increasing or reducing it.
3   In the search for higher profit, central costs should be subjected to examination as searching as the effort to increase profit contributions from products or profit centres.
4   The necessity of covering central costs can easily lead to the maintenance of products which make some gross contribution, even though they fail to make a net – or target – contribution.
5   Raising prices produces such a significant effect on profits that it ought always to be the first option to be explored.
6   The effect of cost reductions will depend upon the cost structure of the product. For most manufacturing companies, this will be the next most effective method of increasing profiits. However, the more efficient the company, the less room it will have for further cost reduction.
7   Improving profits by increasing sales is by far the most difficult method. Sales produce money, but there is an administrative cost involved in procuring them, and it also costs more money to process and supply a greater quantity of orders. So sales revenue needs to be improved by a considerable amount to get a relatively modest improvement in profit.
8   The ideal priority-pattern for improving profits is:

   a.   Get the cost structure right (that is, as low as is consistent with the necessary customer standards of quality).

b.   Decide on the most profitable mix of products and concentrate sales efforts on the more profitable products – if necessary, at the cost of the least profitable items.

c.   Set prices as high as is consistent with the required volume and profit.

d.   Sell more. But note that extra sales effort without the preceding three steps will be less rewarding than it could be.

9   Sales effort can be better directed towards more profitable sales by the use of a profit-weighted incentive system (for example, 'standard units' – using profit-weighted volume – rather than raw sales figures).

10 Those responsible for product marketing must be aware of all the ingredients that produce or influence final profit.

11 In times of inflation, the key to profitability lies in two things: in adjusting the optimum profit mix – frequently, if necessary; and in re-cycling existing products in such a way as to present added values and justify higher prices.

12 All hard times demand a recognition of their particular nature, and a determination to act early – specially where it means taking hard decisions.

13 When markets stand still, the only place from which volumes can be gained is competitors . . . and you are the only place from which they can get *their* gains.

14 Customers always search for maximum benefits at minimum costs. Hard times are good times to emphasize product quality and to make innovative improvements.

15 Particular attention should be paid to the cost and efficiency of marketing activities. Measurable methods of sales and promotion should take precedence over immeasurable or less certain methods at such times.

11

Pricing

Cheat me in the price not in the goods.
 T. Fuller, *Gnomologia: Adages and Proverbs*, 1732

Pricing is only one of the 'direct' elements in the marketing mix. After the product itself, it is arguably the most important.

Although there are many methods which help us to consider the right price to charge, their application is to a large degree an art rather than a science.

11.1 What is price?

Most people view price as an indicator of quality. Two things must be said immediately about this. First, perceptions of 'quality' and 'value' can vary considerably between individuals. Second, something that is of no use to particular individuals has no value for them. Economists distinguish three kinds of value:

- Cost
- Use
- Esteem

The basis on which most companies price their products is still, and quite wrongly, that of cost. Using cost as a basis for pricing is simple: add a certain percentage to your overall costs and you arrive at your selling price. Sometimes, of course, you may have to sell at cost: you do it in order to avoid a loss of course, but why should you do it at all? Well, there can be promotional reasons; or you may wish to keep your resources (including labour) working, and thus avoid the heavier expenses of redundancies and write-offs.

'Use' value is what it is worth to the buyer to have the goods or services. For example, a very high proportion of householders do their own decorating. They place no value on their own time and conclude that it is cheaper to do it themselves than to employ a decorator who will charge for his or her time. However, the value of avoiding nuisance or bother will also enter the calculation. Confidence, too, enters into it: employing an expert may cost more than doing it yourself, but makes you feel more secure.

Finally, what is 'esteem value'? Consider the sorts of reasons why you might choose to fly first class to a holiday destination. After all, you don't get there any faster; the sun won't shine any more brightly, though you may travel more comfortably and receive more attention in-flight. In fact, your decision will contain a large element of this third kind of value. 'Esteem value' is created by the esteem in which an object or service is held. This usually has something to do with scarcity, as in the cases of gold and Ming china. The buyer of a designer dress is guaranteed that there is not another one like it. Amateur buyers of cameras buy a good deal of esteem when they pay high prices for many mechanical qualities that may never be utilized.

How can an understanding of these three sorts of value be put to use in business? Clearly, the lower limit of price is set by costs. The owners of a new and prestigious hairdressing salon in a prime location in London once asked a consultant for advice because their financial difficulties seemed to be getting worse and worse. The place was lavishly furnished on a loan from a bank, and the prices were very high. But the problem was that even if the salon was full all day, every day, it could not make enough money to pay even the rent and the rates! The high failure rate of many small retail businesses is often due to not attracting sufficient customers to pay the basic costs of the business.

Of the three values discussed, the most important one is 'use' value. Unless your customer has a use for your product and values it at a level that affords a satisfactory margin of profit, you simply aren't in business. But it is 'esteem' value which begins to tell us what every experienced marketer knows – that there is a 'right' price at which sales, volume and profit will all be maximized.

Moreover, price may well be higher than cost plus percentage mark-up. Marketing history is full of examples of sales of products which have only really taken off when the price was raised. Why is this? Because people do not have only 'esteem' value, they also have what might be called 'negative esteem' value. It occurs when customers are put-off buying a product or using a service because the price is out of line with its perceived qualities. It provokes reactions such as, 'If it is so good, why is it so cheap?' The psychology of price is vitally important.

11.2 The psychology of price

In areas of uncertainty, price is an indication of quality. The lady who goes to a new hairdresser and is uncertain of standards, or is searching for esteem value, asks for the leading stylist. Faced with two alternatives and no apparent differences, most people will opt for the slightly higher-priced of the two.

Some buying situations are more objective than others, but it is well established that even in apparently emotion-free industrial buying situations, many more things than product quality and price are important. Since many companies are capable of offering the same product, the final decision has to have more components in its favour than quality and price. The psychology of price is associated with the degree of risk involved. The higher the risk, the greater the care that has to be taken. High-priced products tend to be seen as more risk-free than low-priced ones. It is true that at very low prices, people tend to accept the risk and say 'I can't lose much at that price'. Yet, at very high prices, they feel they can justifiably complain and expect recompense if things go wrong – in addition to the fact that it may be perceived as more worthwhile, in financial terms, to use time complaining about defects.

Cost-based methods of pricing (which we will discuss in a moment) could well be dangerous in that they take no account at all of the psychology of the buyer when considering prices. On the other hand, one has to consider what is acceptable in the market; buyers may be only willing to buy at cost-based prices.

11.3 Can you change the price in the market

Whether you can determine the prices in your market, or even initiate changes in the market, depends on several factors, such as:

- the extent of the competition
- how close that competition is
- the strength of demand for your product
- the elasticity of demand for your product
- the price/volume relationship
- the relationship of volume and cost
- psychological factors in your market
- whether you are by tradition a price leader or a price follower.

This list assumes that you are the one initiating the price change; what happens when your competitors move first? If they raise prices, your first reaction should be, 'If they can get away with it, why can't I?' Only then should you start thinking whether there is any marketing advantage to be gained by either not going up with them, or at least not going as far as them. However, that's the easy case. It is not the price increase by a competitor which creates a problem, it is the price reduction. In such a situation, the key questions become:

- Do we have to reduce our prices too? Are there any valid non-price moves we could make?
- If we cut price, what will that do to our image?

If the answer appears to be non-price competition, it pays to simulate the effects carefully. You may like to use the probability analysis described in Chapter 9. In such situations, simulation usually takes the form of: 'If we do this and they do that, what do we do next?' Do remember that most non-price methods are easy to respond to – and that they can be responded to very quickly, if your competitors haven't exhausted their resources in making the price cut. Consider too whether the price cut is a permanent one or a promotional one. Above all else, do not panic. Stop and think. A few days will be well invested thinking through an appropriate response, and a few days won't make all that much of a difference in most markets.

A large number of customers will interpret a price cut as a sign of a company in trouble: perhaps that is why your competitors have gone down-market. Perhaps they will go down, completely: don't let them take you down with them.

11.4 Price elasticity

This is a little confusing: it refers to the market's response to prices moving up or down – that is, the market is not terribly worried about what price is charged for the product or service. In other words, how responsive is demand to price? If you raise your price, say, ten per cent – will demand shrink by a negligible amount, by a marginal amount, by a significant amount or by a substantial amount? Some firms or industries are more concerned about price than others. For large and successful firms, price differentials have to be relatively large before they would consider switching from their established supplier – and then they would often scrutinize your firm carefully to reassure themselves that your lower prices were not going to lead to an early demise for your company. Smaller firms, on the other hand, are often looking for the cheapest source of supply they can get – though longer credit is often a more important consideration.

11.5 Cost-based pricing

There are seven main methods of cost-based pricing, although you may consider some of the differences rather subtle.

MARK-UP PRICING

This is the simplest form of cost-plus pricing. The term 'mark-up' is used because of its wider implications. The mark-up is usually a traditional, habitual or generally accepted percentage. Mark-up pricing is conventional in wholesaling and retailing, but traditional patterns exist in many other industries. Such mark-ups tend to continue unchallenged until it is clear that the level of service or effort provided by every supplier is not the same.

Retail price maintenance occurred in the past largely due to companies being able to buy in bulk at traditionally high discounts, and preferring to increase their volume sales by passing on part of that margin in the form of lower prices. Self-service retailing lowered labour costs and effectively meant that part of the traditional margin was no longer necessary.

ABSORPTION COSTING

Take all the costs, calculate a required overhead contribution, add an agreed profit margin, and the result is an ex-factory selling price (that is, a price before calculation of any margins, discounts, etc.). Thus:

> Direct material costs
> + Direct labour costs
> + Overhead contribution
> = Total product costs
> + Agreed percentage mark-up
> = Ex-factory selling price

Add the costs of the margins and discounts you will need to offer, and you arrive at your retail price.

DIRECT COST PRICING

Also known as 'contribution costing', this system arrives at the price by calculating direct costs, desired profit level, and a contribution to

207

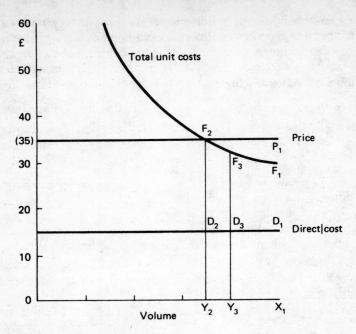

Figure 28 *Direct cost pricing*

cover all other costs (for example, overheads, promotions, etc.). Figure 28 shows how this method works. At an output of X, direct costs (D_1) are £15. Total unit costs (F_1) are £30. The price for output of X_1 for £35 allows a profit of £5. The line F_2, D_2, X_2 shows the volume at which the price of £35 will exactly cover total unit costs.

Suppose that sales fall back from F_1, D_1, X_1 to F_2, D_2, X_2, then the profit margin will fall unless a new price is set. The mark-up used to set the price of £35 was 16.66 per cent. Total unit costs at the lower volume are £33 (at F_3) so that using the same mark-up will produce a new price rounded up to £38.50.

As you can see, this method is not always practical. How many companies would have the courage to raise prices when there is a decline in the market? If volume falls further, prices will have to rise yet again. Nevertheless, despite this obvious problem, the method is a useful way of deciding whether entry into a new market is going to be profitable – at ruling prices or at a range of other prices.

INCREMENTAL LEVELS

This method takes account of the actual extra costs involved in moving from one level of output to another (always remembering that it is possible to suffer incremental costs of *reduced* output too). As a costing/pricing method it makes sure that changes in cost levels are adequately reflected in price. It is particularly suitable for jobbing firms (eg, jobbing printers). Cost calculations generally show the cost advantages of long, continuous, smoothly-programmed orders. Thus, the 'run-on' cost of printing an extra 1,000 catalogues is mainly paper, and makes the cost per catalogue cheaper on a 5,000 run than on a 4,000 run. In this example, incremental costing makes it possible to do the opposite of what the name suggests: it enables the printer to offer a proportionately reduced price on longer runs. Of course, it is possible to think of the opposite kind of case, where increased volume or specifications of quality make for a disproportionate increase in price.

MARGINAL COSTING

This is a form of incremental costing, and it has its dangers. The 'marginal' cost is what it actually costs to produce and sell one extra unit or batch. Its dangers are seen most clearly when marginal costing overrides a standard costing system. The temptation is to remove all the standard costs you can to justify a price that will secure sales. There's nothing wrong with this – provided you can be 100 per cent certain that the cost can be wholly removed and the order genuinely represents extra business.

Nine times out of ten, however, it is not wholly justifiable to remove all of a standard cost. You assume no delivery cost because a van is calling in any case. However, if there is no van calling on the day you need to deliver, then there has to be a special delivery . . . and so it goes on. And what if the marginal deal you do is with Tesco and it draws volume away from nearby Gateway outlets? In this case, part of the fully-costed sales to Gateway, which went towards supporting your deal with Tesco, will have gone. So use marginal costing only with *extreme care*, deliberately taking into account all ramifications of a sale to this customer, and all the things which might go wrong.

OPPORTUNITY COSTS

If the same plant can be used to make two products, manufacturing one could mean foregoing the profit that could be earned from the other. A notional value – or opportunity cost – is put on the cost of producing A rather than B, or B instead of A. This notional value may seem to be a perfectly valid way of dealing with the demands of the two products, but the *real* opportunity cost is not always obvious. There may be a discrepancy between short-term profit and long-term opportunity, for example.

As a pricing method, it works best with one-to-one situations and therefore tends to be widely used in the professions. If a fully-employed barrister earns £100 per hour, the 'opportunity cost' of his or her round of golf may be £200–£300. The chance of a brief at £150 per hour through that round of golf might justify paying someone else £120 per hour to take over an existing brief at £100 an hour.

TARGET PRICING

This method is often described as 'profitable pricing'. The company sets the price that will give the required rate of return at various levels of volume. Figure 29 shows the kind of break-even analysis used to determine price. At a volume of 50,000 units, total costs are £400,000. If the required rate of return is 20 per cent, the profit which must be earned is £80,000. Price per unit will be:

$$\frac{£400,000 + £80,000}{50,000} = £9.60 \text{ per unit}$$

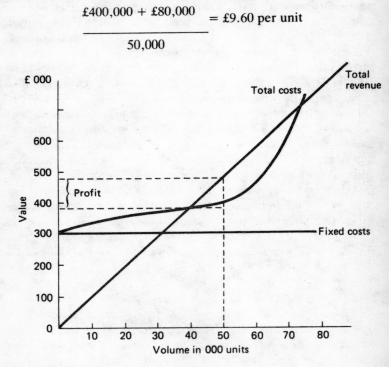

Figure 29 *Target pricing break-even chart*

This too is a cost-based method because demand is ignored: price is determined by hypothetical levels of volume. No attempt is made to determine what price is *necessary* in order to sell at all, and whether that volume of sales is reasonable to expect.

11.6   Break-even pricing

Figures 28 and 29 indicate two uses of break-even analysis. Chapter 10 indicated another use. Figure 30 shows a relatively detailed use of break-even analysis. Break-even volume is shown at BE, where revenue exactly earns the required rates of return on investment after meeting all costs and contributions. However, the definition of 'required return' varies enormously between competing companies. The company looking for a 30 per cent return on total assets will have to set a higher price than the one looking for 15 per cent. That means that it will probably have a smaller clientele and smaller volume sales – though, as has already been pointed out, this is not necessarily true. It is a matter of assessing your market.

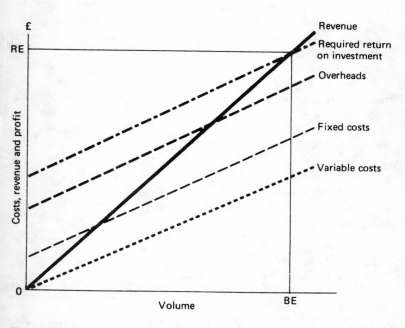

Figure 30   *Sophisticated break-even analysis*

The big danger with a slavish use of break-even analysis is that when times are bad, and revenues are reduced, prices will have to rise; conversely, when times are good, revenues rise, as the result of higher volume and prices will then be reduced. Both reactions maybe the opposite of what is required in such situations.

Additionally, there is nothing in break-even analysis itself that allows competitive reaction to be taken into account. In theory, if your competitors lower their price and steal some of your volume, you will then have to increase prices even more – which means, of course, that they take even more of your volume!

Break-even analysis has its uses but should only be used with great care. It can become a useful discipline if probabilities are assigned to the chances of achieving the necessary volumes at various price levels (see Chapter 9). Break-even charts are specially useful in calculating by how much sales will have to rise to offset lower prices (or by how much they would need to fall to outweigh the advantages of higher prices).

11.7 Demand-based pricing

This system of pricing works on the principle of going by what the market will bear. In theory, this is clearly the best way to price, although it is not always easy to discover the correct level, and some painful experiences may be gathered along the way. 'Charging what the market will bear' usually comes down to segmenting the market and producing different prices for each segment. In other words, price differentiation. This is so common – by customer, by time, by place, by volume and by value – that it passes without comment. We do not expect all seats in a theatre to cost the same. Even though a child occupies one whole seat on a train, we expect to pay less for the child than we do for an adult.

DIFFERENTIATION BY CUSTOMER

There are at least six criteria for charging different prices to different customers:

1 Degree of price responsiveness
2 Intensity of demand
3 Level of knowledge of product
4 Level of awareness of market prices
5 Urgency or timing of demand
6 The belief that prices indicate levels of service, quality and expertise.

DIFFERENTIATION BY TIME

Price differentiation by time may be possible where there are peaks and troughs of demand – and especially where costs remain level through the sales variations. Thus, hotels charge more at peak holiday times but at off-peak times may be prepared to accept low prices that merely make a contribution to the necessary costs of keeping a hotel ready for business. Public utilities too have off-peak, reduced-rate tariffs: for example, 'Awayday' fares on British Rail make a contribution to getting the trains in position ready for the peak (full cost) travel hours. A problem with differentiation on the basis of time is that it could lead customers to adopt new patterns: those who can delay their departure until cheap fares come into operation will do so.

DIFFERENTIATION BY PLACE

First-class berths on ships, hotel rooms with a bath, a balcony overlooking the sea – these are all examples of differentiation by place. So, too, are products sold ex-works, delivered, FOB (free on board). The price is higher for the customer who involves the supplier in the most cost or effort. Profit can be greatest where customer estimates of scarcity or esteem value are greatest.

DIFFERENTIATION BY VERSION

If you take two versions of a service or product, and calculate the difference in their cost price, the result is two different prices, though the difference is probably not all that large. The policy of pricing differentially by version means that a higher or lower price is assigned to the two versions than is justified by the difference in production price. This is best seen in different versions of what is basically the same car from a manufacturer.

Another version of this pricing policy might be called 'bundling'. For example, you can buy a 35mm camera and a standard 50mm lens separately, but many manufacturers encourage you to buy both together by making the price of the packaged version distinctly cheaper than the price of the two separately. This ensures that the maker's lens is sold with the body, and means that the sale is not lost to a rival.

DIFFERENTIATION BY VOLUME

This is the most common form of price differentiation, specially in relationships between manufacturer and intermediary, and between one business and another. Discounts on volume and on

213

quantity are common in sales to the public, for example where consumers might be offered a giant pack at less than the price of two packs which make up the same quantity.

The effect of this type of differentiation is to create different final net prices for customers buying different quantities. Normally, the prices charged reflect the advantages of higher volumes of manufacture or delivery, or the effects of various cost plateaux. There is only a marginal difference in cost between transporting a container (or truck, or ship), whether it is full or empty. A form of reverse differentiation is also practised because of the difference in handling costs, such as when a minimum order quantity is fixed, or there is a charge for small orders.

DIFFERENTIATION BY VALUE

You might say, for example, that you will offer a ten per cent discount if customers buy goods worth more than £100. The trouble with this system is that £100 buys less and less in terms of actual goods as time goes on. Therefore your profit margin on the goods worth £100 will shrink with time. The result: you will soon be out of pocket, unless you either reduce the percentage or increase the limit on which you offer ten per cent. Whichever you do, the result will be customer dissatisfaction, because they will feel less well rewarded than previously.

Moreover, history shows that it is very difficult to remove a percentage allowance. The best use of this form of differentiation is therefore in short, sharp bursts as a form of special promotion.

DIFFERENTIATION IN INTERNATIONAL TRADE

Selling in another country normally involves additional costs which must be recovered through higher prices, if profits are to be maintained. However, different countries place different values on products. So a foreign market can be more profitable than a domestic one.

11.8 Competition-based pricing

There are three main systems of competition-based pricing, as follows.

THE GOING RATE

This is sometimes called 'pleasant pricing' or 'follow the leader'. In well-established markets with traditional prices, it is usually wisest

214

to enter at, or very close to, the ruling rate unless you present significant added benefits. It means that you need similar cost structures and that you must keep very careful control of costs. It also tends to mean that you cannot alter your price until the price leader in the market does so.

PLATEAU PRICING

An extreme form of the going rate, it is still found in international trade, particularly with commodities and raw materials. Price is often maintained at the plateau by government subsidy and/or control by buffer stocks. Although price cartels are officially banned in most parts of the world, 'gentlemen's agreements' exert the same influence on prices in many industries.

SEALED BIDS

Many companies operate in businesses where there is no option but to tender against competitors, known and unknown. Companies in such businesses would be well-advised to study the expanding literature on bidding. The best place to start is Marsh's book, *The Art of Tendering* (see Further Reading list). Most such books make extensive use of probability analysis in order to estimate possible success rates against different competitors and the outcomes of various bids.

11.9   Pricing new products

There are four key factors which need to be taken into account when setting new prices:

1   How much money you have available for investment in market research, testing, distribution deals, advertising and the rest.
2   The degree of competition that is likely and the extent to which you are protected from it.
3   Your perception of how responsive customers are likely to be to price levels and changes in price.
4   Which method and/or price will produce the better net result, according to your calculations: high price low volume or low price high volume? That is, penetration or skimming.

Of the five major ways of setting prices for new products, the first two raise again the most critical decision relating to the fourth factor above – are you going to try to build up the market as fast as possible at a low price, or will you aim at slower growth but at a high profit?

PENETRATION PRICING

A low price is set and this, together with heavy promotion, is designed to ensure a rapid take-off and deep penetration of the market. We are all familiar with new FMCG products which are launched with massive television advertising, door-to-door couponing or sampling, and further cut-price activity at the stores.

This is a typical example of both the pricing technique and the way the marketing mix is involved in supporting the price strategy. The reason for the strategy is that the price has been set to achieve volume, and it requires a lot of volume to justify it. Further, substantial economies of scale will be achieved at those volumes. It is assumed that the market is going to be price elastic. That is, more will be bought at a lower price. It is also hoped that the low price and the supporting marketing activity will discourage competitors. Indeed, any competitor is likely to be forced to enter at the established going rate.

MARKET SKIMMING

Since the full title of this method is 'skimming the cream', it will hardly surprise you to learn that it is also known as 'creaming'. If the previous method assumes that the market is capable of rapid growth, this second method assumes the opposite. Moreover, it requires a considerable lead-time over competition.

The principal practitioners of skimming are the ethical pharmaceutical companies who, under the provisions of the Sainsbury Committee rules, are allowed seven years to exploit a new market before competition can enter. Price is set very high to recoup the heavy investment in developing the product. The aim is that high profits will be earned while the period of protection lasts, so that when competitors enter, the first company has the option of: switching to a penetration policy to deter them; staying where it is and relying on the reputation it has built up; moving down but preserving margin; or simply waiting to see what the competition charges and meeting it.

Clearly, the company that can use a skimming policy is presented with a range of options. Perhaps the best is that it has a period in which it can establish a price/quality relationship that may prove to be detrimental to new entrants at lower prices. It is possible to compromise between penetration and skimming, and this is often done by industrial companies who have high investment to recover but do not wish to limit the development of the market by setting too high a price. So they set a sort of 'mid-way' price.

EARLY CASH RECOVERY

Both the methods described have early recovery of investment as part of their aim. This third method aims at quick cash returns. Often, such an aim can indicate a lack of real confidence in the product or the market. If so, it is vital to use a method that guarantees rapid cash recovery and profit. If you work in a market characterized by short life-cycles, like certain parts of the confectionery market, you need to be sure of getting your money back before the market declines.

PRODUCT LINE PROMOTIONAL PRICING

This method is seen at its clearest where the use of one item is dependent upon the use of another. For example, you could price copying machines very low but charge a relatively high rate for the paper needed to operate them. If the copiers you manufacture can utilize plain paper, then of course, you can't use this system. Instead, you may want to lease rather than sell your machines, and charge a rental based on metered paper usage. 'Conditional pricing' is often used to describe these very close relationships. King Gilette was a pioneer of this method when he gave away razors that only his blades would fit. Retailers use 'loss leaders' in a similar way: a low price offer brings people into the store who then buy higher-margin items.

RATE OF RETURN

It is possible to employ this method with any of the cost-based methods of pricing; the most widely used is the one that we referred to earlier as 'target pricing'. Clearly, a company that has developed a new product or service will have invested in it and will require a return on it. By the use of break-even analysis, it is possible to arrive at prices at various volumes that will satisfy the rate of return desired, assuming that the particular volume is achieved.

11.10 Summary

Setting the right price is a critical decision for any business. As with all aspects of marketing, the right price is the one which is acceptable to the customer. It is easy to discover when a product or

217

service is *over*-priced, but it is extremely difficult to discover when it is *under*-priced. The psychology of price is important in discovering customers' views of the relationship between price and value. Attitudes to price also relate very closely to the amount of risk the prospect feels is involved in the purchasing decision.

For all these reasons, cost-based methods of setting prices can be very dangerous. Their real value lies simply in determining the lower limits of the price. Which system of pricing you use will depend on your judgment of what is conventional, what is appropriate in the marketplace, and what the customer is likely to perceive as acceptable.

11.11 Checklist

1 Next to the product itself, the price is the most important element in the marketing mix. Indeed, customers can only rate a product in relation to a price. Without a price, there is no real indication of value.

2 Something which has no use to an individual, has no value for him or her. Whatever value is placed on a product or service is entirely individual and usually based on subjective, and possibly emotional, reasons.

3 There are three dimensions of value in any product: cost, use and esteem.

4 Cost-based pricing methods:

- *absorption costing* takes account of all costs plus a profit margin
- *direct costing* price is calculated from a break-even chart; theoretically, every time volume declines, price must rise, and vice versa
- *incremental costing* takes seriously the costs of moving from one level of output to another
- *marginal costing* is the cost of one extra unit or batch. Can be dangerous to use unless the extra costs are realistically assessed and the extra volume generated is not going to offset sales elsewhere
- *opportunity costs* are the costs of foregone profits when taking one course of action rather than another. This is very difficult to calculate, except where scarcity of resources makes the choice obvious
- *mark-up pricing* is widely used in the wholesale and retail trades; this consists of adding a standard mark-up after all costs have been taken into account

- *target pricing* sets the price on the basis of the required rate of return.

5 Break-even analysis is not a good way of setting prices, but it is a useful way of determining minimum price levels and of calculating the effect of price changes.

6 Demand-based pricing is based upon charging what the market will bear and involves differentiation by:
   a. customer
   b. time
   c. place or position
   d. version
   e. value
   f. nation or region

7 Competition-based pricing must take account of the following factors:

- the going rate in the market. In many markets, one is forced to accept that rate or something very close to it
- plateau pricing is most commonly supported by governments and international agencies. That support may take the form of subsidy or buffer stocks, especially in trading commodities and raw materials
- sealed bids are common in certain types of industry. Not all bids are accepted on the basis of the lowest tender, though a surprising number are. It is important to discover as much as you can, legitimately, about the committee or group which will eventually make the decision, as well as about the criteria on which they will function.

8 Pricing new products: the first decision is whether to penetrate the market or to go for a skimming policy. Not all companies will have an option; the conditions for skimming are arduous and essentially require a lengthy period without effective competition.

   Early cash recovery is a necessary strategy in some markets but can be seen as a sign of lack of confidence in the product or the market. Of the cost-based methods, target pricing is the most appropriate.

   The pricing of new products must always be seen as part of the total marketing mix and there are appropriate mix strategies for each pricing technique.

9 Promotional pricing can be used for the launch of items in a product line. Forms of conditional pricing are specially suitable for

9   product lines where the use of one item is dependent upon the purchase and use of another.

10 Price elasticity describes the proportionate effects of a change in price in one direction and changes in volume on the other. Because it is difficult to calculate precisely, a feel for the elasticity of demand in any market determines whether or not you are able to extract maximum profit out of price changes.

11 Price is an important indication of quality to most people. The psychology of price in any purchasing or market decision must always be considered most carefully.

12 The ability of any company to initiate price changes depends upon the extent and closeness of the competition; upon what acceptable substitutes are available; upon the strength and elasticity of demand; upon the relationship of price, volume and costs; upon psychological factors; and upon the tradition of the company as a price-leader or price-follower.

13 Reactions to competitive price changes may depend on the ability to respond by non-price means and the best estimate of the effect of price changes on the image of the product – and on the image of its quality.

14 Non-price reactions can often be copied quickly by competitors, leaving you no better off than you were.

15 If a change is unlikely to damage the product's image, you can match the competitors, beat them or go part-way towards their prices.

16 Try to understand why your competitor has changed tactics or strategy; whether it is a long- or short-term move; what it is costing them; and the depth of their purse as well as their resolve if it should come to a price war.

12

Chiefs, Indians and the rest of us

Not everything that goes by the name 'Marketing' deserves it. It has become too fashionable. A grave-digger remains a grave-digger even when called a 'mortician' – only the cost of the burial goes up.

Peter Drucker, *Managing for Results*

Marketing is primarily a state of mind. Although there are numerous techniques that can be used to improve our marketing ability, they can do nothing if there is no understanding of marketing and no commitment to it in a company. That was why we began by emphasizing the place of understanding and action from the very first chapter. Without the right sort of understanding the right action is unlikely. The question is: do we need any marketing assistance?

12.1 Why have a marketing department?

You can adopt the marketing philosophy without a marketing department. Often, chief executives may be personally committed to, and even highly skilled at, marketing; and there are situations where the other calls on their time may not prevent them from exercising an executive function in the marketing area.

There are also occasions when the size of the business will simply not stand another specialist. Nevertheless, it is somewhat strange that any business can 'afford' not to have someone to look after the customer-creating process, when it has someone to look after the product-manufacturing side. The reason for this strange state of affairs is that nearly everyone claims to know all about advertising and selling: it is rather easier to justify not employing a dog when you fully intend to bark yourself.

The considerations that lead to the appointment of a separate

221

marketing specialist (with or without a department) are exactly the same as those that lead to the appointment of any other specialist. If there are any differences between marketing and other professions, they are (negatively) that marketing is less tangible, more subjective, and (positively) that marketing can co-ordinate the activities of the whole business from the viewpoint of the customer and can help to ensure that total quality-consciousness and controls are firmly established.

Specifically, if yours is a business which needs continual and close analysis of the customers of your goods and services, or if your business needs to apply some of the more specialized techniques of market research, advertising, sales promotion, public relations, selling, and so on, then there is a very strong case for a marketing function – even if it consists for the moment of only one consultant upon whose services you call as needed.

TIME

A fair proportion of the marketing task can be done by all reasonably intelligent managers, if they have some training and the time in which to apply both the philosophy and the techniques. From this book's simplified explanation of the basic elements of marketing, it will be clear that considerable chunks of unbroken time need to be devoted to considering the ramifications of possible courses of action. Trained and experienced marketing executives are more likely to be able to do this sort of thing much more quickly, quite apart from freeing busy senior managers for other productive work.

ATTITUDE

Training and experience can change attitudes, but some people will always think more creatively than others. In today's fast-moving times, it isn't good enough to get there eventually, you have to get there fast – and, if possible, get there first. You want the best minds working for you to help you get there.

SKILLS

Good marketing people are 'generalists' as well as specialists; Jacks-of-all-trades but also masters of one. They can master any of the marketing techniques discussed in this book: you will, of course, need to choose someone who specializes in an area most appropriate to your business. If you spend heavily on promotion, someone with experience and skills in advertising may be

222

advantageous. If industrial market research is the key activity, that sort of specialization may make sense. In either case, a pre-requisite for the job will be knowledge of where to buy the best services. That knowledge by itself is an enormous saver of time and resources.

MANAGEMENT

In many companies, the marketing department will be quite sizeable, especially if it includes the salesforce. But whether large or small, a marketing department (like any other well-run unit) needs detailed management and guidance. A marketing director or manager has to perform all the personnel and training functions that any departmental head does, and nothing disturbs any specialized skill or talent more than reporting to an uncomprehending and unsympathetic management.

RESPONSIBILITIES

For all the reasons outlined above, chief executives frequently choose, and should at least consider, delegating all detailed work, and consideration of all policy questions to specialized marketing departments, which can think about alternatives, examine the possible effects, outline all the ramifications and then make recommendations. If a particular recommendation is accepted, they may be asked to take executive authority for certain sections of the plan, working to targets and under budgetary constraints similar to those of other departmental managers. And the areas over which they are likely to exercise this delegated responsibility are those we detailed in Chapter 1:

- Assessing markets
- Specifying products and services
- Pricing policy
- Sales and distribution policy
- Advertising and promotion
- Co-ordination
- After-sales service
- Quality control

12.2 What kind of person is a marketer?

Good marketing people have lively and active minds, with a wide range of interests. From the esoteric to the commonplace, they seem to know rather more about a bigger range of unrelated things than the average manager. What used to be called 'the common touch' is usually a sound recommendation for the high frequency mass markets. In any case, marketers need a balance of those apparently contradictory qualities – sound analytical abilities and pronounced flair. Too much creativity may result in a certain wildness in the schemes they propose, while too much analysis may lead to a loss of opportunities.

Courage and commercialism are essential ingredients. Marketing people are usually good with people and at risk-taking: although the marketing philosophy and some of the techniques can be applied to non-commercial undertakings, a marketing executive thrives in a business setting. All marketers need an eye for detail since that is essential to the enhancement of quality, to co-ordination as well as to quality management.

Where there is a fairly large marketing department, it is possible to be more flexible and to choose a wider range of complementary skills and abilities. However, marketing departments work best when individuals have delegated responsibility for all that concerns a client, a product or a service. Such individuals are called product managers. It is generally best to ensure, therefore, that you employ only well-rounded marketing people in a company – specialists can always be hired on a temporary or contract basis.

12.3   The concept of product manager

A product manager has full delegated authority for the overall performance and conduct of a product or group of products. Such people tend to be quite junior, yet appear to possess an enormous amount of power. So much so that a particular product manager was once exaggeratedly defined as 'the managing director of his brand'. Any power which is possessed by product managers is not their own but is delegated to them. Moreover, their power covers, at best, only the areas of co-ordination and quality. Though they may have delegated responsibility for ensuring that sufficient product is available to achieve agreed plans, for example, they do not run the factory. They have no responsibility or authority over the personnel. They cannot authorize capital expenditure.

Product managers are almost certain to be the highest ranking people in an organization who know all about the affairs of a particular product area. There are others above the product manager who also know what is happening to a product or brand, but they don't attend to detail.

224

How necessary is the product manager? That depends very much on the complexity of your operations. Generally speaking, the role is seldom necessary in companies with very few products or services. Product managers are needed where it is necessary to prevent management overload from simply being transferred from the chief executive to the senior marketing manager, or where that senior manager will be unable to give needed attention to all product areas.

A major problem with the introduction of the product manager system is that the early needs are likely to be far greater than the later ones. If a company were to staff-up to carry out just the analysis suggested in this book on a large range of products, it would almost certainly require at least twice as many people initially as it would require in two years' time.

This makes a very good case for using consultants as a task force in the early stages, under the close direction of the person who is going to run the final department. That will take care of most of the necessary once-only work, and help ensure that the right-sized department is established when the time is ripe. It may also help other managers to understand the role of brand managers when they arrive, for the concept represents an organizational anomaly in all sorts of ways.

12.4 Some problems of marketing departments

Essentially, there are two kinds of marketing department: one includes the salesforce under the wing of the marketing director or manager, while the other does not. The only really good reason for not combining them is a management one, and they should be put together as soon as the management problem is solved. To keep them separate is rather like asking accountants to produce the annual results without giving them the figures. It is not a question of marketing becoming ascendent over sales, or vice versa. Sales people generally have more people-management experience and, other things being equal, should make better departmental managers than the people with the best marketing abilities.

But the separation between sales and marketing is largely artificial. Marketing is a sort of federal government in which specialized functions like selling, advertising, public relations and market research are like states. Some of these states are more important than others at different times. Some are unnecessary in certain kinds of company. It is difficult to co-ordinate the efforts of truly separate functions when inter-related ones are themselves artificially divided.

There are various other possible types of administrative arrangement. Some companies keep the public relations function, for example, outside the marketing department. In many companies, there is probably more of a case for this than there is for other kinds of separation between marketing and its constituents. Where the public relations function is essentially oriented towards personnel, welfare, relations with institutions, local and central government or other non-sales work, it is not necessary to keep it within the marketing department. However, where it is concerned with product promotion, enquiries, complaints, trade relations and general customer satisfaction, there is no valid case for keeping it outside the marketing department.

Advertising is sometimes outside the marketing department, too, specially in large technical companies which need a good deal of technical literature. Is it conceivable that any chief executive could even think of asking one manager to make plans, another to promote the product and a third to sell them, without ensuring that there is adequate overall direction and co-ordination? To separate advertising and marketing is to separate strategy and execution. If the separation is rigidly enforced, as it frequently is, it results in advertising agencies receiving inadequate and incomplete briefs – with the inevitable results.

Such arrangements always compound the anomalous position of the product manager: the advertising manager has power without responsibility over part of the area where the product manager has responsibility without power! The only situation where a separate function is justified is where the needs of a strong corporate image make demands which transcend individual product identities.

The case for an in-house advertising production department is harder to argue, though some companies maintain that they have special needs: if you can justify employing specialists, it may pay you to have them under your own roof. Generally, overheads can make this option cost more in the long run than putting the work out. Generally, too, the difference in cost would permit you to buy the services of really top-flight creative talents on a one-off basis for individual jobs. The half-way house of employing an experienced buyer of creative services, with possibly a small in-house studio for day-to-day use, is much more desirable, less costly and more efficient. It is increasing in popularity as a result of the greater familiarity with the potential of desktop publishing systems.

Market research can be a problem, although the attitude of market researchers is much closer to that of product managers: actual difficulties arise far less often than they do with selling and advertising.

Problems can arise because market research involves so many very narrow specializations that most brand managers find this the area where the gap between vocabulary and practice is greatest. That is where market research managers can help, though the problem is this: do those managers simply act as buyers, advising on techniques for problems and recommending suppliers, or do they decide on needs, commissioning work and feeding results to product managers as well? You will find that companies work both ways. By and large, opinion favours the market research advisor/ buyer role, while practice has the market research manager and the product manager working together without friction and achieving the better points of both alternatives.

12.5   Recent emphases in marketing

The world grows increasingly complex, and so does marketing. Until recently, you would have found books on marketing concerned only with the identification and satisfaction of consumers' wants and needs. However, there have been several forces which are changing marketing, particularly:

- sustained and profound criticism of marketing
- the consumer movement
- moral and ethical issues.

CRITICISM OF MARKETING

There has been increasing and powerful criticism of advertising for some years. Why? Because of the way in which marketing encourages people to be greedy; because of the materialism built into the way in which industry and marketing are presently organized; because of the environmental damage caused by industrial products; and so on. In some circles, the word 'marketing' has become identified with a number of wrong practices, ranging from dishonest trading to over-enthusiastic advertising claims.

Criticism of marketing takes place at two levels. First there is the level of details: market research which intrudes on individual and family privacy, deceptive packaging and labelling, and so on. Second is the level of society as a whole and the direction in which marketing is propelling it: for example, marketing, say its critics, is wasteful; helps to create monopolies; and therefore limits customer choice; produces advertising aimed at children; and so on.

THE CONSUMER MOVEMENT

From the 1930s, there has been a strong consumer movement lobbying for the rights of consumers. It began by concentrating attention on the first level mentioned above (that of product and business detail), though nowadays it focuses attention at least as much on larger issues, such as food safety, industrial pollution, urban congestion, material waste and ecological imbalance. The relentless drive for safe products, for good quality products, for 'green' or environment-friendly products, has recently brought new products and services into the market, just as it has over the years helped bring forward increasing legislation designed to protect customers.

ETHICAL AND MORAL ISSUES

There are three levels at which ethical and moral issues make an impact on marketing: that of the individual, that of the place of an individual in an organization and that of marketing (and indeed of business and society) as a whole.

From an ethical point of view, marketing is a double-edged activity. Some people describe it as 'neutral'. But it is not neutral. Like science, it is powerful, and therefore capable of good as well as ill. Science can save a child's life as well as abort it. Marketing techniques can be used to sell unpalatable and even untrue statements on behalf of political parties, just as they can be used to sell the need for helping people in difficulty or distress. Confectionery, cigarettes, alcohol, fashion garments, atomic weapons – these are examples of areas where individuals, and some whole sections of society, have moral questions.

Entertainment and bribery are other areas which often come up in discussions of marketing and ethics. In all these matters, you – and your company – will be greatly helped by thinking through where you stand. Would you personally, for example, feel happy helping to market all the things named above? Think about your attitude, as a customer, to goods and services. There are some you clearly enjoy; you may not feel too strongly about others. Yet others you may dislike for reasons of quality; for their effect on the environment; for their effect on other people; and so on (for example, there is now widespread concern about the poor

228

conditions of workers in tea estates and people supplying the fashion clothes industry). If you feel uneasy about some products, how would you feel about being involved in helping to get them to more people?

It is worth writing down a list of those things which you would feel unable to market. The interesting thing is that it is possible to steer clear of any products or services you may feel uneasy about, even if you work in the marketing department of a company which is involved, among other things, with those products. (Of course you would have a problem if the company dealt in nothing except goods which you felt uneasy about.)

It is also possible that though you have no objection to a particular product, you dislike the way in which it is marketed: the hard-sell methods of some encyclopaedia firms and some double-glazing firms have given the whole of those fields a bad name. You may feel that, if you were asked to market some such products, you would be able to do a good, as well as ethical, job of it. You may indeed be able to bring about such a revolution, but don't underestimate the strength of market forces – and remember that not every shark in business started out that way: some, at least, (however rightly or wrongly) felt themselves forced to go the way of the world for the sake of survival.

Individuals are often under intense pressure in organizations because of a conflict between loyalty to their organization, friends and colleagues, on the one hand, and, on the other hand, being true to their own conscience and to society at large. Recent years have seen numerous examples of leaks and revelations from individual employees of large organizations. Such individuals are traitors from one point of view, heroes from another. Whatever our view, we must recognize that individuals who dare to disclose deceit or danger to the public, usually at the risk of their own career and financial security, have had to choose between their corporate loyalty and their personal ethical code.

Whatever it might cost the organization in terms of bad publicity, such action is always going to cost the individual far, far more. There must be thousands of people who live with profound moral and ethical dilemmas unresolved, because they cannot bring themselves to pay the cost of blowing the whistle.

Such enormous pressure, and such costly decisions, would be entirely unnecessary if organizations were as they should be. Inconsistencies in behaviour or attitudes will eventually cause an organization to be labelled untrustworthy, devious or unreliable –

and to lose out in the marketplace as a result. Though it must be admitted that it is very hard for individuals to be consistent, there is every reason why it should be much easier for organizations.

This is not to deny the need for continual watchfulness. There is a temptation to take the moral high ground either at home or abroad, but not in both spheres; some people are outraged by the suggestion that they give an 'introductory payment' to a Middle Eastern official but will happily spend ten times that amount entertaining a key customer or official in Britain. There are, even today, organizations which have a plush showroom for their products and a dirty café for their workers.

Every company has a sort of 'personality'. This emerges as much from the customer talking to his or her friends in the pub after work, as it does from expensive TV advertisements, glossy annual reports, sheaves of press releases, and the chairperson's speeches and interviews.

Most people appreciate a high standard of ethics most of the time, but it is also easier in practice to maintain clear high standards than it is to try to see that a more uncertain line is adhered to.

Why is it necessary for pressure to be exerted, inside and outside an organization, for it to adhere to moral standards? Part of the difficulty is no doubt that in a largely materialist and secular society, there appears to be no single authoritative source of moral guidance. The churches, professional associations, schools and other institutions do their best, of course, but where the basis of morality is now merely personal conscience – and where personal consciences don't get much nourishment or exercise – it is not surprising that there should be widespread confusion about what is right, and even about what is acceptable.

Professional codes of conduct, company codes of practice and even individual conscience wilt under the constant unexamined pressure of the multiplicity of customs and practices which abound.

It requires all the pressure that we can bring to bear, as individuals and as organizations, to keep organizations, companies – and indeed governments – on the uncomfortable and difficult path of quality, honesty and consistency, which will always pay in the long term, and which marketeers are bound to welcome, since it contributes to the overall image of an organization and to the satisfactions it is able to offer customers. It also contributes to the business environment, the human environment and the ecological environment in which we all, after all, have to live.

The application of marketing philosophy and techniques to social

230

problems must also be welcomed for similar reasons. Such social problems as poverty, illiteracy and disease on the one hand, and the over-development of the industrialized world on the other, are now receiving the attention of people trained in marketing philosophy and techniques. This cannot harm any legitimate individual business, and can only accomplish good on behalf of all of us.

Having said that, it must be pointed out that companies themselves are going through a profound transformation. Where they used to be concerned only with making a profit within legal means, there is much more of an expectation nowadays that commerce and industry will be socially responsible. Of course, it is possible that companies may revolt against the increasing burden that is being placed on them. In Britain, they are being expected to give money to every good cause, support schools and inner cities, provide people to run everything from hospitals to the arts – the list is endless.

At the end of the day, companies still have to make a profit before they can survive long enough to do any of these worthy things. But even if there is such a revolt, I fear that there will be no going back from the overall principle that companies have responsibilities other than mere profit.

Free societies have many disadvantages; they also have many advantages. One of them is that public opinion cannot be squashed, even though it can be manipulated and deceived for certain periods. But everyone can't be deceived all the time, and public opinion has now matured into firm favour for those companies which are seen to be doing their duty for society as a whole. It is part of the responsibility of marketing to ensure that its parent organization is, and is seen to be, ethically and socially responsible in terms of its products and services, its dealing with competitors and its internal policies and practices.

12.6 Summary

A marketing department isn't absolutely necessary, but in many cases, it will be justified by ensuring adequate attention to all the details of quality control, social responsibility and customer creation and satisfaction.

People trained and experienced in the application of the marketing philosophy reduce the lead-time in creating customer-satisfying strategies, and have the knowledge and experience to apply the appropriate techniques in the best way for the company. Ideally, all those techniques will be under one person's control and any apparent exception to that rule will be properly questioned and accepted only if justified.

It may make very good sense to use outside task forces to deal with the initial heavy workload of a marketing department, and to delay full staffing until continuing needs can be assessed. This will also assist decisions regarding the appointment of managers to individual products or product groups, and related questions about whether they should be responsible for each of the technique areas on that product, or whether some things should be the responsibility of product managers.

The marketing department has a special responsibility to ensure that the company is concerned about quality, ethics and environmental and social responsibility. These are the new frontiers of business today. Companies which fail at these levels are not going to last long. Companies which take these dimensions seriously will gain the competitive edge.

12.7 Checklist

1 A marketing department isn't necessary to the adoption of the marketing philosophy. So far as marketing techniques are concerned, you can buy them in on a temporary, part-time or occasional basis.

2 The decision to employ marketing specialists involves the same factors as those which are used to consider whether the employment of any other specialist is justified.

3 From a chief executive's point of view, the key reasons for employing marketing specialists are that they have:

- the ability to reduce the *time* taken to make decisions and implement them, and can release time for other senior executives
- training in a discipline that always puts customers first in satisfying profit objectives; this means that the heart of the business (*quality*) will be well cared for
- the skills to assume delegated responsibility for the definition and *co-ordination* of all the commercial aspects of a business
- breadth of *knowledge*, as well as one or more areas of specialist knowledge; knowing what can be done, how to do it, where it can be obtained, and so on
- the experience and ability to help provide an *effective management style* throughout the organization.

232

4 Where there are many products requiring special attention, each of them may benefit from having a product manager. Such a person is, ideally, profit-responsible for the product(s) assigned, knowing about all that may affect that product, and co-ordinating the separate departments involved.

5 Product management is most necessary where there are many products, where they use different resources and where they involve different methods of reaching customers.

6 In the early stages, the workload may be far greater than in later stages. So it may make sense to buy-in a task force to handle work which may not need to be repeated.

7 Ideally, all functions aiming at the same objective or customer should be under common control. Under no circumstances should responsibility for tactical planning be divorced from the responsibility for strategy.

8 There has been powerful and growing criticism of advertising. Research these criticisms to assess their validity in the light of your own experience.

9 It is helpful to think through and clarify where you stand on a range of moral dilemmas in marketing, so that it will be easier for you and for your company when you are actually at the pressure points where you have to make difficult decisions.

10 You may wish to explore opportunities in which you can promote high standards on the basis of their commercial benefit – in your own personal life, in your company, in your particular profession, in the sector of industry in which your company operates, in business and society as a whole.

11 Do you have clear written policies on how the company should respond to complaints from employees and customers? Devise ways of keeping an eye on how your organization responds in practice: it is not unethical to 'create' a customer complaint (for example, by having a friend write or telephone) simply to track how the matter is dealt with. Make the results of your experiment known to everyone within the organization, whether those results are good, bad or indifferent. Such tests are evidence of the seriousness with which you take the matters you test. The fact that such tests are run from time to time will encourage people to deal with complaints and moral matters much more seriously, though you must take care not to victimize any individual if it is a whole system (or department or procedure) that needs attention and improvement.

13

Techniques in sequence

True science teaches, above all, to doubt and to be ignorant.
Miguel de Unamuno, *The Tragic Sense of Life*

This chapter looks at two areas: marketing as a whole, and the deployment of marketing techniques in the best possible way.

13.1 Scientific marketing

Marketing is not a science. Science formulates hypotheses, and then investigates them to see if they are true or untrue. In other words, it verifies or falsifies ideas. Another cardinal principle of science is that it is repeatable. When a particular explanation meets these criteria, we call it a law.

Even the things which are apparently verified and repeated sometimes go tragically wrong, because we can't possibly test for all the variables that might be present. For example, a relaxant drug was submitted to all the tests that seemed appropriate and was duly certified by the relevant health experts. It seemed to be the drug the world was waiting for – until it was administered to expectant mothers. Then it was discovered that Thalidomide causes abnormalities in a small proportion of unborn children. A small proportion, but a tragic result.

In marketing, there are few cases where we can even begin to approach the relatively stringent standards of science. These cases occur most often in the field of market research, where the laws of probability can be applied. However, commercial factors force us to move away from the ideal of random sampling, for example, to which those laws apply. We retreat instead to more affordable samples, where few could consider the results reliable in any absolute sense. So marketing techniques are not necessarily academically rigorous, though they are practically useful – and they are improving all the time in precision and sophistication.

For these reasons, the results of advertising campaigns or sales efforts cannot be accurately forecasted in relation to the precise amount of effort or money involved.

However, as one of our definitions of marketing so memorably put it, techniques take the guesswork out of hunch: marketing cannot eliminate risk, but it can help reduce the risk which is inherent in all commercial decisions. None of the individual figures produced by a marketing technique may be entirely trustworthy, but when used along with other marketing techniques in a carefully ordered sequence, they generate a mass of data, specifically on direction and mood. The picture which emerges provides a useful indication of market attitudes, response, and so on. This information can contribute significantly to the reduction of business risk.

You can see that the term 'scientific marketing', which has become popular in a number of circles, is a bit of a misnomer. But it refers to the fact that there is a best order in which the techniques can be employed, so that one successively eliminates uncertainty and ensures that customers' needs are understood and catered for.

In what follows, certain steps may not be required by every business. For example, if your company does not use advertising, then it will clearly not need to test any advertising copy; nor will every company need to test its goods or services in a representative part of the country.

Not all the elements described in the list have been discussed in this book in any detail. If the list encourages you to seek more detail, you will find that the Further Reading list is a good place to start looking.

But let us begin at the beginning. If we were starting a business, we would work through the following steps in relation to marketing:

1 Define possible consumer needs which you might be able to meet

2 Research these markets to establish whether suitable consumers exist in a sufficient quantity, and are willing to pay the sort of price which is necessary for you to establish a viable business

3 Test your concept or product

4 Make any necessary alterations to the concept/formulation/performance/price/blend/flavour/service, and so on, to best serve customer needs

5 Test the modified product or service again

6 If necessary, repeat steps 4 and 5 till you are satisfied that a market does or does not exist

7 Develop forecasts

8   Test your advertising/packaging/promotional concepts to see if they are effective

9   Improve, refine or redesign your advertisement/packaging/promotion on the basis of step 8

10 Repeat steps 8 and 9 till you are satisfied that you have the most effective forms of advertising/packaging/promotion you can have

11 Decide the next step: will you have a national launch, or will you test market? – that is, enter a small but representative section of the country in order to contain costs and provide indicators of the likely extent of success

12 Design and undertake the actual launch on which you have decided, being careful to check that you have paid sufficient attention to the timing of it

13 Monitor and measure key variables, such as: sales in, sales out, customer off-take, usage, frequency of purchase, etc.

14 Evaluate your success against your forecast in step 7

15 In the light of step 14, modify (if necessary) your service or product, as well as your advertising, packaging and promotion

16 Develop a new forecast: decide on the variables you are now going to monitor (remember they must be relatively controllable and/or predictable); make simple correlations (that is, what goes with what); as well as complex correlations (using multi-variate analysis to examine the inter-relationship of several apparently related variables)

17 'What went wrong?' Examine all departures from your forecast against the controllable or predictable variables for causal relationships; question the validity of your planning assumptions

18 Revise your forecast

19 Repeat the appropriate step for any development or variation of your product or service. For example, if a product has been reformulated, test the new version with customers. If advertising copy has been changed, test its communication effectiveness. If there has been increased promotional activity, review the sales forecast.

20 Follow this with the planning sequence described in Chapter 7.

13.2　The forecasting sequence

It is now possible to look at the sequence that enables us to use the range of marketing techniques to best effect. Figure 31 (page 238) portrays three broad categories along which data can be explored. In every case, the stage furthest away from the forecasting 'box' represents one of the simplest methods. The stage nearest the box represents a level of sophistication which will not be demanded by every situation. However, if the methods you are using are not providing satisfactory answers, it is possible that you should be moving nearer the box. The greater the number of stages that you use in conjunction with each other, the fewer the risks that you will run in forecasting, and the greater will be your ability to evaluate what is happening.

The three categories examined are sales, demographics and attitudinal/sociological factors. The section above the 'box' indicates what you should be examining; the section below the 'box' indicates the means of doing so. In every case, the final stage just below the 'box' enables attempts to be made to predict the results of alternative courses of action.

The sales category begins by looking at your own performance, and asks you to examine your sales figures. To look at competitors' sales, some method must be found to measure total market performance as well as the performance of named competitors within that market. Examination of the sales figures leads to an audit of the whole operation at the retail and consumer levels. Simple and complex relationships can then be identified and analyzed by the various methods indicated.

Demographics is concerned with the description of buyers – by location, importance, age, sex, class, size, lifestyle, and so on. The stages above the 'box' are the same as for sales, simply substituting the closest parallel. The cheapest way to discover such facts is to pay for your questions to be included in a larger piece of research, in order to share the overhead costs of contact and fieldwork. Consumer audit is the final stage in this stream: in some cases, demographic information can be regarded as a by-product of the consumer sales audit, while in others it is the basic reason for its use.

Consumer audits can be rather general or specially structured to study changes in buying behaviour; how much sophistication you get depends on how much money you want to spend. The Tea Council in the UK has subscribed to such research over a very long period, being especially interested in the usage of tea by different age groups.

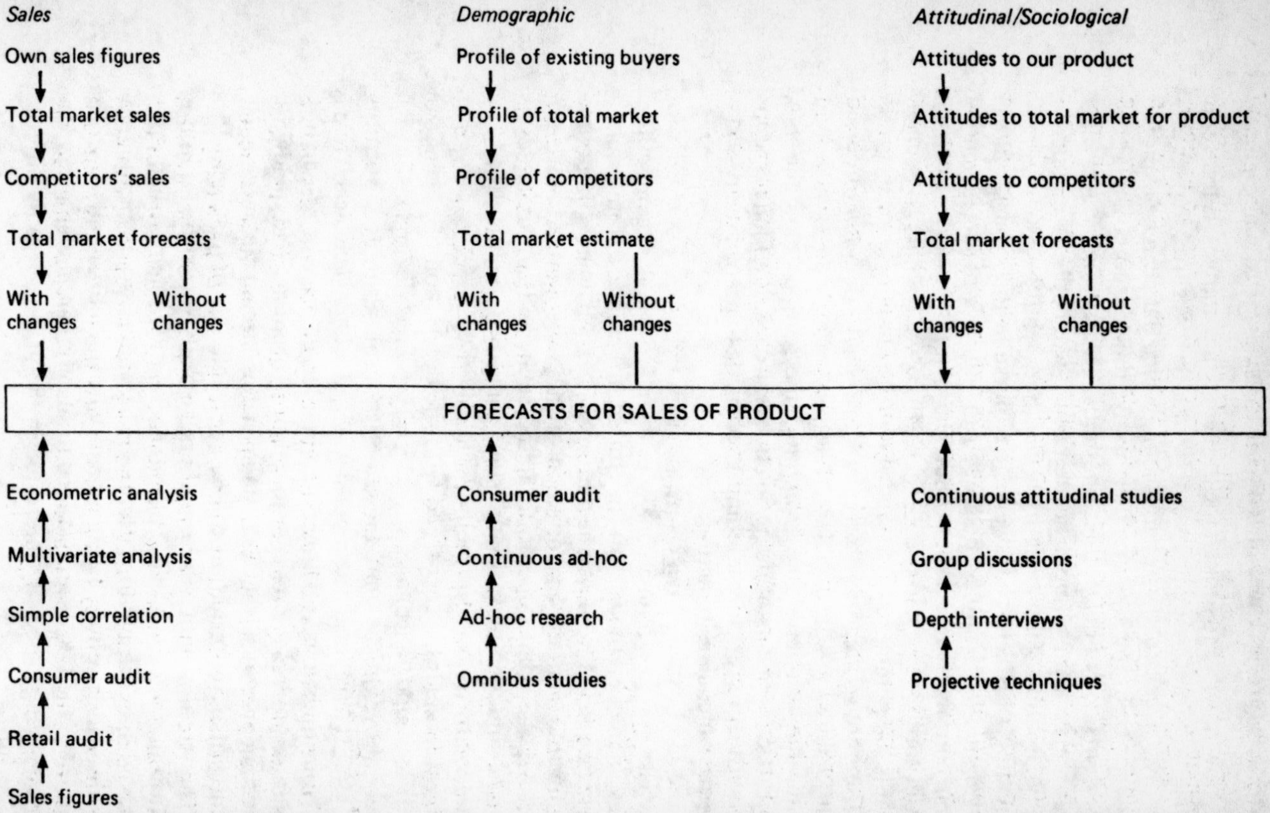

Figure 31 *Three routes to market forecasting and evaluation* (Distance from 'Forecasting' box indicates simplicity;

Sales

Own sales figures

Total market sales

Competitors' sales

Total market forecasts → With changes → ← Without changes

Econometric analysis

Multivariate analysis

Simple correlation

Consumer audit

Retail audit

Sales figures

Demographic

Profile of existing buyers

Profile of total market

Profile of competitors

Total market estimate → With changes → ← Without changes

Consumer audit

Continuous ad-hoc

Ad-hoc research

Omnibus studies

FORECASTS FOR SALES OF PRODUCT

Attitudinal/Sociological

Attitudes to our product

Attitudes to total market for product

Attitudes to competitors

Total market forecasts → With changes → ← Without changes

Continuous attitudinal studies

Group discussions

Depth interviews

Projective techniques

238

Attitudes are much more difficult to discern and consequently expensive to measure, but they are essential to marketers. Information on attitudes can be collected by using direct questions, word association, sentence completion, story completion, cartoon techniques, interviews, and so on. One example of these interesting methods is where people are shown pictures of domestic situations, and asked to describe what sort of people would live there and what brands they might buy. From such methods, attitudes to brands and companies are elicited. Interviews should be detailed, and probe reasons for answers. Group discussions reduce the amount of time that would be taken by talking to one individual at a time – but they also have the advantage that much more information, and different sorts of information, emerges in group discussion, than in single interviews. Continuous studies of such sorts often go hand-in-hand with consumer audits, in an attempt to discover which attitudes lead to what kind of purchasing behaviour.

A further step can help us analyze whether any particular groups of people are open to being influenced – perhaps by advertising – and thus amenable to change.

13.3 Summary

Marketing is neither an art nor a science. It provides a relatively rough but practically useful guide, based on some art and some science. The art has to be used all the time; the science (such as it is) can be used from time to time. But, by marrying the two, and using techniques in a carefully ordered sequence, risk can be reduced and business improved.

13.4 Checklist

1 The number of variables likely to influence any marketing situation is too great to permit scientific accuracy, or to enable us to discover precisely how people will respond to a particular advertising message, or to any particular sort of packaging.
2 The trends, and the rough understanding of the market, revealed by marketing techniques can acquire considerable force as evidence if used in the suggested sequence, with each subsequent activity being used to test the most useful bits and patterns of information dug up by previous activities in the sequence.

3   Three routes to better market forecasting and evaluation are:
- sales analysis
- demographic study
- attitudinal and sociological probing.

4   Each route begins with examining our own product or service, then looks at the total market and at competing products in order to provide total market forecasts for each aspect examined.
5   These final forecasts are made assuming changes from present conditions as well as no change – that is, using 'What if?' scenarios.
6   The main techniques associated with each of the three aspects are described in Figure 31. In each case, we begin with the simplest and cheapest method, and then move step by step to the most complex.
7   Very few companies will need to employ each technique along any particular route, though the most complex market situations will require the majority of them.

Further reading

How to find your way through the reading list
The list may look long, but it is meant to contain the most important or interesting books and articles, so that you can know where to start looking for further information on any of the following subjects.

You don't need to read all these materials. In fact, you don't need to read any of them – unless you are interested in the particular area they cover.

If there are particular areas about which you wish to find out more, you can start with any one of the books or articles listed.

How can you decide which of the books or articles on a particular topic you should read first? There are two simple principles, and you can use any one of them, or both:

1 Begin with the briefest publication, and
2 Begin with the latest publication.

Enjoy finding out more about marketing – and practicing it!

General reading
Ansoff, H. I. *Implementing Strategic Management*, Prentice-Hall, 1984
Baker, M. *Marketing*, 4th edition, Macmillan, 1985
Bureau, J. R. *Brand Management* , Macmillan, 1981
Kotler, P. et al. *The New Competition*, Prentice-Hall, 1985
Levitt, T. *The Marketing Imagination*, Free Press, 1983
Ohmae, K. *The Mind of the Strategist*, Penguin, 1983
Porter, M. E. *Competitive Advantage: Creating and Sustaining Superior Performance*, Free Press, 1985
Porter, M. E. *Competitive Strategy: Techniques for Analyzing Industries and Competitors*, Free Press, 1980
Van Mesdag, M. *Think Marketing*, Mercury Books, 1988

Consumer behaviour

Ehrenberg, A. S. C., Goodhardt, G. J. and Foxall, G. R. *Understanding Buyer Behaviour*, Wiley, 1988

Engel, James F. et al. *Consumer Behaviour*, 5th edition, Dryden, 1986

Foxall, G. R. *Consumer Behaviour*, Croom Helm, 1980

Industrial marketing

Buckner, H. *How British Industry Buys*, Hutchinson, 1967

Chisnall, P. M. *Strategic Industrial Marketing*, Prentice-Hall, 1985

Hakansson, H. (Ed). *International Marketing and Purchasing of Industrial Goods*, Wiley, 1982

Hill, R. and Hillier, F. *Organizational Buying Behaviour*, Macmillan, 1977

Marsh, P. *The Art of Tendering*, Gower, 1987

Marketing services

Cowell, D. W. *The Marketing of Services*, Heinemann, 1984

Donnelly, J. and George, W. R. (Ed). *Marketing of Services*, American Marketing Association, 1981

Langeard, E. et al. *Service Marketing*, Report no. 81–104, Marketing Science Institute, August 1981

Marketing small businesses

Green, P. E and Tull, D. S. *Research for Marketing Decisions*, Prentice-Hall, 1978

Longenecker, J. and Moore, C. 'Marketing and Small Business Entrepreneurship' in Hill, G. E. et al. (Eds). *Marketing and Small Business Entrepreneurship: Conceptual Research and Directions*, International Council for Small Business, 1980

Marketing non-profit organizations

Blois, K. J. 'Marketing for Non-Profit Organizations', pp 405–413 in Baker, M. J. (Ed). *The Marketing Book*, William Heinemann, 1987

Market analysis

Piercy, N. *Low-Cost Marketing Analysis*, MCB, 1978

Piercy, N. *Marketing Organization: An Analysis of Information Processing, Power and Politics*, Allen & Unwin, 1985

Pricing

Gabor, A. *Pricing: Principles and Practices*, Heinemann, 1979

Brown, W. and Jacques, E. *Product Analysis Pricing*, Heinemann, 1965

Marshall, A. *More Profitable Pricing*, McGraw-Hill, 1979

Promotion

Adams, J. R. *Media Planning*, 2nd edition, Business Books, 1977

Broadbent, S, and Jacobs, B. *Spending Advertising Money*, 4th edition, Business Books, 1984

Lovell, M. and Potter, J. *Assessing the Effectiveness of Advertising*, Business Books, 1975

Selling

Lidstone, J. *Negotiating Profitable Sales*, Gower, 1981

Lidstone, J. *Training Salesmen on the Job*, Gower, 1986

Computers and information technology in marketing

Parkinson, S. T. 'Computers in Marketing', pp 188–203 in Baker, M. J. (Ed). *The Marketing Book*, William Heinemann, 1987

Index

In the following index, 'marketing' is abbreviated to 'm'

246

247

248